Property of **Communists**

Property of

COMMUNISTS

The Urban Housing Program
from Stalin to Khrushchev

Mark B. Smith

NORTHERN ILLINOIS UNIVERSITY PRESS

© 2010 by Northern Illinois University Press

Published by the Northern Illinois University Press, DeKalb, Illinois 60115

Library of Congress Cataloging-in-Publication Data

Smith, Mark B.

Property of communists: the urban housing program from Stalin to Khrushchev / Mark B. Smith.

   p.   cm.

 Includes bibliographical references and index.

 ISBN 978-0-87580-423-1 (clothbound : alk. paper)

1. Housing—Soviet Union—History. 2. Housing policy—Soviet Union—History. 3. Home owner-

ship—Soviet Union—History. 4. Real property—Social aspects—Soviet Union—History. 5. City and

town life—Soviet Union—History. 6. Communism—Social aspects—Soviet Union—History.

7. Soviet Union—Social conditions—1945–1991. 8. Soviet Union—Social policy. I. Title.

HD7345.A3S57 2010

363.5'85094709045—dc22

2010004819

Contents

Charts

Tables

Acknowledgments

I would like warmly to thank the organizations whose financial support made possible doctoral research and the writing of this monograph. The Arts and Humanities Research Council of the United Kingdom funded my doctoral award. Additional costs were met by the School of Slavonic and East European Studies, University College London, where I worked on my PhD. I subsequently held an Economic History Society postdoctoral fellowship at the Institute of Historical Research, London. The History Department of the University of Durham, under the direction of Professor Philip Williamson, was a very pleasant place to spend a year, not least during the long summer days when I finished this book in the comfortable office of Professor David Moon. I corrected the proofs in my new professional home at the School of History of the University of Leeds, and I thank my new colleagues for their support.

Some of the book's arguments and evidence appeared in a different form in an article and a book chapter: "Individual Forms of Ownership in the Urban Housing Fund of the Soviet Union, 1944–1964," in *Slavonic and East European Review*, and "Khrushchev's Promise to Eliminate the Urban Housing Shortage: Rights, Rationality, and the Communist Future," in Melanie Ilic and Jeremy Smith, eds., *State and Society under Nikita Khrushchev*. I thank the publishers for their permission to redeploy this material.

My principal academic debts are to my PhD supervisors, Professor Geoffrey Hosking and Dr. Susan Morrissey. Geoffrey made the whole project possible; like many others, I have benefited enormously from his great contribution to the study of Russian history. Susan much expanded my view of Soviet history and rigorously appraised every detail of my work. It was a privilege to work with them both. The late Professor Lindsey Hughes, who acted as my backup supervisor in the earlier part of my research, provided much valued support, advice, and ideas. Dr. Stephen Lovell and Dr. Jeremy Smith read my work with both care and insight, helping me considerably. I am also indebted to Professor Lewis Siegelbaum and Dr. Stephen Bittner, whose detailed feedback enriched my understanding of these matters and allowed me to improve the manuscript distinctly. As an undergraduate at Christ Church, Oxford, I was introduced to the advanced study of modern European and Russian history by Dr. Katya Andreyev, to whom I remain grateful.

The following dispensed specialist knowledge, key suggestions, practical help, morale-boosting kindnesses, or scholarly comradeship—and/or facilitated the indispensable employment that helped underwrite the project at crucial moments: Dr. Lesley Abrams, Dr. Scott Anthony, Dr. Martin Conway, Rob Dale, Dr. Sarah Davies, Professor Julian Graffy, Dr. James Harris, Daniel Levitsky, Dr. Shaun Morcom, Dr. David Priestland, Professor Lyndal Roper, S. A. Sedykh, Dr. Simon Skinner, Anna Solev'eva, and Dr. Chris Ward. The team at Northern Illinois University Press, including Amy Farranto, Susan Bean, and Julia Fauci, have been truly excellent from start to end. Errors and infelicities are of course my own responsibility.

Research was principally undertaken at the State Archive of the Russian Federation (Main and RSFSR branches), the Russian State Archive of the Economy, the Central Archive of the City of Moscow, the Russian State Archive of Social and Political History, the National Archives at Kew, the British Library, the Library of the School of Slavonic and East European Studies, the Library of the London School of Economics, the Library of Congress, and the Russian State Library. I thank the librarians and archivists of these institutions and am especially grateful for the kindness, good humor, and specialist advice that met me in the Russian archives.

I would like to thank my mother-in-law, R. A. Shikova for her kindness and hospitality; my sister, Gillian Lockyer, and her family; and my brother, Dr. David V. Smith, for reading the manuscript and for sharing insights over many years. My much-loved wife, Larisa, helped to create the conditions in which I could complete this book, not least by being a wonderful mother of our daughter, Sonia. Sonia has inspired me and been my source of delight since her birth during those sleepless weeks just before I submitted my dissertation. My parents, Brian and Dorothy Smith, have always and without hesitation given me far more support of all kinds than I surely deserve, and I dedicate this book to them with love and admiration.

d.	*delo*, file (located in given catalogue of given archival fund)
domkom	(pl. *domkomy*) house committee
domoupravlenie	house administration
f.	*fond*, archival fund (collection)
GARF	State Archive of the Russian Federation
GlavAPU	Main Administration of Architecture and Planning (Moscow Soviet)
Glavmosstroi	Main Moscow Construction Trust
gorispolkom	city soviet executive committee
Gosplan	State Planning Committee
Gossnab	State Committee for Material and Equipment Supply
Gosstroi	State Construction Committee
krai	large territory (administrative unit)
kvartal	neighborhood district
l.	*list,* folio page in archival file
mikroraion	housing "microdistrict"
obkom	oblast' party committee
oblast'	province (administrative unit)
oblispolkom	oblast' soviet executive committee
op.	*opis*, catalogue of archival fund

Presidium	the redesignated Politburo between 1952 and 1966
propiska	(pl. *propiski*) residence permit (stamped in the internal passport)
raion	city district
raisovet	city district soviet
RGAE	Russian State Archive of the Economy
RGASPI	Russian State Archive of Social and Political History
shosse	highway (chaussée)
sovnarkhoz	council of national economy (major Khrushchev-era regional economic/administrative unit)
Sovnarkom	Soviet of People's Commissariats; replaced by the Council of Ministers as the chief organ of central government after the Second World War
subbotnik	day of voluntary work (on a Saturday)
tipovoi proekt	(pl. *tipovye proekty*) standardized construction design
TsAGM	Central Archive of the City of Moscow
Tsekombank	*Tsentral'nyi Kommunal'nyi Bank*, Municipal Bank
TsSU	*Tsentral'nyi Statisticheskoe Upravlenie*, Central Statistical Administration
ulitsa	street
val	street (historically, "rampart")
vedomstvo	"department"/agency of state
voskresnik	day of voluntary work (on a Sunday)
ZhEK	housing-operation bureau (*zhilishchno-ekspluatatsionnye kontory*; pl. ZhEKi)

Limits of Sacrifice

While . . . you were building your dacha in the Moscow suburbs,
the Black Marias were ceaselessly darting from street to street, and
the secret policemen were knocking at doors and ringing bells.

—**Aleksandr Solzhenitsyn,** *The Gulag Archipelago*

[W]e cleansed ourselves of the crimes Stalin committed and
showed that affirming Soviet power and the ideas of Marxism-
Leninism did not demand such bloodletting.

—**Nikita Khrushchev, memoirs**

During *perestroika*, an activist from the Memorial pressure group developed a new
archaeology of the city of Moscow. With vociferous precision, he catalogued the
killing fields and burial sites of the Great Terror, places such as Butovo and Strogino,
the Donskoi Monastery, the Kalitnikovskoe Cemetery.[1] Yet the old backdrop and
the evidence of violence had often disappeared. Instead, a contrasting cityscape
tended to encroach, dominated by the vast apartment blocks that had transformed
urban space and popular conditions since the 1950s. Architects had built welfare
on terror—and durably so. The policies behind their projects sustained the Soviet
Union for nearly forty years after Stalin's death. Scratching Moscow's concrete
exposes the contradictions that kept the system going.

The history of the Soviet Union as a whole, like that of its capital, contains several defining paradoxes, and perhaps the biggest is this: the party-government that
viciously terrorized the population also protected and fostered its progress. From
its earliest days, the revolution unleashed terrible violence—and constructed new
frameworks of individual possibility. Stalinism became the bloodiest of Russian

epochs, during which the basis of the Soviet welfare apparatus was hewn out. Later, under Khrushchev and then his successors, citizens had access to the most universal of welfare systems, but their rights, overall, were partial and unanchored, and the possibility of a reasonable life was uncertain. These successive stages of Soviet rule were separated by qualitative shifts, just as they were bounded by underlying continuities. Though never resolved, the historic paradox at the core of Soviet rule became more workable as time progressed.

Soviet history's cardinal fact is the willful destruction of human life on an epic scale. Yet terror and catastrophe cannot be explained without reference to the liberations, enlightenments, and material improvements that were equally inherent to the project as a whole. Stalinist rule (1928–1953) was ruthlessly progressive. Its reasoned sacrifices were most barbarously expressed in the camps of the Gulag, where the security services simultaneously terrorized prisoners and established a functioning environment of Sovietization. Here prisoners were subjected to the most terrible conditions in order, apparently, to create a new world.[2] After the Great Fatherland War (1941–1945), sacrifice was increasingly sidelined as the motor of policy, and the construction of better living conditions steadily resulted. Late Stalinism (1945–1953) was an arbitrary and cruel system, and post-Stalinism retained some of its characteristics, but both were, as time went on, increasingly (if always inconsistently) more beneficent than wartime and prewar Stalinist rule. Over time, the aims of the party-government were thus several. Its attempts to raise living standards in the 1950s were as purposeful as its deliberate sacrifice of earlier generations. The Soviet system begat welfare and terror with equal logic, though after 1945 it increasingly sought to improve popular conditions for their own sake.

This book concerns one of the most revealing and extensive of the resulting Soviet welfare measures, the mass urban housing program. It was one of the greatest social reforms of modern European history, though it is only starting to attract the attention of historians.[3] Between 1956 and 1963, per capita housing construction in the USSR was by far the highest in Europe, transforming the Soviet cityscape and improving the lives of tens of millions of citizens. New apartments were occupied by single families, so they were "separate" and not "communal"; they had a bathroom, a kitchen, a hallway, and, most typically, two multi-use rooms. As perhaps four or five family members shared forty square meters or so of total space, the dwellings were cramped and functional, and often of low quality, but their proliferation still amounted to an extraordinary upswing in the well-being of the population. Prefabricated apartment houses—often five stories, and broader than they were high—were constructed across the Soviet Union. They were built quickly from concrete and preassembled parts, their exteriors hastily whitewashed, their stairwells narrow and badly lighted, and lacking elevators. Known as *khrushchevki*, they presented a forbidding similitude that created one of the most recognizable signatures of the Khrushchev era (c.1953–1964).[4] Yet it was precisely their economical modesty and mass replication that made possible an unprecedented improvement in living standards. The program's social impact, epoch-defining qualities, and structural deficiencies were each greater than those of the new National Health Service in Britain.

For historians and contemporaries alike, the housing program exemplified the material culture and socio-ideological changes of the Khrushchev era. Yet the rudiments of an urban housing program actually took hold during the closing stages of the Great Fatherland War, as a barely avoidable response to the mass destruction of that conflict, and then advanced substantially during the years of late Stalinism. In this book, the purpose is to ask how and why the program was launched in its particular scale and form between 1944 and 1964. At the core of the answer lies an unexpected phenomenon: complex property relations as an essential driver of the program and, more broadly, as a central dynamic of the Soviet system. This neglected approach makes possible a new analysis of the impact of the Great Fatherland War and the death of Stalin on the Soviet Union.

In Kira Muratova's acclaimed film of 1971, *The Long Goodbye*, the female lead, Evgeniia, declares to a group of acquaintances, "Make yourselves at home. It's not our house . . . but it's our house all the same."[5] Ownership rights had attained an ambiguous, complicated, but workable structure by the end of the Khrushchev era—one that is conjured up in passing by Muratova's Evgeniia—and would broadly persist in such a form until the end of the Soviet Union. This complexity stands in contrast to customary views of the great simplification that apparently marked Soviet property relations. Private property had, after all, been abolished in a series of measures between 1917 and 1922.

New legal tenures and informal arrangements replaced their capitalist and conventional predecessors, however, and at their heart the citizen's status as an individual owner persisted and even flourished. The Soviet urban housing fund was always divided into several tenures; it was never somehow "nationalized." There even existed the tenure of "personal property" (*lichnaia sobstvennost'*), which allowed a citizen to own his home, legally, albeit within novel constraints and on the terms of "socialist morality." Local soviets and other state institutions such as industrial enterprises also owned housing space. Yet their tenants, who would become the majority of the population, often claimed to enjoy a form of ownership over their space, thanks to their increasingly secure and particularly Soviet rights of occupancy. All Soviet tenures thus allowed the resident to exercise a substantial share of de jure or de facto ownership. This share would strengthen during wartime and late Stalinist reconstruction and during the Khrushchev-era mass housing program that followed. With officials deliberately manipulating the extent and substance of individual ownership as a tool to increase the volume of housing construction, a fundamental expansion in the individual's possibility of ownership took place. Individual ownership helped to navigate the wartime emergency and to push forward the grand project of Khrushchev. Governing principles motivated by beneficence and the pursuit of paradise facilitated this approach.

Three motifs were encoded into the ideology of Soviet urban housing: "sacrifice," "beneficence," and "paradise," which contingent circumstances would in turn make the drivers of policy making. The dogma of sacrifice, according to which living conditions were ruthlessly subordinated to the fulfillment of industrial, military, or prestige priorities, was the force that made crash urbanization and industrialization possible. It produced a housing profile in the 1930s that was dominated by barracks and hostels, with pockets of luxury for the elite. The dogma of beneficence was manifested by the ruling order's self-conscious determination to improve living conditions immediately and for their own sake. It generated some of the revolutionary housing reforms that immediately followed 1917, and also made possible the very high level of housing construction under Khrushchev. The dogma of paradise—using housing to create a way of life appropriate to communist ideals—gave rise to the promises to abolish private property from 1917, the isolated experiments in model communal living of the 1920s, and the consciousness-changing aspects of the mass housing program at the high-water mark of the Khrushchev era, when housing was a mechanism for pushing society from socialism to communism. While paradise was always the ultimate goal, it was the explicit and immediate target only in the third stage of this scheme.

This tripartite framework can be compared with Vladimir Paperny's dualistic concept of the two cultures of Soviet architecture: culture one and culture two. Paperny argues that the history of Soviet architecture, especially in the 1920s and 1930s, proceeded according to a binary dynamic. The 1920s architecture of "culture one" was characterized, for example, by forces that were "horizontal" (that is, internationalist), "uniform" (or spatially universalizing and democratic), and "collective." Stalinist "culture two" was the opposite: it was "vertical" (or nationally inspired), spatially "hierarchical," and "individual."[6] Although Paperny's main discussion ends with the death of Stalin, he shows that post-Stalin architecture had some features of "culture one." Beneficence and paradise form a rough match with culture one, and sacrifice would be an aspect of culture two. The three motifs of sacrifice, beneficence, and paradise, deeply embedded in Soviet ideology and rising in turn to determine the housing program's practical course, reflect some of the dynamic of Paperny's argumentation. Exploring how (and determining when) one motif replaced another as the motive force of policy lightly structures the argumentation of this book. This framework also illuminates the prehistory of the urban housing program, from 1917 to 1941.

Origins of the Origins—The Prehistory of Soviet Mass Housing

The notion of an urban paradise, and specifically of a housing stock that existed for the good of the proletariat, was encoded into Soviet ideology from the start. Marx's precept—"From each according to his abilities, to each according to his needs"—was the self-conscious principle of the housing redistribution that began in 1917 and might have been inscribed on every identical *khrushchevka*.[7] *The Communist Manifesto* of 1848 placed the legal precondition of the future housing program at the heart of the Communist approach: "the theory of the Communists may be summed up in the single sentence: Abolition of private property." Engels elaborated the principle in *The Housing Question* of 1872, as did the Bolsheviks' first party program in 1903.[8] Lenin's utopian text of 1917, *The State and Revolution*, looked to "the letting of houses owned by the whole people to individual families," that would ultimately be "rent-free." Private property was abolished shortly after, following the revolution, and the redistributions of that period—sometimes spontaneous, sometimes directed by officials—conformed to such a vision of paradise.[9]

That most characteristic form of revolutionary housing, the communal apartment, resulted. This was a new departure in modern Europe. Residents "packed" themselves or were "packed" into former bourgeois dwellings or other redesignated housing spaces, which were managed by residents, municipal employees, and party representatives.[10] In the communal apartments that resulted, workers would receive one room per family (if they were lucky) and share the bathroom, kitchen, and other common spaces with strangers. This represented a radical improvement in the fortunes of some workers, and a cataclysmic decline for the former property owners. The first flush of revolutionary transformation made the communal apartment seem a figment of paradise. Meanwhile, the idealistic but very peripheral experiments of house communes (*dom kommuny*) in the 1920s were a striking innovation, the purest expression of a would-be urban paradise. Their explicit aim was to release a new kind of communal consciousness and to reduce class differences in a highly conditioned but benign environment. Original architectural designs included A. S. Fufaev's Dukstroi housing cooperative in Moscow (1927–1928), and the communal housing complex of the People's Commissariat of Finance, which was completed between 1928 and 1930 according to the blueprints of Moisei Ginzburg and Ignatii Milinis.[11] The latter building was particularly celebrated; its five stories combined the sharp lines of constructivism with equally experimental open-plan interiors. Its shared facilities were the result of careful and innovative design rather than a by-product of shortages. But these experiments were little more than monuments to the revolution. Tiny numbers of people lived in them.

The very exceptionalism of the house-communes emphasized that paradise was far off in the future. Founding ideology and Bolshevik policies thus recognized the need not only for such visions of paradise but also for simpler improvements before paradise would come. The beneficent housing reforms that resulted were revolutionary in comparison with the tsarist past, but their immediate goal was not the transformation of consciousness. Instead, they required the straightforward material improvement of housing conditions on principles of radical equality. The second party program (March 1919) demanded that the revolution should "strive for the improvement of housing conditions of the working masses; for the elimination of overcrowding and unsanitary, old housing quarters; for the elimination of unfit housing." Calling also for "the rational resettlement of workers," this amounted to a better life for workers, rather than a communist experiment.[12]

Mass redistribution was legally founded on new tenures. These tenures were revolutionary, but their precise form still reflected unavoidable compromises, and their ruling principles derived from beneficence, not paradise. "Personal property," by which up to half the urban housing stock was owned during the 1920s, was the outstanding example of pragmatism in property relations.[13] In the context of the semi-marketized New Economic Policy (NEP) of 1921 to 1928, these tenures bonded individual energies, personal motivations, and citizens' own resources onto goals that were partly universal and collective. These compromise tenures existed because state bodies lacked the capacity to effect an immediate and proto-communist improvement in people's experience of housing.

Similarly, communal apartments were the result of practical, legal, and ideological compromises. They might have been born in the shadow of paradise, but their ongoing existence in the 1920s (and indeed throughout and beyond the life of the Soviet Union) resulted from chronic shortages. Families shared housing space because it was scarce; and it was scarce because of the failure to build new housing on a substantial scale until the 1940s. Despite common assumptions, there is simply no convincing evidence that communal apartments were deliberately designed as instruments for transforming urban dwellers' consciousness, or regulating their lives through mutual surveillance.[14] Yet these apartments still illustrated a newly redistributive and superficially equitable attitude to the allocation of dwellings. By aiming, however crudely, to make adequate living standards more widely available, the entrenchment of communal apartments was driven by a beneficent approach that grew out of the revolution. The motif of mild beneficence thus replaced that of paradise as the imperative of housing policy during the NEP. By the end of the 1920s, it had given way to sacrifice.

During the industrialization program that began in 1928 and continued until 1941, housing conditions were sacrificed utterly to the higher needs of the five-year plans.[15] In contrast to the period 1917–1928, the party-government was simply not interested in the housing conditions of the masses. While the construction industry expanded in the 1930s, urbanization proceeded much more rapidly than the provision of housing for new migrant workers, and the greatly disproportionate focus on expensive luxury apartment houses for elites was entrenched. The result was the miserable sacrifice of the workforce's living standards. To be sure, the paradigm of sacrifice had earlier origins and expressions: Lenin's *The State and Revolution* was based on the premise that, while the proletariat would enjoy an immediate rise in standards of living after a revolution, the current generation as a whole must endure great sacrifice in order to guarantee the revolution's viability. Stalin pursued this blueprint with terrible literalness. The consequences for living standards were drastic and often tragic; most prosaically, the urban housing profile was flattened, as the number of inhabitants per room rose from 2.71 in 1926 to 3.91 in 1940.[16] John Scott, an American steelworker in Magnitogorsk, remembered that housing "construction was always behind schedule. It was 1933 before the first house was occupied. The quality of the work was very bad. The roofs leaked, as did the water pipes. Foundations sank, walls cracked." For Scott, industrialization was premised on sacrifice: "Money was spent like water, men froze, hungered and suffered, but the [plant] construction work went on with a disregard for individuals."[17]

Across the Soviet Union, as peasants flocked to new factories and the urban population grew rapidly, workers often found themselves living in tents, cellars, unheated barracks, boiler rooms, corners of their workplaces, perhaps having no more than the same bunk—and sheets—as a coworker on a different shift. And yet official rhetoric at this time constructed a different world. A Central Committee decree of June 1931 insisted that as the five-year plan unfolded, "the questions of the urban economy (housing, water supply, street lighting, heating, sanitation, transport, external amenities, bath houses, laundries, communal dining) acquire the strongest significance."[18] This was entirely false. Yet the worked-out notion of a beneficent urban improvement, in which housing was a principal component, was so embedded in Soviet ideology that it infected policy pronouncements even when the direct effect of policy was actually its reverse, the sacrificial.

This situation persisted during much of the 1930s. The end of the Terror in 1938, however, marked the onset of a more rational approach to politics and administration. Such rationality caused a modified approach to housing policy: sacrifice began very tentatively to give way to beneficence as the underlying determinant of urban policy. Section 4 of the third five-year plan, approved by the eighteenth party congress of March 1939, made a more sober assessment of urban conditions than before and adopted the more realistically calculated promise of an additional 35 million square meters of urban housing space for 1938–1942.[19] This political and administrative rationality was the basis of the beneficent approach. The post-Terror, prewar shift to more regularized and predictable administration might locate the immediate origins of a beneficent housing policy in 1938 or 1939. Statistics for Moscow gathered by Timothy Colton show that the average amount of housing space built in the three years between 1938 and 1940 was 68 percent higher than the average for the preceding three years.[20] A film of 1957, *The House I Live In*, shows a building site on the eve of war, soon reduced to rubble.[21] The war ended the third five-year plan, and the shift in planning was largely confined to paper.

Such a brief burst does not make a housing program. In terms of housing policy at least, it was the war that changed Stalinism. Thanks to the war, the ideological motif of beneficent improvement, and later that of paradise, would emerge from the confines of rhetoric in order to influence the specific formulation of policy. That foreshadows one of the book's indispensable frameworks: the interpretative problem of periodization.

Borders of Stalinism—Periodization and the Creation of the Program

Soviet history divides conveniently into periods associated with political leaders. Many historical problems seem naturally to fall within their boundaries. The urban housing program has long been associated with the Khrushchev era. Yet an obvious hypothesis is that wartime destruction must have led to an immediate reconstruction drive of significant proportions or else complete urban breakdown would have resulted; that a "proto-program" must have existed or Khrushchev could not have created his program so quickly; that, in sum, immediate postwar reconstruction must have been intimately connected to the mass housing program of the Khrush-chev years.

This hypothesis compelled a search for historical evidence across a twenty-one-year period from the onset of reconstruction early in 1944 to the fall of Khrushchev late in 1964, and then the pursuit of argument against the grain of conventional periodization. Yet historiographical attitudes to this conventional boundary between Stalinism and post-Stalinism—to the newly significant question of how much 1953 represented a fundamental disjunction in Soviet politics and life—have already changed, and enough work has already been done to derail the old certainties. Drawing on long immersions in the archival record, historians of the postwar Soviet Union now argue that the impact of the Great Fatherland War was as significant as that of Stalin's death, and that some Khrushchev-era policies originated in the period before 1953.[22] Aleksandr Pyzhikov and Aleksandr Danilov have posited that the parameters of a reformed Soviet polity emerged after 1945 and would persist, in part, to the 1980s thanks to the new international configuration of superpower rivalry.[23] Pyzhikov has also located in the late Stalinist years the origins of specific reforms that are conventionally associated with Khrushchev;[24] and Rudol'f Pikhoia has presented aspects of the same case.[25] Yoram Gorlizki and Oleg Khlevniuk have drawn a careful picture of late Stalinist politics, which contains evidence of officials drafting reforms: reforms that would be routinely shelved, either before or after they reached Stalin's desk.[26]

Scholars have probed the 1953 disjuncture in varying degrees of detail to explore such issues as trade policy,[27] official approaches to science,[28] the emergence of a new party program,[29] and urban planning.[30] Others, led by Elena Zubkova, have explored popular moods and opinions, revealing that some of the cultural and social varieties assumed to have been released by Stalin's death were actually locked into people's experience of late Stalinism.[31] The research for this book built on some of these arguments and proceeded in parallel with others but its approach is distinctive in using a raft of archival material to explore a particular topic with precisely equal attention (year for year) paid to the late Stalinist and to the Khrushchev eras. It thus forms an original case study of the comparative effects of the war and of Stalin's demise on the USSR.

The most tangible characteristic of the war was its intense physical destructiveness, with the loss of as many as 27 million soldiers and civilians, the total or partial elimination of tens of thousands of settlements, and the severe dislocation of industry and communications.[32] While "desertification" accompanied the German retreat,[33] mass destruction was coincident with all stages of the fighting, and its effects spread far beyond the zones of combat. Among the most important results was the terrible urban housing shortage, which was so acute that the country needed unprecedented construction merely to return the housing fund to its miserable prewar size, and thus to ensure a basically functioning urban economy. This was in turn the minimum pre-requisite for fulfilling such priority postwar tasks as the rebuilding of heavy industry.

The major systemic motivation for a new kind of housing policy was the perpetuation of Stalinism itself, but this was a modified form of Stalinism, one that was decisively different even from its tentatively reformed post-Terror incarnation of 1939–1941.

During the extreme emergency of the war, administration and popular experience were partly based on new forms of flexibility and freedom, and necessity ensured that the relationship between ordinary people and Soviet power became more collaborative. New expectations flowed from the war to the "late Stalinism" of 1945–1953. Recent research makes it difficult to sustain the stark contention that a fierce clampdown followed the victory, though some major historians still maintain that a primary continuity in Stalinism outweighed any postwar changes. Amir Weiner argues that while the war was the revolution's purgatory, relegitimating the Soviet project and providing people with the networks of patronage and sociability to facilitate their postwar lives, it was also one of several Soviet episodes marked by the common desire to purify and control the population. The urge to "excise" undesirables and enforce uniformity united the subperiods of Stalinism more than anything else might have divided them; it drove, for example, both the Terror of 1937–1938 and the anti-Semitic campaigns at the end of Stalin's life. More concisely, Robert Service argues that, after 1945, "Stalin's mind was like a stopped clock," stuck in the 1930s.[34]

Yet victory encouraged officials of varying seniority to seek modifications in the Stalinist system. The goal was to learn from the tumultuous policy experiences of the 1930s and the war, to take into account popular expectation and wartime experience, and thus to make the system unshakeable. From time to time, and always when Stalin was on vacation, even members of the Politburo fruitlessly mooted shifts in policy and approach.[35] The war empowered some officials—a cross section of medium-ranking and senior cadres in the central machine, working across various areas of policy, but much less those at the apex of power or those running the localities—to rethink the relationship between the "state" (specifically, themselves) and the population.[36] With varying degrees of explicitness, they argued that a new moral imperative existed as a result of the war: that socialism, and thus 1917, only made sense if people's wartime service was acknowledged in material terms. Their numbers might have been small, but it does not seem unreasonable to mark out a newly enlightened strand of Soviet officialdom.

Between 1944 and 1950 these officials developed new housing policies that were more beneficent than sacrificial, and thus different in kind from those of the 1930s, but these policies lacked a statement of coordinating intent and were fragmented in their details. Immediate postwar reconstruction delivered an unprecedented increase in the urban housing fund, but still one that was highly inadequate. Late Stalinist power pondered the improvement of popular living standards yet remained arbitrary and violent, treating the population with contempt. Between 1951 and 1954, the development of policy, technology, and expertise accelerated as officials better understood the extent of the ongoing emergency. But developments went largely unimplemented, and the enhanced capacity remained latent. It took

Khrushchev's leadership to make radical use of this existing potential. The single greatest moment was the introduction of the housing decree of July 1957, in which the party-government promised to eliminate the shortage by the end of the 1960s.

Such a revised periodization demands an interpretation of the genesis and development of the urban housing program that cannot be reduced by the metaphor of "thaw" and does not really fit the paradigm of "de-Stalinization." Contemporaries, commentators, and historians have long described a post-Stalin thaw, in which a Stalinist winter gave way in 1953 to a new Soviet spring or at least to milder political and sociocultural weather. This "thaw" continued to 1956, in some accounts, and to various endpoints in the 1960s, in others. The term was coined by Il'ia Erenburg in his eponymous novella of May 1954 and has enjoyed an unlikely afterlife; "the thaw" became a routine designation for the Khrushchev era, or for the period from 1953 to 1968. Yet while historians' use of the metaphor has sometimes been reflexive, it has often been highly self-conscious. Scholars and Khrushchev's contemporaries alike have exploited its multiple implications, analyzing the subtleties of change during the period with reference to unpredictable weather, to variable climatic cycles, to thaws and freezes of different lengths. Historians have probed these consequences of the political temperature in sometimes inventive ways, finding new elaborations of the old metaphor.[37] Even the most subtle and skeptical deconstructions of "Thaw" have been predicated on its continued use and ongoing evolution.[38]

A different possibility remains: the enterprise can be abandoned.[39] Historical periods are not usually given metaphorical labels, though they sometimes are; and historical knowledge is now such that the Soviet 1950s and 1960s can no longer be conceptualized with a single metaphor, however venerable or adaptable. A term that seemed adequate for the study of cultural forms, intelligentsia responses, and episodes in high politics—on which much early scholarship on the period was focused—cannot now explain even these aspects, let alone a fuller range of historical developments. The argument here does not use the old term or seek a substitute but engages, however, with "de-Stalinization," a concept with more analytical potential.[40] In this study, de-Stalinization is a tool that opens up the border between Stalinism and post-Stalinism for historical exploration, but the concept is not in itself adequate to explain the post-Stalin period. The origins of the housing program lay in late Stalinism, and the program responded to Stalinist economic imperatives, but it only assumed mass dimensions after Stalin's demise, when rights and respect could at least partly structure the discourses and practices of society and politics. This was a reform whose success depended on Stalinism and de-Stalinization alike.

Citizen Autonomy and Totalitarianism

Neither "thaw" nor de-Stalinization can explain one of the most important drivers of the urban housing program: citizens' autonomous activities. In the absence of adequate state capacity, late Stalinist housing policy deliberately empowered citizens to take positive and autonomous actions to improve their own conditions. Expressions of permitted autonomy by individual citizens remained important—though less a matter of life and death—even in the context of the massive state inputs of the Khrushchev era. Officially forbidden but practically permitted activity by citizens was thus systemic to the urban housing economy throughout the period 1944-1964. Neither de-Stalinization nor (still less) "thaw" adequately conceptualizes the jagged evolution of these particular forces after 1953. By contrast, the rich historical scholarship on Stalinism and especially its 1930s variant provides an essential set of analytical tools with which to clarify the extent of individuals' autonomous activities from the 1940s to the 1960s.

A simplified scheme isolates two broad scholarly attitudes to citizen autonomy in the Stalinist system. Each attitude is somewhat catholic and brings together only generally similar approaches. First, the "neo-totalitarian" branch of historiography pioneered by Stephen Kotkin clarifies the existence of autonomous citizen responses inside a tightly restrained, limiting, repressive, but productive form of social organization, though this scholarship develops a model of state power that ultimately seems overdrawn. Kotkin coined the phrase "speaking Bolshevik" to headline his argument about the tight discursive frames within which Soviet citizens operated in 1930s Magnitogorsk.[41] These frames were not just a form of repression but also bound a linguistic universe to which citizens adapted for reasons of belief or pragmatism; people expressed themselves using the terms of the regime in order to seek out what they needed. Weiner, meanwhile, argues that people often "made sense" of the Great Fatherland War as robust individuals, who had become more substantial and personally authoritative as a consequence of their wartime experiences, but who were still confined and directed by set patterns of Soviet perspective.[42] These two historians therefore acknowledge that forms of individualism could be expressed in what was a powerfully totalitarian polity. The least compromising neo-totalitarian scholars minimize this possibility, arguing in some of their work that the revolution and Stalinism acted so powerfully on individuals as to make subjectively undesirable any thought or behavior that was outside the totalizing discourse.[43] It is the more expansive views of citizen autonomy developed by Kotkin and Weiner that are more convincing and evidentially reasonable, though, and which illuminate (without ultimately explaining) the range of behavior and attitudes of ordinary people and officials contained in the sources used here.

Citizen autonomy modulated by an intrusive state is clarified from an opposite angle by those social historians (of whom Sheila Fitzpatrick is the most influential example) who reject the notion of a totalizing ideology, and hence the capacity of regime-imposed discourse to control perceptions and condition outcomes.[44] For Fitzpatrick, the Stalinist regime could repress, kill, and destroy; it was capable of such feats as the collectivization of agriculture, which showed the extent of its brute power. Yet individual citizens were constantly capable, on an everyday level, of rejecting the spirit and detail of official propaganda; they might engage with its categories in order to exploit them, or they might obtain the things they needed to survive by other means.[45] This is a practice-driven approach that implicitly sets up state and society as two interacting but separate partners.[46] Research on Soviet trade between 1917 and 1953 reveals the necessary existence, for survival reasons, of black markets and private sectors.[47] They had nothing to do with ideology, and their basic importance to people's survival chances flourished independently of official discourse. Patterns of popular discourse have been discerned that were governed by motifs entirely outside state direction, such as "us" (the people) and "them" (the boss class in the broad sense).[48] A revised Marxist approach finds a "working class" shattered and atomized by a simultaneously overbearing and ineffective state, coping with emergency conditions with little help.[49] In Moshe Lewin's "quicksand society" of the first five-year plan (1928–1932), a chaotic citizen autonomy, inflected by the new urban workers' surviving peasant attitudes, existed inside a would-be totalitarian order that flailed at its objectives.[50] Meanwhile, in particular situations, such as Ivanovo Province (oblast') in the 1930s, genuine resistance and even anti-"regime" collective action took place.[51] In one way or another, these various interpretations and arguments depict a high level of citizen autonomy that existed in ways that the regime did not desire.

For all their intrinsic interest, however, examples of full-scale resistance cannot be a source of generalization, while everyday resistance explains only some aspects of people's experience and only some of their transactions with authority. Popular disjunction from an officialdom that was motivated by a different set of interests also does not explain the dynamics of Soviet urban housing by the 1940s and beyond. Meanwhile, in the urban housing economy of the late Stalinist and Khrushchev eras, the state lacked a totalizing aspiration, much less ability, though ordinary citizens sometimes continued to adopt official discourse and behavior in order to promote their own self-interest. Ritualistic conformance was hardly more important than instinctive everyday survival (and was not the same thing). Instead, by 1944, housing policy deliberately engaged the autonomous input of citizens in a natural, increasingly predictable, and systemically consistent process. A largely organic development, it required collaboration and compromise.[52] State agencies of different capacities and strengths sought to harness the chaotic and variably effective survival strategies of individuals, families, and groups of neighbors or coworkers. Some citizens' practices chimed with official discourse, while others operated outside it. "State" and "society" meshed as they faced the housing crisis between 1944 and 1964; the former did not only try to control the latter, and the latter did not only operate independently of the former. Their boundaries were so fluid that they utterly infused each other.[53] This did not make the Soviet Union a totalized monolith, nor did it define the Soviet way of doing things, but it illustrated a single example of collaboration and shared interest. By contrast, Stalin's collectivization and Khrushchev's party-government reorganizations were major examples of how the center frequently imposed unnatural-seeming changes on lower structures—sometimes viciously, sometimes just disruptively.

Various scholars have shown that party and government recognized the urgent need to engage with the population during the war, and not crudely direct it, thereby releasing a flow of autonomous and effective popular responses.[54] When it came to developing a policy for the reconstruction of urban housing, at a time when resources were scarce and the construction industry was particularly enfeebled, it was natural that the party-government would seek to mobilize the resources and energies of the population in the reconstruction of their own housing stock. Explicit cooperation between "state" and "society," by which the former enabled the autonomous responses of the latter, underpinned one of the most important reconstruction measures: the May 1944 decree that granted state credits to individual citizens who wanted to construct their own house. Relative citizen autonomy was also the context in which citizens made use of the legal system and the patronage-based possibilities of appeal that surrounded it in order to regain or retain control of housing whose possession had changed hands during the war. The official requirement of individual initiative persisted during the Khrushchev era, though by then it was more tightly regulated, and the much greater extent of state construction made it less crucial. Individuals' construction of their own houses continued on a major scale until the end of the 1950s; and shareholding in cooperative housing, an activity that located citizen autonomy perfectly within the ideological and practical organization of the system, was revivified in measures of 1958 and 1962.

The system tolerated unofficial, even illegal, individual survival strategies and effectively built them integrally into the urban housing program. Examples include the retrospective legal formalization of houses that citizens had built without any kind of authorization during the postwar emergency or the tolerated combination of official and illegal methods used by citizens to exchange apartments, which took place on an expanding scale in the early 1960s. The systemic immanence of these processes and their evolution within limits is further exemplified by patronage. During late Stalinism, people often sought the protection of powerful patrons, however tenuous their connection to them, in order to acquire or retain housing space. They used recognized channels, such as correspondence with Supreme Soviet deputies, to seek out the highest patrons of last resort. Under Khrushchev, by contrast, people were increasingly aware that systematized contact with their trade union (supplemented, admittedly, by favors from acquaintances or support from one's workplace collective) could yield the desired result.[55] Moreover, Stalinist realities of patronage and clientelism were often overwritten by a discourse of gratitude and gift,[56] which was antipathetic to the Khrushchev era's increasingly voiced discourse and practice of rights. This makes for a seemingly organic blend of permitted autonomy and tolerated but unauthorized behavior, which changed over time but whose basic characteristics explain important parts of the urban housing program's course between the war and the fall of Khrushchev.

Welfare, Property, Rights

In the context of this collaborative relationship, citizens' rights of "ownership" and welfare reinforced each other. According to neo-totalitarian scholarship, one consequence of the post-Enlightenment trajectory common to Russia, the USSR,

Western Europe, the United States, and elsewhere was the welfare state. It was a crucial component in their universal modernity.[57] Characteristically, Kotkin argues, "because the welfare state rested on a certain social logic and a number of transferable social practices, it was viable in a variety of political settings, including Stalin's Russia." Scholars of all stripes seem to accept the label and the logic of the "Soviet welfare state."[58] But the comparative history of welfare reveals cardinal differences as well as similarities between socialist and capitalist variants of modernity, and the Soviet Union was never a welfare state. The combined system of rights that governed Soviet citizens' access to housing—derived in turn from the relationship between property and welfare—was antipathetic to that which underwrote the welfare states of the West, from which in this sense the USSR was different in kind. Paradoxically, the USSR derived far more of its property relations, and less of its welfare system, from a common European history than scholars have tended to acknowledge.

According to Asa Briggs's classic definition, a welfare state is characterized by the guarantee of minimum incomes, regardless of market imperatives; the alleviation of conditions during, for example, old age or unemployment; and social services of high standards that are available universally. In other words, a welfare state is a state in which both a "minimum" standard of life is guaranteed and equal access to "optimum" standards of social provision evolves.[59] Such a coherent and well-developed condition did not exist either in Kotkin's Magnitogorsk or indeed anywhere else in the Soviet Union in the 1930s, when material conditions were explicitly sacrificed to the higher needs of industrialization. It was no part of late Stalinism either.

Meanwhile, the post-Stalin system went far beyond the scope of Western welfare states, which were still constrained by free markets and private property, and became something quite different: the all-people's state. The Soviet project adopted this label at the height of the Khrushchev era, following the assertion at the twenty-first party congress in 1959 that socialism was victorious, and that the transition to communism could begin. It was a stage marked by popular participation, revived Leninist idealism, and state investment, making possible, apparently, a newly vigorous attempt to modify the consciousness of the Soviet person while improving all aspects of his standard of living.[60] This ambition was exceptional, and brief, though not without results. It ensured that the Soviet system of welfare genuinely applied to much of life—not just to specific areas such as education, healthcare, and pensions, but to jobs, leisure, and housing; and everyone in principle had access to these goods, not just those who were unable to provide for themselves. At the height of the Khrushchev era, this depth and universality were founded on the supposition of impending paradise. While Nazi Germany and Fascist Italy also had welfare systems of unusual reach, they retained strongly limiting characteristics that contrasted to the Soviet Union's.[61] The prewar system of Soviet welfare was thus so feeble that it simply did not qualify as a welfare state, while the post-Stalin system was so universal that it went far beyond qualification, outstripping the criteria and becoming fundamentally different in kind from the welfare states of capitalist countries.

Briggs's definition makes it possible to draw one line of distinction between the USSR and Western welfare states. But it makes for a reductive approach, effectively counting up the benefits and assigning the polity a value. Instead, therefore, of arguing that when an unspecified critical mass of welfare is obtained, a state becomes a welfare state, it seems more promising to contend that the welfare states that emerged across Europe after 1945 were different in kind from what had gone before. They were not just made up of exactly the same entity, writ large. Bismarckian Germany was in its core different from the Federal Republic; the reforms of Asquith and Attlee were made of a different substance. Welfare states existed inside a postwar ideology of citizenhood that offered universal access to unprecedented norms of material well-being, based on a democratically substantiated system of rights.[62] By contrast, a Stalin-era discourse of rights, which became more widespread as a consequence of the war, was never given plausible, testable meaning. The late Stalinist polity remained arbitrary and flexed itself spasmodically, with caprice and cruelty. People's access to welfare was modulated accordingly.

This changed under Khrushchev. The aim of the housing program was redefined as every family's right to occupy a separate apartment within about a decade. Processes of application, distribution, and appeal were regularized and regulated in such a way as to make for a predictable system in which rights were an indispensable component. From the vantage point of 1964, these rights might well have seemed fixed, legitimate, and of undoubted durability. In fact they would survive until the collapse of the Soviet Union. They were so central to the entire system that it cannot really be imagined without them. But they coexisted alongside other areas of political, social, and economic activity where rights were absent, and they were imposed by a dominant and only murkily answerable center. Although everyday local life included a practical "democratic" component during the Khrushchev era and thereafter, the lack of overall democratic norms and the sometimes violent power of authoritarianism ensured that access to the USSR's vast welfarist scheme was not constitutionally predictable, citizen-backed, or democratically accountable in the way it was in contemporaneous welfare states in the West.

Another area of difference between these welfare states and the USSR was the purpose of welfare policy. On one level, the political reasons for the introduction of welfare measures were similar. The governments of the USSR and the countries of the West used welfare both as an end in itself, to improve the conditions of the people, and also for calculated political reasons, to maintain the stability of the system and the position in power of certain groups. Claus Offe, effectively following Marcuse, has argued that the postwar capitalist "peace formula" consisted in the obligation by state agencies to pay welfare benefits to citizens in need, and in trade unions' systemically integral role. Class struggle was therefore dissipated and an existing structure of power maintained.[63] This contention might be reductive and skewed, but it still throws light on the pragmatic compromises between power interests in welfare states, perhaps most explicitly in the West German corporatist settlement. Such influential theory was a ubiquitous background for

Cold War Sovietologists, even those of the Right. They tended to argue that a post-Stalin welfare settlement was simply a more efficient means than terror for the Communist Party to keep power: buying off the people rather than killing them.[64] Other scholars of the 1960s accepted that the entrenched Communist elite was exercising an interest but, being more coolheaded, these scholars argued that the precise moral motivation of its interest was not clear.[65]

Welfare systems existed in both the West and the USSR, therefore, for some broadly common political reasons. But the USSR used welfare for additional purposes. This was especially true during the late 1950s and early 1960s. Attempts were made to activate the potential of welfare policy to alter behavior and advance consciousness. In the sphere of housing, communal structures of everyday organization were promoted in the local housing microdistrict (or *mikroraion*). The Soviet approach also deployed surveillance as a built-in component of housing policy, in a range of highly particular supervisory mechanisms, which were as important under Khrushchev as they had been under Stalin. These powerful and sometimes violent tendencies far outpaced the capacities of state technologies in the contemporaneous West.

After Stalin, a highly particular set of welfare rights governed people's access to housing. These welfare rights reinforced property rights and did not diminish them. This powerful relationship between the two sets of rights has been neglected by historians of the Soviet Union. It is correct to argue that the mass housing program was only possible because private property had been abolished at the outset of the revolution. State agencies thereafter owned a high proportion of the housing stock, while land was owned in common by the people. Local soviets could manage the use of land, and central organs could push an ideological vision, avoiding external constraints of private power and wealth. If the statist basis of Soviet housing turned housing space into a welfare good and eventually a welfare right, it also generated a set of tenures that gave the individual citizen real rights of ownership over his dwelling. Unlike in the West, welfare and property explicitly strengthened each other.

The abolition of private property was not the same as the eradication of individual forms of ownership. These persisted in the urban housing funds of the Soviet Union. Local soviets and other agencies of the state had never been able to organize the requisition, administration, and maintenance of all urban housing. Tenurial arrangements were thus established that made the Soviet urban housing economy more consistent with the European tradition of property than historians allow for. Tenure was split into two general categories. Agencies of the state (broadly conceived) owned "socialist property," while individual citizens could own "personal property."[66] Soviets (the organs of local government), "departments" (*vedomstva*, or ministries, industrial enterprises, trade unions, academies, higher education institutes, and so on), and cooperatives could hold socialist property. Cooperatives were added to the housing stock between 1924 and 1937, and then again from 1958. They were often composed of employees of the same institution, who became shareholders in the cooperative, and their occupants had considerable legal rights over their own separate apartment but were not the formal owners (the cooperative itself was). Personal property in housing was something akin to a medium-term leasehold largely stripped of any cash-generating potential, and for much of the period covered by this book one-third of the urban housing stock fell inside this category. This was certainly a de jure form of individual ownership. It was not private property, because it was only for consumption with no capacity for raising revenue, acting as collateral, or dividing the population into competing economic interests. But the citizens who lived in state housing space could also claim a de facto form of individual ownership, and as the already secure terms of occupancy became ever more robust during this period, this came close to a watertight possession. Some of the jurisprudential principles and organizing practices on which this "possession" depended fell directly inside the European tradition and were part of a historical line that included Aristotle and Locke. The implications of how the property-welfare nexus was responsible for much of the organization, impetus, and lived experience of the urban housing program are profound.

Sources and Outline

All-union and uniform in its ambition, the housing program had diverse and varied effects. This book is based on largely untapped archival sources that cover the USSR as a whole, the Russian Republic (RSFSR), and the city of Moscow. It contains a new explanation for the origins and course of the program on an all-union level, which is also sensitive to republican and local variations. The focus is entirely on the urban part of the program (which was by far the most important) and usually stops at the front door; the domestic interior is significant here only insofar as it illustrates broader concerns about the development of the program.[67]

The argument derives from a wide range of sources, of which the most important types are evaluated at appropriate points in the book. A few general points might be made at the outset, however. The work draws on numerous archival documents, whose varied genres include correspondence drafted by ministers, reports written by local officials, statistics gathered by the Central Statistical Administration, and letters sent by citizens. Such sources were composed and archived by different bureaucratic sectors and bodies: city soviets in the regions and republics, the State Planning Committee (Gosplan), the Construction Committee of the Council of Ministers (Gosstroi), trade unions, ministries, the Councils of Ministers of both the USSR and the Russian Republic (RSFSR), and various others bodies. Carefully read, these sources release the voices of people of different stations; properly evaluated, they contain a considerable amount of new and useful information.

Yet they all represent an action by or encounter with some kind of agency of the state. At minimum, an official has filtered the contents of each document or selected it for further use in another part of the bureaucratic machine. This applies to the letters of citizens as much as to the notes of ministers. Addressed to state agencies or leading political figures and preserved by the bureaucracy, citizens' letters were often formed of standard discursive components and designed to attain characteristic objectives.

All these sources thus say a great deal about the Soviet state—but they also reveal much about the housing program. The range and extensive volume of documents, and the variety of sometimes competing state agencies from which they originated, facilitate crucial comparisons and cross-checks. Placed in the context of thousands of other documents, the experiences and words of non-state actors—of individual citizens—can be weighed for plausibility. Published Soviet sources such as newspapers, professional journals, and scholarly writings provide another type of evidential control, as does Soviet cultural production, including movies and novels. External voices—the archived comments of foreign diplomats, CIA reports, the writings of Western novelists and travelers—provide further evidence, to be used cautiously on its own terms and as a "control" on the most crucial foundation of this book, the Soviet state documents. Statistical evidence from archival sources, meanwhile, is famously problematic, subject to the distortions of central planning.[68] Historians have no choice but to make use of these figures and must find ways to compensate for their flaws. Controls on statistical evidence are imposed here by using data from different archival collections, gathered by different state institutions, and by drawing on plausible international comparisons.

The argument is divided into two parts and five chapters. Part 1 presents a chronological analysis of the program, in which the chronological division of the chapters is itself a statement of argumentation; and part 2 is a conceptualization of the program in terms of its unique nexus of property and welfare. The three chapters of part 1 are separated by two major turning points. First, in 1950–1951, officials recognized that the wartime and postwar measures they had put in place to tackle the housing shortage were inadequate and needed to be strengthened; then in 1957, the keynote housing decree on housing construction formally launched the program.

Chapter 1 (1944–1950) analyzes the extraordinarily destructive impact of the Great Fatherland War on the already existing housing crisis in the Soviet Union and explores the development and effect of reconstruction policies. These policies were numerous, sometimes major and sometimes minor; they included the individual housing construction scheme, the promotion of the technologies of standardized construction, and sporadically, the rationalization of the construction industry. These policy developments are placed in the context of a general approach to housing districts that promoted separate housing space while sometimes requiring communal participation: a formula that might be assumed to be Khrushchevian. While all this was sufficient to generate new levels of housing construction and reconditioning, policies remained uncoordinated and lacked the direction of political leadership. They benefited millions of people directly and up to a point, but their primary importance consisted in the architectural, technical, economic, and policy-making legacies that were passed on to a period when their latent qualities could be invigorated. These years from war to peace also bequeathed to the 1950s new malfunctions in the extreme economic centralization of Stalinism, with constraining and ultimately self-defeating consequences, which are analyzed in the closing section of the chapter.

In Chapter 2 (1951–1957), the launch of the urban housing program is presented as a process that straddled the last years of late Stalinism and the first four or five years following Stalin's death. The first year of this period was a crucial time, when authorities faced up to the postwar housing crisis in a more focused and systematic way than before. Adequate investment, however, did not follow until the mid-1950s, when existing capacity was consolidated and implemented, thanks in significant measure to Khrushchev's political leadership. The transitional period of 1951 to 1954 is explored in the first part of this chapter, and Khrushchev's longstanding personal role is analyzed next. Khrushchev's achievement was symbolized by a major decree of July 1957 that marked the formal launch of the housing program, promising to end the housing shortage within twelve years. At the end of 1957, housing policy seemed to be progressing along the rational, output-focused course demanded by the decree; the launch seemed to have culminated in success. The rational parameters within which the housing program now started to unfold are assessed in the second half of this chapter. They were characterized by factors that included the relative supremacy of technocrats such as Vladimir Kucherenko (the chairman of Gosstroi), the willingness to learn from foreign best practice, and a flexible approach to tenure. Yet, the rational content of the decree was immediately challenged by the inherent irrationalities of post-Stalinism—illustrated by such problems as how to house former prisoners recently released from Gulag camps and evidenced especially by the economic paradoxes embedded in the twelve-year promise.

These paradoxes are assessed at length in chapter 3 (1958–1964). The political ambition dramatically embodied in the twelve-year promise ensured successes in the housing program, and these are straightforwardly illustrated with numbers. For most of the rest of the Khrushchev era, per capita housing construction was decisively higher than anywhere else in Europe. Given the complexity of the tasks that it set about solving, this really was the greatest housing program in the world. It produced a cityscape that was replicated across the complex breadth of the Soviet Union. Yet, the impetus resulting from the twelve-year promise was offset by the excessive emphasis on the construction of square meters above all. This caused the neglect of necessary social and economic infrastructure and, sometimes, the disregarding of quality. The second half of the chapter shows how this partly self-defeating dynamic was exacerbated by Khrushchev's attempts to use housing policy not just to improve material conditions but to alter consciousness, most notably in a new proto-communist approach at the level of the "microdistrict." This extends into an analysis of how policy, ideology, and cityscape combined to create a new type of "communist living standards."

Part 2 is organized in conceptual rather than chronological terms. Here the housing program across the whole period from 1944 to 1964 is defined as occupying a nexus of property rights and welfare rights. In chapter 4, an attempt is made to define what individual ownership meant in the Soviet Union by drawing on notions of Soviet citizen autonomy and a range of historical comparisons. This generates an analytical map for chapter 5 that focuses more precisely on the late Stalinist and

Khrushchev eras. Here the expansion of individual ownership is seen as a consequence of, in turn, wartime destruction, the death of Stalin, and Khrushchev's short-lived push to the communist future. The expansion is also placed in the context of attempts by state agencies to limit property "rights" through two devices in particular: the rules of *propiska* (a residence permit stamped in the internal passport) and the housing space allocation or "sanitary norm." The depth and scope of individual ownership increased further as housing cooperatives came to replace individually constructed houses during the peak of the Khrushchev period, and as conventional state apartments, rented to tenants on increasingly advantageous terms, proliferated on a mass scale. As a result of these processes, rights of occupancy became so secure and widespread that they represented a powerful form of ownership. By then, property rights were bolstered by welfare rights, in a unique and mutually reinforcing combination that explains much of the course of the urban housing program. That nexus between welfare and property is the subject of the final section of the chapter.

This is to run ahead of the story, however, for the direct origins of the program lay amid the catastrophe of wartime destruction. The most convincing place to start is the year 1944.

PART ONE

From Sacrifice to Paradise

Reconstruction and Its Legacies, 1944–1950

On its arrival, my family found itself in a very difficult situation.
The house I had lived in before the evacuation had been destroyed,
everything that remained of the possessions had been looted.

—An inhabitant of Stalinskaia oblast' on his family's return
home, January 1944

In the wake of the most terrible war in history, a leader of legendary charisma promised to solve the housing crisis. He thundered that the people would never go back to how they used to live, then he acted on his promise. New estates emerged in old cities. Thousands moved into new housing. A standard was set for ongoing improvement.[1]

If Lloyd George could achieve this in Britain after the First World War, why could Stalin not do so in the Soviet Union after 1945? The possibilities in a workers' state, after all, seemed more propitious. A conventional answer suggests that Stalin had no interest in popular housing conditions because his primary concern after the war was not in how people lived but in how securely his government exercised permanent and even total power. His priorities were the recovery and further construction of heavy industry, the pursuit of prestige projects, rivalry with the United States, the extension of Soviet influence in Eastern Europe, and the renewal of state violence against categories of the domestic population. This conventional explanation of the neglect of the housing crisis contains many truths.

It is an incomplete answer, though. The late Stalinist system was capable of generating policy proposals and technological advances in housing construction, all of which had a beneficent potential. These developments achieved a modest though radically inconsistent improvement in the social conditions of the population. For all their considerable faults, they contributed to a partial shift away from an approach to the housing problem that had by definition required the sacrifice of living standards. Yet the late Stalinist order was incapable of making the resolution of the housing crisis into a priority, by coordinating an adequately funded and coherent response by agencies of the state. The achievement and the shortfall are both partly explained by the reliance on autonomous activities by citizens. These were always an essential component of the urban housing program but were particularly indispensable before 1950. From 1944 to 1950, people were sometimes permitted to resolve their own housing problem as they thought best, without support or hindrance from agencies of the state; at other times, these agencies provided people with the financial, legal, and practical help that made an autonomous response realistic. Citizen autonomy was built into the urban housing program from the beginning. It is an essential element in explaining the emerging, splintered beneficence that directed the new housing policies in this period and, more widely, the troubled status of the individual citizen in the late Stalinist USSR.

Although the reconstruction policies of 1944–1950 made possible a newly substantial and extensive approach to housing questions, they were still negligent and inadequate. Their most significant effects were delayed: four legacies that were activated during the 1950s. These legacies can broadly be conceived as political, architectural, sociocultural, and economic. In the immediate shadow of the war, the relationship between citizens and politico-administrative organs was reconfigured, as the expectations of both changed, generating a new policy and a particular way of implementing it. Connected to this were advances in technologies of prefabrication and standardization, whose exploitation would become widespread under Khrushchev. While the housing shortage was acute, the aspiration to occupy separate housing was nevertheless consolidated in official culture and rhetoric, once again foreshadowing an apparently Khrushchevian innovation. Housing policy of these years contributed to many of the features of the later mass housing program, but it also suffered from a virulent double bind of fragmentation in the making and implementation of policy and overcentralization in central planning. The inheritance not only enabled mass construction but defined the dysfunctional economic mechanism by which it would ultimately be fulfilled.

Party-government, Population, and the Housing Crisis

If the Soviet housing fund was extremely inadequate before 1941, then the extent of the housing crisis precipitated by the war was unprecedented in modern history. Before the war, Novorossiisk contained 533,100 square meters of housing space; by the time the Germans had gone, there were 293,327.[2] The decline in Minsk was from 1,070,000 to 415,800.[3] In Voronezh, the city soviet's housing fund collapsed by 83.1 percent between 1940 and 1945.[4] In Smolensk, at 87.9 percent, it was still worse.[5] Meanwhile, at war's end, demobilized soldiers, returning evacuees, and rural in-migrants ensured that demand hardly fell.

These unpublished statistics, from areas subject to occupation or battle, have not been gathered in this form before, but their pattern is familiar. Less well-known are the dreadful strains placed on the housing funds of urban centers far beyond the front line. The incoming tide of evacuated civilians and industrial plant, combined with the general economic disruption of war, led simultaneously to a radical upswing in demand and a decline in urban budgets committed to construction and maintenance. In November 1944, the chairman of the Cheliabinsk oblast' party committee (*obkom*) wrote that the urban population of the oblast' was up 45.6 percent on 1939, while municipal facilities and housing had hardly advanced.[6] In Molotov oblast', the authorities very rapidly expanded the coal industry of the town of Gubakha, thanks to the exigencies of war demand. Consequently Gubakha's population grew from 28,000 to 44,000; these workers and their families shared the same 120,000 square meters of housing space, reducing the average space per person from 4.3 to 2.7. Much of this was in "dilapidated" barracks. Access to public services was desperate.[7] In December 1944, the Chief Architect of Novosibirsk noted that the city had been forced to construct emergency accommodation "of the most primitive type," and he called for recognition of the demands made on such cities.[8] Housing was constructed during the war, but in small quantities and generally temporary form, and was usually of extremely low quality.[9]

In Moscow itself, the urban economy had suffered from both bombardment and neglect. The capital seemed frozen in a time of backwardness and suffering. An American journalist writing in May 1947 used a Cold War tone that did not mask a realistic picture: "The capital city of one sixth of the world's land area is not . . . merely pocked, like Washington, with slums; it is a slum."[10] In 1950 Zdeněk Mlynár, who would become a senior Czech party official, came to Moscow as a student. He recalled a primitive cityscape filled with "wooden cottages."[11] In 1953 an Australian diplomat reported, "even within a range of two miles of the Kremlin there are thousands of single- and double-storey houses, practically none of which have been painted or repaired for an entire generation."[12] Paint was the least of the residents' problems, which were exacerbated by an overcrowded, unhygienic, badly supplied, and decaying housing stock.

Misery resulted. I. V. Vol'nyi, who had held a responsible position in the oil industry in Baku before the war and lost his leg at the battle of Königsberg, ended up in Moscow. He lived with his family—his wife, his mother, and three children aged fifteen, twelve, and only six months—in a room of ten square meters. He wrote in a petition of 1947 that while others were celebrating the eight hundredth anniversary of the founding of Moscow, "my family has no happiness, but grievous woe. . . . I just do not have any strength left."[13] Such situations robbed people of pride and confidence in themselves, let alone in their victory. Lieutenant-Colonel A. K. Pakhomov served during the war, while his apartment in Leningrad was destroyed; between 1944 and his appeal of 1948 he worked as a test pilot in Moscow, first roughly housed in the Novo-Moskovskii hotel and then with his wife's relatives in a space of seven square meters. With the district soviet lacking the resources to solve his problem, he wrote a pleading letter to Georgii Malenkov, his Supreme Soviet deputy: "I don't even have an apartment, that which is most necessary for life for everyone, regardless of his professional specialty or social position. . . . It would be difficult to find more unbearable conditions for a pilot."[14]

Similar cases unfolded far from the battle lines. K. P. Tarasov had been transferred to Kuibyshev from Kovrov, together with his factory, in October 1941. After the war his factory remained in Kuibyshev and shifted to civil production. He succeeded in moving his family there, but the factory management did not provide them with housing space. Tarasov rented space for them in a hostel, but the arrangement was unsustainable, and he had to send them back home. This made for an expensive and lengthy encounter with bureaucratic caprice. He appealed for help in arranging his own transfer back to Kovrov. "In the end my family and I have to live together," he wrote, desperately. "The family is badly supplied in material terms, it needs help, but from here I can't help them."[15]

Knowledge of such suffering molded the attitudes of some officials. Technocratic cadres were becoming more effective and more deeply embedded in the governing order, and their numbers included some who were more outward looking, more anxious to solve social problems, and better equipped to find technically feasible solutions.[16] Not only did the war expand the practical reach of such officials, but it changed the views of some of them about how they should relate to the wider population. The extent of the postwar crisis, apparent in prospect of victory as well as after 9 May 1945, proved beyond question that the reality of housing was catastrophically different from that promised by the original revolutionary settlement. Twin foundation myths (those of 1917 and 1941–1945) demanded a new approach to housing. In this context, a typical order to complete a set of capital repairs on apartment houses in Moscow in time for the thirtieth anniversary of the October Revolution assumed a newly acute importance.[17]

In devising measures that sought directly to connect people's wartime experience with the allocation of housing, some of these middle-ranking and senior central officials even exposed themselves as a stratum of "enlightened officialdom."[18] The scope of their actions was still narrow, but their revised approach to Soviet life brought some new focus to housing policy.[19] In May 1945, R. V. Maiorov, head of the urban economy department of the Moscow Soviet, claimed, "Housing works must without interruption improve the living standards of the workers of the capital. House repairs are not only an economic but [also] the most important political task."[20] Khrushchev, who was then running the Ukrainian republic, commented in 1945 that housing construction "has a huge political and economic significance."[21] This approach required some measures that at least formally favored veterans and their families.[22] In September 1945, it was decreed that 10 percent of distributed housing must be set aside for war invalids, the families of those killed, and the demobilized themselves.[23] A Sovnarkom decree of March 1946 allowed for the construction of comfortable housing specifically for demobilized soldiers in Iaroslavl'. Each apartment in these houses was to have three rooms plus a kitchen and a hallway, an unheated terrace and cupboard space; each of the apartment houses would have a large plot with a garden and an area for growing vegetables.[24]

Ordinary people, meanwhile, tended to lay claim to housing by referring to the war. Among those who had lost the most or endured the worst, a broad sentiment existed that the consequence of victory should be better living conditions.[25] For the people who continued to suffer because of the inadequacies of reconstruction, their experience of the war—loss of limbs or family members—was the reason they deserved better. Although a public discourse of "homes fit for heroes" did not exist, people generated one of their own in their letters of complaint to the authorities. One V. I. Chaiko appealed for the resolution of her desperate case by emphasizing, formulaically, "I am the wife of a Red Army soldier, who from the first days of the Fatherland War was mobilized into the RKKA [Workers' and Peasants' Red Army] and was killed." She defined her wartime experience, the basis of her case for better housing, by not just blood sacrifice but outstanding service: "From the very start of the war, during all the blockade of Leningrad, I worked for the defense of the Motherland, fulfilling my norm by two hundred percent." The conditions, she wrote modestly, were "difficult," but she had all the documents to back up her claims.[26] Yet, in those cities where construction or repairs were proceeding particularly slowly, some layers of public opinion rejected completely the notion of a new relationship with the party-government or the existence of an urban beneficence, and they expressed the rejection in terms of the war. They even saw their wartime effort as a pointless waste because the system did not reward it; they deemed that no closer relationship with the party-government resulted (from which a beneficent housing policy could have flowed). A Stakhanovite from Magnitogorsk petitioned angrily in 1947, "During the war my comrades and I fulfilled our norms by 318 percent. I've already fulfilled my norm for this year." He saw no return on his labor; the officials on whom he depended had failed him, and he wrote, "the relationship of the leadership with people like us is extremely poor. There's no kind of support. I've already lived in a wrecked apartment for a long time, and despite my requests, no one has given me any help. They won't even do any repairs."[27]

Such disillusionment was well founded. Evidence gathered by trade unions suggests that, of their various welfare responsibilities, the bosses of industrial enterprises could be especially neglectful of housing provision—at a time when many of them would have continued to enjoy dwellings of relative luxury.[28] Housing policy would hereafter depend on a mutually reinforcing interaction between the contributions of ordinary people and the boss class, but many among the former soon lost faith in the latter.[29] This trend was obvious enough for the CIA to notice, in a report of January 1947, that "There are increasing signs of apathy, and even unrest, among the populace. Shortages in food, housing, and consumer goods have created widespread dissatisfaction. The vigorous campaign of 'ideological cleansing' indicates the concern with which the Kremlin views the situation."[30] While perceptions and policies had changed, the gulf between elites and people that was characteristic of the 1930s persisted. The (relatively) enlightened officials of the late Stalinist years were usually central policy makers rather than local officials; their numbers are difficult to judge, and their actions were limited by the demands of Stalin. Presidium moderates such as Khrushchev and Aleksei Kosygin were leading examples, but men in the ranks below such as Maiorov and Vladimir Kucherenko (soon the chairman of Gosstroi) were less compromised in their pasts and more systematic in their approach.

Yet their view of how people lived was hardly firsthand. Even official literature, such as Iurii Trifonov's Stalin Prize–winning novel *Students*, delicately suggested that well-meaning forays by the privileged could meet with the incomprehension of workers.[31] Moreover, for every official who apparently recognized that construction should be focused on housing and should be a domestic political priority, there were others such as Maiorov's boss in the Moscow Soviet, Georgii Popov, who argued (implicitly or explicitly) that if construction were politically important, its importance lay in the international arena, and that the function of construction was primarily to showcase the might of the USSR. Talking about the new Stalin skyscrapers, Popov exclaimed at a party meeting in January 1947, "Let [the Americans] come to Moscow and see what sort of houses we have, let them gasp."[32] Writing ritualistically of Leningrad, an architecture scholar perhaps unwittingly placed priorities in order. "Even before the violent sounds of war had been silenced, reconstruction work was started at the Admiralty, State Hermitage, the Kirov Academic Theatre of Opera and Ballet, and other public and housing buildings that had suffered as a consequence of the blockade," he declared. Then he added, in a much more minor key, "A program of house construction both in new districts [*raiony*] and old quarters of the city was started."[33] Visitors to Leningrad noted the same phenomenon. Hugh Trevor-Roper wrote to a correspondent in July 1957 comparing popular housing conditions with reconstruction priorities since the war.

> Here we are staying at the Intourist Hotel, the Astoria, where we find ourselves in a large suite, consisting of a bedroom, a bathroom, a dining room, a drawing room and a study, all richly and heavily furnished with bronze statues, ferns and huge ormolu clocks. (In the city of Leningrad, as in all Russian cities, the housing shortage is acute, and few families have apartments to themselves.) Everywhere around us the thing which most impresses the visitor is the immense respect paid to "culture." All the old palaces and churches have been restored, repainted, re-gilded, quite regardless of cost: never, since they were first built, can they have looked so splendid.[34]

He was looking at the results of late Stalinist construction priorities. By definition, such restorations and new constructions, which also gilded other hero-cities such as Stalingrad and Minsk, sacrificed people's living conditions in pursuit of Stalin's higher cause.

Cruelty and greed tempered enlightenment most especially among local elites. Evidence of this in literary works such as Vladimir Dudintsev's *Not by Bread Alone* prompted Vera Dunham's thesis of a "big deal" between the consolidating managerial class of the technocracy and the Stalinist regime, somewhat at the expense of the mass of the population.[35] Recent archival work has to some extent borne out her arguments and is especially convincing on the gulf between suffering and power inside provincial towns.[36] The relationship between ordinary people and governing elites was troubled, for sure, and perhaps inadequate to the task of major housing reconstruction.

This task was so enormous ás to deflect any quick solutions: more than the selfishness of some officials, the *extent* of the postwar crisis made reconstruction difficult. Yet, the amount of housing constructed in the Soviet Union in the ten years after 1945 was much higher in comparative European terms than in the ten years before 1940 (see chart 1.1). Mass housing was certainly born in the wake of the war and as a result of the war, although these early results were imperfect and uneven. At a time of acute crisis, how could any government introduce policies that would rapidly deal with such complex practical problems whose sum was a suffering, grieving, and

CHART 1.1. IMPACT OF THE WAR: NEWLY CONSTRUCTED DWELLINGS PER ONE THOUSAND INHABITANTS IN FOUR EUROPEAN COUNTRIES, 1930-1955

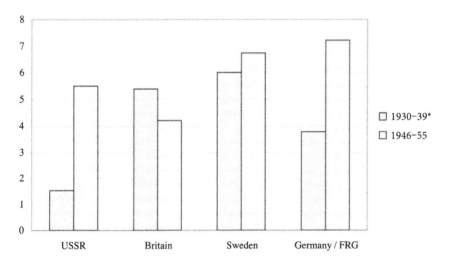

□ 1930–39*
□ 1946–55

*The years 1931–1940 in Sweden.

Note: Each column represents a mean year's construction during the given decade and, given the varied sources of the data, should be considered an approximate representation.

Source: Calculations based on data in *Narodnoe khoziaistvo SSSR 1922-1982*, 425; *Narodnoe khoziaistvo 1956*, 17; John Erickson, "Soviet War Losses," 256; Anne Power, *Hovels to High Rise: State Housing in Europe since 1850*, 213, 159; Stephen Merrett, *State Housing in Britain*, 239; B. R. Mitchell, *International Historical Statistics. Europe 1750-2000*, 4, 7; *Statistisk Årsbok för Sverige 1971*, 222.

miserable society? Housing construction during this period should be assessed in the context of the scale of the crisis. While the response was inadequate, fractured, distorted by a focus on prestige cities and projects, and in parts neglectful of basic humane considerations, elsewhere it was relatively and comparatively substantial.[37] It began in 1943, with detailed planning for the reconstruction of Stalingrad, for example.[38] For the most basic and unavoidable reasons, new housing policies simply had to be instituted to confront epic overcrowding and the crisis of mass destruction. But the government did not face up to the housing crisis with the systematic approach that would have come from sustained interest at the top. The evolving relationship between party-government and population was still too marred by exploitation and distrust to generate a decisive change from sacrifice to beneficence in housing policy. Yet some officials had set a new direction, even if their conveyance thither was underpowered.

Emerging Policies—Fractured but Unprecedented

The Soviet Union experienced a profusion of housing policies between 1944 and 1950. No overall statement of intent acted as a clarion call, in direct contrast to Khrushchev's call in 1957. Stalin allowed no unifying decree and was vague or platitudinous in public utterances. In a rare address of November 1943, he announced "the regeneration of the destroyed towns and villages, industry, transport, agriculture and cultural institutions" and promised "the creation of normal living conditions for the Soviet people who have been delivered from fascist slavery."[39] His spare comments lacked coverage as well as detail. Population and officials alike learned nothing of Stalin's plans for the country's housing crisis, arguably its most urgent domestic calamity. More famously, during the Supreme Soviet election campaign in February 1946, Stalin claimed that the priority of the new five-year plan was a general reconstruction whose aim was to improve people's standards of living. He cited some specifics: "rationing will be abolished (stormy, extended applause), particular attention will be paid to increasing the production of consumer goods (stormy, extended applause), and to establishing all types of scientific-technical institutes (applause)."[40] Once again, and here despite the promise of a reorientation of economic priorities, he failed to mention housing. Even rhetorical hints would have helped to unify policy and to make more effective the considerable effort that people, industry, and administration expended in the housing reconstruction efforts of 1944–1950. The fact that Lloyd George managed such a rhetorical feat in 1918 in the midst of a quite different type of general election campaign, and Stalin did not, exemplified the way that late Stalinist political culture did not require coordinated declarations of policy outside the industrial and strategic areas of maximum priority or the marginal cases of particular populist concessions. Housing policy was left to flutter in shreds, which only in occasional moments deceptively resembled a banner.

Late Stalinist housing solutions were generally piecemeal and incoherent. Officials proposed expedient measures to tackle sudden manifestations of the ongoing crisis or worked on longer-term policies that they could implement only sporadically. Most aspects of policy were really ad hoc measures, formed in response to specific events or problems, frequently in one city. In April 1946, for example, the Council of Ministers (USSR) drafted measures designed to improve the organization and effectiveness of construction, reconstruction, and repair in the towns of Gor'kii oblast', as well as the functioning of municipal services. Of particular significance was the formation of a new construction-assembly trust (*trest*) for the oblast', a necessary stage in the industrialization of construction.[41] Though influential and effective, the rationalization of trusts was a carefully considered measure that was not applied in a universal, transparent, or consistent way; instead it leaked out in separate measures, like this one for Gor'kii. Other decrees just listed targets. The city of Kalinin was a typically unfortunate object of the megaphone of republican government in November 1948.[42] Moscow could shout targets at local officials without providing the means or the guidance to fulfill them, or indeed the sense that these targets were part of a comprehensible program. Moscow-based makers, implementers, and communicators of central policy, working in the agencies of either the all-union or the republican councils of ministers, seemed unable to decide whether to keep their distance or to engage in micromanagement. The expansive Kalinin decree contrasts with a constrained and precise decree of the same month, perhaps surprisingly the business of republican government, that concerned itself with "the completion of the construction of two [apartment] houses in Sverdlovsk and Nizhnii Tagil."[43]

During this period, republican councils of ministers were sometimes able to give political direction to local leaders as well as to central ministries, and sometimes to harness their own administrative capacity in order to kick-start highly complex housing construction tasks, but only at the level of a particular city, and then only in short episodes. In August 1948 the Council of Ministers set out logically unified policies for the city of Molotov, delineating the roles of various ministries and other organs connected with housing, defining particular improvements in associated areas such as road- and school-building, and listing a raft of specifically measured targets.[44] Similar examples can be isolated for Tomsk, Penza, and Krasnodar.[45] Integrated policy was a transient phenomenon in many places, gone before it had much effect, but it showed the intentions of the most farsighted officials and provided examples for a more balanced approach in the future.

Such examples of coherent policy were only unpredictably replicated. Across the union, vitally important questions were not answered. Nobody made clear, as a matter of policy, whether all resources that were set aside for urban reconstruction should be devoted to the provision of shelter. If they were, then it would take years to rescue the population from its plight, but it would take even longer if resources were balanced with the reconstruction of such infrastructure as water supplies, transport links, and kindergartens. But if, say, water pipes were not expensively rebuilt, the consequences would be immediately catastrophic; and if transport were not improved, then housing reconstruction would in turn proceed more slowly. It was to clarify such tricky issues that decisive political leadership was necessary, for despite their humble sound, these were actually some of the greatest questions that the Soviet Union had ever faced. Hence a tone of desperation colors a Council of Ministers (RSFSR) paper of 1946: "At the present time the situation regarding the water supply in Velikie Luki is exceptionally tense."[46]

Despite these inadequacies of policy, the bureaucratic structures of late Stalinism were becoming more regular and responsive, though the orders of the dictator remained unpredictable, capricious, and yet, in "neopatrimonial" terms, crudely logical.[47] Officials oversaw an urban housing economy whose administration was at least somewhat smoother than before. In Moscow, the Housing Administration of the city soviet passed various orders in 1947 that recorded responses to citizens' complaints, implying at least some level of systemic reaction to popular need within the housing economy (albeit a reaction that was modulated by patronage).[48] Bureaucracy was cumbersome, as architects and others noted.[49] But its different branches did check each other. The results of such bureaucratic mutuality fitted roughly inside the paradigm of beneficence. In November 1948, N. S. Leonov, a deputy of the Moscow oblast' soviet, wrote to Georgii Malenkov, the deputy chairman of the Council of Ministers (USSR), about the case of an employee of the Ministry of Procurement (USSR), I. K. Stepanova, who lived in a communal apartment in a house owned by the ministry. She experienced "extremely difficult conditions" in her room of five square meters, which lacked light, heating, and ventilation. Leonov sent Malenkov a pack of documents showing "that the Ministry of Procurement has not taken measures to improve the housing conditions of Citizen Stepanova, of forty-five years' service and failing health."[50] The bureaucratic chain was certainly slow-moving and convoluted, but it was not entirely unresponsive.

Immediate postwar reconstruction was boosted by one particular policy of enduring value, which consolidated similar prewar measures with new levels of investment and political priority. In May 1944 a decree was instituted that authorized easy state loans for the self-built construction of individual houses. This provided a crucial legacy for the 1950s of pragmatic policy making and the nurturing of state-backed citizen autonomy as means for tackling the housing crisis. A citizen could acquire an extended lease for a plot of urban land from the local soviet and build a house. He would own the house himself, according to the tenure of "personal property."[51] The scheme entitled him to apply for credit at the Municipal Bank, usually via the enterprise for which he worked.[52] He might obtain assistance from his trade union in formalizing the legalities.[53] Other help—with the procurement, assembly, and transportation of parts and construction materials, and the provision of standardized plans (*tipovye proekty*)—should be provided by the enterprise.[54]

The results were, of course, diverse. Rough-and-ready shacks, perhaps of a single room and built entirely by the resident, contrasted with houses that were constructed to professional blueprints, and with professional help. Most individual houses were wooden, especially where forest reserves were accessible. An individual builder might cut down the wood himself or have it delivered as timber from his workplace. Meanwhile, incongruous-looking materials, obtained through informal channels, were indispensable; these ranged from badly fitting panes of glass to rusting sheets of metal. As time went on, more owners had access to a range of prefabricated parts, both large and small. Blueprints of the standardized individual houses show verandas and largish interiors, though contemporary descriptions in both state documents and the published writings of observers suggest that badly built, overcrowded, sometimes squalid—though functioning—shanties were more common.[55]

As a policy, the scheme's effectiveness was as varied as the physical traces it produced. The director of the Moscow Region Municipal Bank, Comrade Iurkin, lauded the scheme publicly in January 1945, giving as an example the half million rubles that the bank had disbursed to the workers of an unnamed armaments factory. This allowed "several dozen" of them to become the individual builders (*zastroishchiki*) of their own dwellings, thanks also to the help from the factory management in "the acquisition of materials as well as the actual building." Iurkin praised the Moscow river port, the "Paris Commune" factory, and enterprises of the People's Commissariat of Communications. He criticized (for "using credit badly") the factories Krasnyi Blok, Komega, the Stalin Car Works, and the Mikoian Meat Combine.[56] This is how the authorities sought to present the scheme to a popular readership, striking a populist note—and underscoring its significance—by ritualistically humiliating industrial managers who failed to implement it adequately.

By contrast, one of the few historians to consider the scheme, Donald Filtzer, has characterized the process of acquiring the state credits as time-consuming and excessively bureaucratic.[57] Such criticism is not unfair, but workers in most parts of Europe did not have any access to equivalent "mortgages" at this time (though their living conditions were usually less desperate). Archival sources provide examples of successes and shortcomings. Trade union (*profsoiuz*) reports, a major source, indicate a failure to meet plan targets, but their evidence is partly colored by institutional self-interest; in presenting failures, they propose a greater involvement of their own organs in the process. By September 1944, four months after the decree, management had distributed 17.2 percent of the loans budget at the Red October factory in Stalingrad; 115 people had been given loans, but only twenty had completed the construction of their dwellings.[58] Three years later, the corresponding annual plan for 1947 had only been fulfilled by 34.1 percent by the end of August.[59] In the Crimea, meanwhile, Municipal Bank inspectors hinted at corruption infecting the scheme in 1947, and in Kerch, loans to employees of the bank itself were misused, for "personal needs."[60]

These are not isolated cases, and results across the union were mixed. Yet evidence showing the success of the scheme in both financial and construction terms is more plentiful. Success depended on the effectiveness of local soviets, enterprises, trade unions, and Municipal Bank departments, as well as the energy or urgency of the local population. For every instance where the plan remained unfulfilled, the archives contain more examples of the opposite. By August 1945, the city soviet of Rostov had distributed all the credits for individual construction that the Municipal

Bank had granted them; its chairman then appealed for an additional 50 percent of the annual budget. Leningrad made a similar request in the same month. The scheme was expanded in Magnitogorsk from the end of 1945.[61] Monies for the ultimate use of individual constructors were the lion's share of Municipal Bank credit lists in the RSFSR in 1947.[62]

The all-union stock of urban housing owned as personal property rose by 69.1 percent between 1944 and 1950, an acceleration that was in many but not all cases the result of the scheme. During the same period, the volume of housing in the hands of local soviets grew significantly more slowly, by 23.4 percent.[63] Credit provision for individual house construction was a flexible mechanism, moreover, that officials found useful in the consolidation of other areas of policy. The Ministry of the Municipal Economy pushed for union-funded loans for wartime orphans who had completed three months at an enterprise or building site.[64] This gave priority to a category of the population that needed special help to obtain state credits, while providing particular recognition of wartime service, sacrifice, or loss. Historians might have taken little note of this conspicuous policy of state-backed individual construction, but contemporary observers noticed its extent and influence. A pioneering Western scholar even described the policy as a "new NEP in the sphere of housing relations."[65]

Considered in administrative and political terms, headlined by the individual housing drive, and assessed in terms of construction output, the period from 1944 to 1950 saw the first substantial government-directed housing construction policy in either Soviet or Russian history—far more significant than the much more piecemeal construction of the 1920s and 1930s. This was in every sense a consequence of the war, and while it amounted to a limited but still partially successful reconstruction, much its greatest significance consisted in the crucial foundation it laid for the later mass housing program.

Yet it should still be considered in its own terms. Archival sources make it a complex task to measure construction output between 1944 and 1950. Detailed fragments of evidence combine to create an unfinished but generally clear picture. The stock of housing owned as personal property rose fastest, reflecting the input of the individual housing scheme. More broadly, from the end of the war in 1945 until 1950 the total state housing fund (the stock owned by agencies of the state, soviet plus departmental tenures) grew by 28.9 percent (from 149,180,400 square meters to 192,408,252).[66] This was considerable in international terms, but much of it was the result of repair and reconditioning rather than new construction. Builders often failed to meet targets. Only 33.8 percent of the 1946–1950 plan for housing construction in the RSFSR had been realized by the end of 1948.[67] Such failings were compounded by regional variations. Table 1.1 takes six sample cities—two prestige cities substantially damaged during the war, two typical if large cities that were almost destroyed, and two that were far from the fighting—and compares the total housing funds (all state tenures plus personal property) in 1940, 1945, and 1950.

TABLE 1.1. COMPARING POSTWAR HOUSING RECONSTRUCTION IN
SIX SOVIET CITIES

	1940	1945	1950
Minsk	1	0.39	1.03
Leningrad	1	0.87	0.92
Smolensk	1	0.19	0.52
Voronezh	1	0.39	0.76
Omsk	1	1.17	1.37
Novosibirsk	1	1.27	1.50

Source: Calculated on the basis of RGAE f. 1562, op. 14, d. 2767 (Minsk); d. 2707, l. 2 (Leningrad); d. 2726, l. 2 (Smolensk); d. 2695, l. 2 (Voronezh); d. 2718, l. 2 (Omsk); d. 2717, l. 128 (Novosibirsk).

The raw data exaggerate some achievements. For example, the new housing space in such cities as Omsk and Novosibirsk would have been consumed by the swollen wartime and postwar population, and it was often of exceptionally poor quality, including hardly renovated space in buildings not designed for human habitation. The data also overstate the recovery of major prestige cities. In Leningrad only a very low standard of what was fit housing could have defined 87 percent of the prewar stock as extant in 1945. Chart 1.2 provides additional evidence of these tendencies, with extra examples.

Underlying the evidence of varied outcome in the graph is the fragmentation of policy. True, fragmentation could imply flexibility. Central government agencies were sometimes quick to respond to emergencies and willing to shift additional resources toward those urban areas that had suffered most during the war. The distribution of Municipal Bank credits for individual construction by oblast' in 1947 shows a focus on war-damaged areas. Smolensk oblast' obtained 20,000,000 rubles, while Primorskii krai, thousands of miles away on the Far East coast, was awarded 1,200,000.[68]

But it is the weakness engendered by fragmentation that is more compelling. The lack of major declarations of intention made it possible for local soviets to pursue their own priorities, or for the center to impose on them apparently foolish judgments that derived from the incidental irrationalities of central planning. In March 1949 the Ministry of Finance made an apportionment to the "housing" budget of Kalinin oblast'. Here housing deprivation on a mass scale produced grinding suffering, as the research of Kees Boterbloem has illustrated.[69] The Ministry of Finance granted 4,276,000 rubles for the reconstruction of 6,000 square meters of

CHART 1.2. HOUSING RECONSTRUCTION TO 1950
IN TWELVE RSFSR CITIES

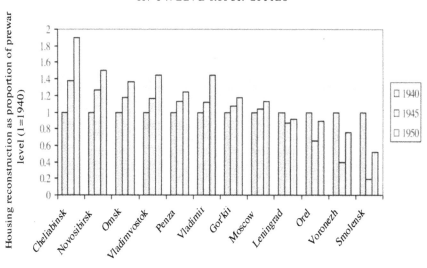

Source: RGAE f. 1562, op. 14 (1940) d. 2686, l. 2; d. 2693; d. 2695, l. 2; d. 2696, l. 2; d. 2707, l. 2; d. 2710, l. 2; d. 2712, l. 2; d. 2717, l. 128; d. 2718, ll. 2, 74; d. 2719, ll. 2, 146; d. 2726, l. 2; d. 2731; (1945) d. 1212, ll. 1, 6; d. 2686, l. 2; d. 2693; d. 2695, l. 2; d. 2696, l. 2; d. 2707, l. 2; d. 2712, l. 2; d. 2717, l. 128; d. 2718, ll. 2, 74; d. 2719, ll. 2, 146; d. 2726, l. 2; d. 2731; (1950) d. 2031, ll. 7, 11, 15, 19, 23, 25, 45, 77, 141, 157; d. 2032, ll. 53, 61, 67, 109; d. 2686, l. 2; d. 2693; d. 2695, l. 2; d. 2696, l. 2; d. 2707, l. 2; d. 2710, l. 2; d. 2712, l. 2; d. 2717, l. 128; d. 2718, ll. 2, 74; d. 2719, ll. 2, 146; d. 2726, l. 2; d. 2731.

housing—and an astonishing 1,572,000 for the completion of a Hotel Moskva.[70] The fragmentation of city housing queues persisted during this period, thanks to the shift from control of housing by soviets to ministries and departments (and hence local enterprises) that the 1946–1950 plan foresaw for the state housing fund. Yet even within their more limited role, soviets had managed by the end of 1948 to meet their construction target only by 17.4 percent.[71] The downgrading of the soviets in housing provision made less likely a central city housing queue and equitable distribution; it magnified the caprices of factories' housing departments, as would be acknowledged, to some extent, in the late 1950s. So while housing reconstruction was indeed underway, and the switch to beneficence had started, and this was the most rapid spurt of housing construction and improvement hitherto in Soviet history, the housing policies of 1944–1950 amounted to only a partial and highly variable reconstruction effort, nothing more. The malign effects of a fragmented policy were exacerbated by the overcentralization of the planned economy. It was the contours of policy rather than its direct accomplishments that were the real effect of housing policy between 1944 and 1950. This provided a usable legacy, a particularly visible aspect of which was architectural.

Architecture and Construction Technology

If the war changed the preconceptions of the people and the party-government, however inconsistently, the same pressures acted specifically on architects. At the All-Union Architectural Conference of December 1944, a Belorussian architect asserted, "to build as we built before the war is impossible today."[72] More poetic and influential, Moisei Ginzburg, who had been at the top of the architectural profession since the 1920s, stated at the Union of Architects in August 1943, "Can one imagine that the colossal hardship that our motherland has undergone, the floods of blood that have been shed by our best sons for the motherland, will have no influence on the creative work of any of us? It is a monstrous thought that it will have no influence on our work." Ginzburg called for a new "socialist humanism" in architecture; he criticized Moscow's Gor'kii Street, in whose prewar remodeling he had been involved and for which he now declared atonement, for its "pomposity" and "triumphalism," as well as for its failure to consider people's needs for sufficient space and amenities.[73] Such apartments, he thought, were too big to be consistent with "socialist humanism," because the allowance of housing space per person (the sanitary norm) resulted in their being divided between "five or six families per apartment," which turned family homes into communal apartments. Ginzburg died in 1946, an architect grandee, convinced that a universal and immediately applicable beneficence should guide Soviet architecture. The motif of beneficence united his career; the paradise that marked such communally inspired housing designs as his houses on Moscow's Chaikovskii Street (1928–1930) was not reductive or blind to personal comfort, and he effectively apologized for the sacrifices implicit in Gor'kii Street.

Few of his colleagues could develop such an independent vision; Ginzburg was ahead of his time. The social, propagandist, and artistic functions of Stalinist architecture remained entrenched. During most of the Stalinist years, from the 1930s to the 1950s, a grand and bulky neoclassicism was the architectural idiom of distinguished apartment houses. Members of elites, including senior architects, were often allocated large separate apartments in the prestigious buildings that were so disproportionately expensive to construct. Typically, the press lauded a seven-story apartment house at 43 Gor'kii Street, completed in 1946, for its "monumentality" and "massiveness."[74] This architecture was hardly beneficent; it sacrificed general living conditions for the benefit of elites and the prestige of the country. Such buildings formed the impressive set-piece centers of many cities, announcing a message about the permanence of the Stalinist order to Soviet citizens and foreign observers alike. By designing these places, architects enjoyed a crucial and prestigious role in Stalinist society. Their authority allowed them to discharge creative independence in their work, provided they operated within the official style. Professional attitudes and systemic imperatives encouraged architects to view their work in creative rather than socially transformative ways. It was still possible for an architect to believe he was an artist casting Stalinism in columns and friezes, rather than a construction professional working to rectify the postwar housing crisis. Original productions of neoclassical grandeur inspired greater interest among many architects than the mass replication of basic apartment blocks. In the discussions of the Moscow Soviet's Main Architectural and Planning Administration (GlavAPU), it sometimes seemed more pressing to re-craft a shrapnel-spattered cornice than to build a standardized apartment block. Dmitrii Chechulin chaired a meeting in August 1944 of very senior architects who discussed at length the repair of a particular apartment house in the Chistye Prudy Boulevard in Moscow, its tower and façade.[75]

Chechulin was at that time an ambitious forty-three-year-old who, after working on a series of grand 1930s structures in Moscow, including metro stations from Dinamo to Komsomolskaia and the Chaikovskii concert hall, was promoted at the end of the war to chief architect of the capital. As a leader of the reconstruction drive, he remained stubbornly attached to sustaining architectural creativity in the expensive Stalinist idiom.[76] His substantial architectural work began too late for his creative sensibility to be tested by the revolutionary innovations of constructivism, while his professional pronouncements during the 1940s were not convincingly inflected with the beneficent concerns that motivated Ginzburg.

Architecture changed after the war, not because of the worldview of its leading exponents but because of the grim imperative of postwar desolation. Architects variously responded to this new reality. The most susceptible to change were the frustrated modernists who had always privately deplored Stalinist neoclassicism, and the more ideologically independent architects who were most conscious of the social function of their profession. Ginzburg was a striking example, but only because of his fame and articulacy. Other concerned professionals discussed policy with some critical autonomy in the semipublic forum of architectural conferences, such as a major all-union event in Moscow in December 1944, and edged toward a more rational and coherent approach than the one apparently encouraged by Chechulin.[77] At such gatherings, professional contact and exchange helped to clarify and advance separate elements of policy, such as prefabrication and the industrialization of construction; discussion was wide-ranging and opinionated. Thus the psychological impact of the war, the exigencies of reconstruction, and the perhaps unforeseen logic of government policy combined to bring about advances in architectural practice with regard to housing in the period 1944–1950. These advances, happening at this stage, were uneven but unstoppable. Without them Khrushchev would have pressed the button to start the mass housing program and it would have clicked hollow.

The core architectural change that made possible the mass housing program was the rejection of neoclassical grandeur and the elevation of prefabricated forms of construction. Historians have generally dated this change to the All-Union Construction Conference of December 1954, when Khrushchev condemned "excess" in architecture.[78] But here Khrushchev was giving public voice and political direction to a major architectural shift which dated back to 1944.[79] That December, at the

All-Union Architectural Conference, standardized construction or prefabrication was not far from the top of the bill. Arkadii Mordvynov was perhaps its leading champion.[80] Since 1943 Mordvynov had been chairman of the Committee of Construction and Architecture of the Council of Ministers (USSR), and in 1950 he became the president of the Academy of Architecture. Three years later, he would hold that appointment simultaneously with the office of vice president of the International Union of Architects.[81] He had already beaten the path to rapid-construction technologies with his designs for housing blocks in Moscow's Bol'shaia Kaluzhskaia Street (1939–1940) and Bol'shaia Polianka Street (1940). At the Congress of Soviet Architects in June 1937 he made a ritualized condemnation of "formalism." Yet in focusing his rhetoric against those architects who, he said, thought more about the impact of their designs on the sentiments of passersby than on the people who lived inside the buildings, and by insisting that architects should meet future residents and hear their views on apartment layouts, he foreshadowed the tone and principles of the early Khrushchev era.[82] The mass destruction of the war gave him the chance to push this agenda closer to official policy.

Yet Mordvynov had to make diplomatic use of his wartime status at the peak of the architectural profession. By its nature, standardized construction depended on advanced technologies that reduced architects' imaginative scope and promoted architecture's social utility at the expense of its creative force. In his leading address at the December 1944 conference, Mordvynov sought to marry these priorities to architecture's autonomous and creative status, vigorously defending the architect's aspirations for originality and aesthetics. He insisted that a successful urban future depended on the economical, standardized approach: "It is impossible to exaggerate the significance of standardized design of housing and public buildings. A large part of the new mass construction will be realized by standardized design." Yet he was also determined that "architectural appearance" and "architectural quality" remain crucial. "A house that has been built according to standardized design," he went on, "must be a high-level architectural production, that is it must be beautiful, comfortable, and convenient for living, and at the same time be economical and answer all the conditions of industrial construction."[83] The architects' dilemma shines in bright lights.

Any shift away from the elite projects to which Stalinism had accustomed them raised the hackles of some. In 1945, talks at the architectural soviet of Moscow's GlavAPU reflected hostility toward new standardized designs. Attendees criticized early models of standardized sections for low-rise apartment houses, which offered access to the bathroom via the kitchen, though they also vented little enthusiasm for seeking out improvements.[84] But Mordvynov's speech still represented a considerable shift from the vision of unadulterated neoclassical grandeur that had dominated the 1930s and from the tense, limited discussions of it in those years. Some other architects expressed support for mass standardization at the 1944 conference without adding riders like Mordvynov's emphasis on architectural creativity; they were more unambiguously aware of their social role. However strong or widespread this change might have been among architects, it was the disruptive professional impact of the war and the urgent requirements of reconstruction that brought it about.

The absence of coherent policy and convincing political direction further confused and discomfited some architects. While there was no official change in architectural policy, with prizes still going to the great neoclassical designs, increasing numbers of government decrees required the use of standardized models for economical construction.[85] Indeed, the major policy initiative on individual construction of May 1944 depended on the production of standardized plans and industrially produced parts and kits for individual builders. At the start of 1945 the Institute of Mass Construction of the Academy of Architecture had blueprints for one-room, one-story houses and was undertaking plans for larger dwellings.[86] The Karachovskii woodworking industrial combine (*kombinat*) was producing the materials for such larger houses a few months later: it offered three-room houses, with veranda, hot water supply, and fence, to be built according to standard "framework construction" in workers' settlements, and especially in war-damaged areas. According to Moscow's evening newspaper, *Vecherniaia Moskva*, mass production was about to get under way at prices "fully affordable for individual builders."[87]

Meanwhile, officials in the Council of Ministers (USSR) in 1946 proposed the use of standard designs for one-, two-, and three-story houses in reconstruction work in Stalingrad, Smolensk, Viaz'ma, Voronezh, Kalinin, Briansk, Orel, Kursk, Rostov-on-Don, Pskov, Novgorod, and Velikie Luki.[88] Another set of correspondence proposed eighteen types of standardized design for the RSFSR during 1948.[89] By 1949, architectural industrialization could deliver prefabricated four- or five-story apartment blocks that might be considered early forms of the super-mass-replicated medium-rise blocks associated with Khrushchev (khrushchevki).[90] The standardization, industrialization, and prefabrication of housing construction were emerging across the Soviet Union.[91]

Such partial projects, would-be programs, and ambiguous proposals were inconsistent and not very thoroughgoing. They fell victim to some ambiguity in policy, but they made possible the qualitative shift in architectural capacity that was underscored by an admittedly incomplete transition from sacrifice to beneficence. These architectural and technological advances form the second of the legacies bequeathed by the period 1944–1950 to the mass-scale program of the 1950s, following the recalibrated relationship between population and party-government and the impact on politics and policy. The third legacy is directly connected to its second. Standardized housing construction implied small apartments, which in turn implied single-family occupancy. This had distinctive ideological, social, and cultural implications that have long been associated with the Khrushchev era. But far from being Khrushchevian, the official respectability of separate housing inside a carefully planned local urban "municipal economy" (or "communal economy," to translate more directly) had deep Soviet roots that were well cultivated between 1944 and 1950.

Separate Housing and the Economy of Communality

A half-sentence summary of the Khrushchev-era urban housing program might go like this: the construction on an unprecedented scale of separate apartments in communal housing districts. The mass building of five-story blocks of independent family apartments in microdistricts (mikroraiony) was a new development and represented a policy that was genuinely worked-out and worked-through. But the basic components within these two elements—the separate apartment and the communal urban community spirit—were not novel. The blend of separate and collective uses of domestic space was particularly productive and influential just after the war, sometimes drawing on the encouragement of the state but also reflecting the drive of individual and group initiative in places and at moments when the state was too stretched or when official interest lagged. This reformed sense of the boundaries of domestic and neighborhood space was a pragmatic wartime and late Stalinist change, whose beneficent basis could be adapted later to the demands of paradise. It was a highly usable legacy for Khrushchev and his policy makers to inherit.

During 1944–1950, communal housing of one kind or another remained the basis of the stock. Barracks for factory workers were perhaps its starkest expression, even though they have attracted less attention among historians than the communal apartment, that Soviet archetype. Barracks accounted for 10.6 percent of total housing space in the RSFSR in 1943 (and 10.7 percent in 1947).[92] Not insignificant numbers of newly built separate apartments were shared, thus becoming communal apartments.[93] Throughout Soviet history, however, separate housing was legitimate and important, though the value placed on it in transactions between the population and the party-government varied. There is no evidence that the proliferation of communal apartments after 1917 was an ideologically driven policy with the aim to break down specifically individual ways of life and establish surveillance. This might have been a welcome by-product, but the principal mechanisms for surveillance in work-driven early Soviet society were focused on the workplace. Beyond the statistically insignificant experiments of the house-communes (dom-kommuny) in the 1920s and the grand dwellings of elites, the form of Soviet housing was always the result of the demands of economy, not of ideological abstraction. It seems unlikely that the party-government opposed separate family dwellings in any serious or sustained way on ideological grounds at any stage of Soviet history.[94] Only during the window of 1958–1964 did the authorities in Moscow switch emphasis and invest considerable resources and pride in creating microdistricts as arenas for the refashioning of consciousness. Under Khrushchev, this and not the separateness of the separate apartment was the crucial ideological innovation in the sphere of housing, though its practical impact was less sure than its expressed intention (see chapter 3).

Separate housing was at least as much a part of Soviet culture under Stalin as was communal housing, though far more people lived in communal apartments, dormitories, and barracks than in enclosed family homes. The cultural centrality of comfortable family living and the misleadingly common image of the separate home in popular publications made the construction of individual houses during and after the Second World War a feasible and indeed probable response to the housing crisis. In other words, the Stalinist separate apartment had a significant social and cultural impact far beyond its few and favored occupants. Elite blocks of separate apartments were a feature of every city and were an object of aspiration; only the best-connected or luckiest workers and their bosses had a chance of obtaining one, but these buildings were architecturally and discursively dominant.

Such blocks helped to intensify the "bourgeois" family values of the Stalin era. Furnishing industries and self-help manuals existed for the use of their occupants, and this "consumerist" infrastructure facilitated the modest decoration of private spaces in communal housing.[95] Even during the war, in January 1945, an exhibition at the Art Salon on Moscow's Gor'kii Street displayed designs for wallpaper and furniture.[96] Two weeks after the end of the war, in an article entitled "Furniture, Wallpaper, Light Fittings: The Development of an Artistic Industry," a journalist wrote, "Great perspectives are opening before the artistic industry thanks to postwar housing construction. Architects, artists, and workers in the industry ought to invest their effort in the creation of beautiful and comfortable things, and in decorating the way of life of the Soviet person."[97] This might have been misty rhetoric about what was really something only for the most privileged, but late Stalinist public culture made such consumption a legitimate aspiration for all. At the Moscow Soviet in January 1949, a speaker complained, "Many people come to furniture shops, but far from everybody gets what they need. The choice of furniture is meager, and the quality is low."[98]

If many people wanted furniture in vain, they were nevertheless aspiring to furnish their own space, whether it was a private room in a communal apartment or even a separate apartment. And although conditions were still more desperate after the war than before, with the common absence of any privacy within housing units, separate space was still discussed in positive terms in the outlets of public culture. Moreover, people created illusions of separate home life wherever they could. Kenneth Straus argues that a family room in a communal apartment, of which there were proportionately more during the second and third five-year plans than during the first, gave much more scope for the development of private space than a bunk in a barracks.[99] Katerina Gerasimova has described some of the strategies that people adopted to make life more private and more bearable in the Stalinist communal apartment.[100] Since the 1930s, even in dormitories, people had looked for tablecloths, curtains, and the rudiments of an enclosed family life, and women's magazines of the 1940s continued to give hints about how to achieve it.[101]

Under Stalin as much as under Khrushchev, people wanted separate living quarters. When it had the resources, and after the isolated examples of communal housing projects of the 1920s had been disbanded, the government had no reason to frustrate this aspiration. It is likely that the Stalinist leadership thought it had nothing to fear from separate housing. Terror and attempts to enforce conformity did not require communal living; Soviet state violence intruded into separate and communal apartments alike, while Nazi Germany was filled with millions of enclosed family dwellings. At the same time, Stalinist society was infused with the rhetoric and practice of collective endeavor and mass mobilization. Having a separate family home or aspiring toward one while actively participating in the collective units of one's housing district or apartment block was entirely consistent in Soviet life.[102] The willingness to conflate aspects of individualism and collectivism—the private and the public—within general domestic space seems reinforced by Soviet and Russian culture.[103] Demands of economy and cultural norms alike made domestic privacy a problematic concept and an uncertain reality: even the separate home was a relatively open space, with rooms having multiple functions, usually occupied by more than one family member, and with substantial interaction between neighbors within the block. This was not a specifically Russian phenomenon, but it had striking analogues in Russian peasant tradition. In short, there was no contradiction between the separate apartment and the collectivist aspiration of official ideology. Khrushchev's favored solution of a separate apartment within a collective housing district was not just a logical development of the Soviet past, it was a direct legacy of the immediate postwar years.

Yet the separate apartment (or improved housing conditions in general) did not represent a good of absolute value: it was an object located within a repressive Stalinist universe, in which rights were absent and people were instructed to be grateful for what their masters gave them. By the post-Stalin era, in contrast, a notion of rights underwrote popular expectation and government delivery. In 1946, when Professor A. P. Kreshkov eventually obtained extra housing space (in line with the law) because some of his work inevitably had to take place at home, he wrote to Malenkov, who had helped him, "From all of my soul I thank you for your attention."[104] An article in *Vecherniaia Moskva* of June 1949 stated, "The Soviet state is generously providing the means for the improvement of the social and cultural conditions of workers' lives. . . . [Apartment] houses are being made of better quality, [and] taller, more comfortable."[105] A later report about the Moscow Kuibyshevskii administrative district (raion) party conference of April 1950 noted, "The collective [of workers] at the Kirov 'Dinamo' factory have received a good present. Today they started to move into a new apartment block, built in the Kozhukhovskii settlement, near the Stalin Car Works metro station."[106] This discourse of gratitude and gift, which has been discussed in other contexts in the historiography of Stalinism, reflected the contempt with which Stalinist rulership related to the population, forcing it to pay obeisance for the provision of hardly lavish shelter.[107] While separate living space was therefore consistent with Stalinism, its physical, social, and discursive boundaries differed markedly from separate family housing as it might have existed in, say, Birmingham or Bordeaux.

Stalinist and post-Stalinist governments, in different ways, distrusted the notion that people who lived in separate apartments were private individuals. In the Stalin-era housing economy, people were repressible separate units in vertical relationships, underwritten by deadly violence, inside the housing economy; and they discursively existed with Stalin in a disfiguring relationship of humbling gratitude. Under Khrushchev, individuals should always be part of wider communities, bound by powerful horizontal ties. The classic urban forum for popular mobilization, the microdistrict, arose in the late 1950s. This ideally self-contained neighborhood can be compared, in principle, to a macro-version of a 1920s house-commune. The Stalinist system distrusted such a space more than it distrusted any notional "privacy," because it encouraged people to organize and form horizontal ties independently of the state. By contrast, the individual housing scheme exemplified how state agencies could enable citizen autonomy in a process that was ultimately facilitated by vertical ties; Stalinist government encouraged people to collaborate in housing projects only when resources were especially scarce or state capacity was particularly enfeebled, notably during the wartime and postwar emergency.

The first published reference to the mikroraion (rather than the neutral word *kvartal*, or housing quarter) probably dates to 1957.[108] It referred to a housing district whose facilities and style of living enabled inhabitants to attain proper consciousness. In September 1945, however, Baburov, the head of the Administration of City Planning and Construction (Council of Ministers, USSR), wrote to architects and architectural officials across the USSR suggesting a coordinated program of experimental construction of microdistricts and asking for practical plans for possible microdistrict developments.[109] The notion was new: he asked them, for example, what they understood by the term *mikroraion*. Responses were not enthusiastic. Erevan's overworked chief architect replied briskly, "Unfortunately, this project coincides with a range of tasks connected with construction."[110] The chief architect of Tallinn gently pointed to its probable irrelevance, emphasizing the city's profusion of separate houses, and the difficulty of finding an appropriate area for the experiment.[111] Nevertheless, republican administrators eventually returned plans together with discussion of what was meant by *mikroraion*. The proffered definitions were rational and technical; no one seemed interested in the remaking of the Soviet person, which would be the official function of the microdistrict twelve years later. One architect gave the proposal ideological weight by remarking that it was evidently a "further development" and "strengthening" of the existing kvartal, which would allow for a greater focus on the common interests and needs of the inhabitants, but even his focus remained on practical aspects.[112] Moreover, the report that summarized this feedback made comparisons with the U.S. "neighborhood unit" (directly transliterated from the English).[113]

It seems that nothing really came of these discussions, in that the word *mikroraion* disappeared from public architectural debate for more than a decade. But the discussions still had consequences. In 1947, for example, the chief architect for Pervomaiskii raion in Moscow described a forthcoming kvartal at Semenovskaia Embankment of "future [apartment] houses with a kindergarten, nurseries, a polyclinic."[114] In 1947, Ivan Zholtovskii set about designs for a new block at Smolenskaia Square in Moscow, whose first floor was equipped with a cafeteria, a children's polyclinic, and direct access to the Smolenskaia metro station.[115] The architectural imagination could thus combine elite apartment houses with neighborhood services, with the whole forming an urban community, albeit one that was often composed only of the privileged, and cut off from the rest. Such places were distant from the ideologized forum of the Khrushchevian microdistrict, and most late Stalinist architects were occupied by a mix of society's urgent practical needs and their own artistic fancies. Nevertheless, these immediate postwar years were crucial in fostering ideas, ideals, and practices that were necessary for the rapid development of the microdistricts in the late 1950s.

In the bitter hardship of war and victory, all forms of housing, either communal or separate, existed inside a complex economy of communality. This was, in part at least, a new departure. The principle by which officialdom encouraged and facilitated limited collective volunteering among neighbors was compromised before the war by the absence of much government interest in the urban housing economy, let alone serious housing policies. True, during the 1930s, collective strategies were necessary for individual survival in the tough hinterlands of Soviet cities, and residents made ad hoc, culturally traditional attempts to organize as collectives in some communal apartments.[116] But the wartime and postwar emergency engendered a new, more focused, and officially sanctioned collectivism. This was partial: the repressiveness of late Stalinism could not tolerate the profusion of semi-independent collective structures that were unleashed in the urban housing economy of the Khrushchev era. Official rhetoric, however, airily declared that the war had brought people together, and it is possible that in some urban communities from about 1944 to 1946 elements of such a spirit did exist alongside the enthusiastic words of politicians and newspapers in a mutually reinforcing relationship. The chairman of the Leningrad Soviet, Petr Popkov, claimed on the first anniversary of the end of the blockade that "hundreds of thousands of Leningraders" were spending their spare time working on the city's reconstruction. He invoked a city patriotism: "If before our slogan was 'Everything for the defense of Leningrad!' then now our motto is 'All our strength for the reconstruction of Leningrad!'"[117]

Public culture between about 1944 and 1946 created at least four categories of urban collective whose function was to bring voluntary labor to the preservation or improvement of the housing stock. The first type of collective was the city as a whole, as celebrated by Popkov for Leningrad, but common elsewhere too: "Stalingraders are applying all their strength to make their town still more beautiful and well appointed than it was before the war."[118] A second category of collective was the city district, or raion. *Vecherniaia Moskva* reported a grand sequence of days of voluntary labor (*subbotniki* or *veskresniki*), in the capital's Zheleznodorozhnyi raion, during which, apparently, "[f]or the last two Sundays, more than ten thousand residents have participated in cleaning yards and streets," as well as in repairing gates, doors, and windows in and around apartment houses.[119] While the practice of subbotniki had a long revolutionary heritage, these events were harnessed now—rhetorically— in a particularly systematic way and for the particular goal of maintaining housing and associated infrastructure. Public culture promoted a third level of collective at the kvartal, or neighborhood district. The same newspaper described ten five-floor apartment blocks, among whose communally inspired population "[o]nly one question is being discussed: in what way and how can every resident help make his house and district better appointed?"[120]

A fourth and final type of urban collective was composed of the residents of a single apartment block or communal apartment. Given the notorious tensions that existed between close neighbors in extremely overcrowded housing space, the presentation of selfless popular participation was here particularly improbable. In a published letter sent to *Vecherniaia Moskva*, a resident of Furmannyi Lane described her voluntary commitment to childcare in her building: "although I myself am the mother of two small children, I've taken this on with great willingness."[121] Another published letter had a more complex message. Correspondents from 29 Gogolevskii Boulevard described how residents had combined (with the particular help of the activists among them and the assistance of the local housing administration) to keep the boiler room going through the winter.[122] Every reader would have known that the necessary supplies of firewood and other fuel could not have been obtained without access to informal networks of supply and *blat* (informal exchange of favors or exercise of "pull"). Although likely fictionalized, the letter indirectly exposes a credible model of cooperation among local state agency, party members, and ordinary residents, combining to keep an apartment block running at some level of basic survivability, partly through resort to the second economy: a precise example of how officials sought to facilitate autonomous activities by citizens within non-state collectives for the protection of the housing stock.

The last example implicitly brings rhetoric and reality into closer alignment, as do official documents. In spring and summer 1944, the Moscow Soviet set about harnessing the voluntary participation of cohorts of male and female workers and employees in "preparing the housing economy for winter."[123] Two years later, officials in the Council of Ministers (RSFSR) looked to the "great political and economic significance" of "patriotic" work by the urban population "in the activity of assisting construction, reconstruction, and improvement of housing." They proposed the provision of better collective facilities for local communities in reconstructed areas, including red corners and wall newspapers.[124] Red corners were the space in a housing management office or local club where propaganda was dispensed and imbibed. Officials discussed how to mobilize local communities (*obshchestvennost'*), a term that could carry an ideological charge. Housing management administrations (*domoupravleniia*), which operated under the supervision of the local district soviet (*raisovet*), were one of the mechanisms. In the era of reconstruction, these administrations were reconstituted, with the aim of better exploiting residents' efforts and labors in the maintenance, repair, and checking of the stock. Housing management administrations also contained paid staff, the most important being the house manager (*upravliaiushchii domom/domami*), who might be responsible for several apartment blocks. In the autumn and winter of 1945, the executive committee of the Moscow Soviet reorganized the city's 2,546 housing management administrations into 2,430 "commissions" with 18,097 members, whose everyday functions were fulfilled by an *aktiv*. This was a hub of enthusiasts and perhaps party members from (ideally) each apartment house, with responsibilities for such matters as repairs, sanitation checks, cultural and educational activities, and the supervision of wall newspapers. Makarov, the minister of Municipal Economy (RSFSR), who used the word *obshchestvennost'* when describing participants in this activity, considered such arrangements to be of "wide help" in reconstruction.[125]

Individuals' lived experience was more tense, brittle, and fractured than its representation in public culture or in more optimistic official papers. There was a sharp variety in the level of service provided by housing management administrations and by house managers. This flowed inevitably from their parlous finances, especially in the earlier part of this period. According to a report on the annual budget of the Housing Administration of the Moscow Soviet, "[t]he financial condition of domoupravleniia in 1944 was extremely strained."[126] In general, 82 percent of the city's 1,532 housing management administrations were running at a deficit.[127] Failure was also caused by incompetent personnel. In August 1948 the Moscow Soviet lambasted a house manager in the Novoslobodskii raion for allowing two wooden housing blocks on Sushchevsksii *val* to fall into dreadful disrepair.[128]

Taking public discourse seriously forces the conclusion that this variation in quality was in part a consequence of the limits of obshchestvennost' and community-mindedness. If people sometimes banded together or worked according to conscience and self-interest to improve the state of their housing, sometimes they did not.[129] In March 1944 the residents of 44 Chkalova Street in Moscow complained about their house manager's complete lack of attention to the upkeep of their building. They cited the lack of running water on the top floors, the long broken elevator, and windows that let in the snow.[130] Their complaint implies a passivity that would have disappointed the minister Makarov and his claims for what obshchestvennost' could achieve.

As has so often been the case in Russian history, the wide gap between people and elites hindered the development of mutually beneficial public activity based on shared interests.[131] This is implicit in the government's disproportionate interest in the reconstruction of elite housing from 1944. Historians such as Elena Zubkova have shown that postwar society was soon fractured in countless places.[132] The great unhappiness that seems such a common feature of the Soviet Union during the immediate postwar years could be caused or exacerbated by a failure of urban community spirit. One female worker in Moscow lived in a hostel after the war, in a room of thirty residents. On 16 January 1947, all her documents, including her ration cards, were stolen. "I live on nothing," she petitioned desperately. "I live alone, I have no family, I earn 300 rubles a month. I appealed to the factory committee and the local trade union committee, I didn't get any help."[133] This is a single case, told from one point of view, but if a person "live[s] alone" in a room of thirty residents and is the victim without remedy for such a considerable theft, the collective has plainly ceased to function. Whatever people might have thought about each other, or indeed about their government, they were obliged to cooperate in and around the housing management administrations. In the closing stages of the war and the years thereafter, these organizations became hybrid formations, funded by the city soviet, combining paid employees with voluntary help.

Postwar Stalinist society was highly traumatized and had many unique and troubling historical features. Forms of urban association and cooperation were expedients of the government rather than elements of civil society. They were neither a check on the structures of Stalinist rule nor an opposition to it. Community-minded voluntarism and mobilization were only sporadically significant, not very deep, and typically marked by a lack of idealism. Individuals seemed prepared to make appropriate efforts if others did, and if the state did too. A polisher at the Stalin Car Works was reported in September 1946 as saying, "I live in a departmental house on Mashinostroenie Street. The plastering is caving in. The glass was broken in 1941, during a German air raid on Moscow, but still hasn't been replaced. We agree to help in the repairs, only let them organize the work [properly]."[134]

Such failures existed everywhere, but local housing management administrations were capable of latching state resources onto voluntary local collectives within which individuals could exercise self-interest. Local officials could mobilize the autonomy of citizens. At least sometimes, the actions of these local officials and the central policies that facilitated them fostered a "communal economy" (as "kommunal'noe khoziaistvo" or "municipal economy," is somewhat literally rendered) in which separate housing could exist. For all its severe faults and limitations, this still amounted to a template that Khrushchev would later use when he took the separate family apartment in the collective housing district as the basis of the mass housing program. Another bridge from the 1940s to the 1950s had a less desirable destination. It was the moonscape of the planned economy.

Central Planning and the Operation of the Housing Economy

Perhaps everybody in Tashkent was waiting for an earthquake. It did not come during the time of war or late Stalinism, when the city was packed out with evacuees from the battle zones. It came two decades later, on 26 April 1966, and swathes of the housing stock collapsed, with tragic results.[135] Back in 1950, the residents of a new apartment house on Navoi Street were anxious about that fate. Their three-story block had been constructed between 1943 and 1948 and was owned by the Ministry of Light Industry of the Uzbek Republic. Residents started to move in during 1947, when the block was unfinished, and they had filled the apartments by 1949. By then, they complained, the building was still not completed and major defects remained. That year, a commission recommended that part of the building be evacuated—but only when the ministry had space to rehouse the residents elsewhere. In December 1950, they were still there, angry about their miserable conditions, and anxious that they might still be living there when the earthquake came.[136]

The Soviet Union was not the only country to prepare inadequately for earthquakes, and it met the consequences of that disaster, when it struck, with rapid construction. It is for another reason that the story of the apartment house on Navoi

Street is significant. The story foreshadows some typical experiences of central planning during Khrushchev-era mass construction: of residents moving in (with or without permission) before a building was completed, because of the unstoppable pressure of demand; and of officials signing off on a building as complete when it was far from ready, in order that it appear on the lists of that year's plan. Like other problems associated with central planning, these practices dated back in principle to the 1930s but took on a particular form in the closing stages of the war and the first years of peace, and they conditioned what happened next. Between 1944 and 1950, the main components of Khrushchev's mass housing program were developed to greater or lesser levels of sophistication, but they were not assembled: the enabling factors were partly put in place, the positive legacies were gathered, but the program was not launched. Particular aspects of central planning and economic organization that would set the course of construction from the mid-1950s also date from this earlier period. They did not always enable mass construction, though; they often prevented it from achieving its potential.

During the fourth five-year plan (1946–1950), enough new resources were diverted to the urban housing economy to change its course. Yet the inputs were far from sufficient, and the mechanisms for distributing them were often inefficient. Central planning was a fluid system, in which a hierarchical management structure from the dictator down to individual enterprises engaged with the prescribed plan. This plan, complex and all-embracing, was a monument as much as a reality: it was based on partial information provided by industrial enterprises, which manipulated data for the sake of their own advantage, and Gosplan's targets were seldom attainable.[137] Both before and after the war, the plan favored heavy industry, but even in this sector the insistence on speed created slack in the system; projects fell behind time and were often left incomplete.[138] And as the goals of the system became, however modestly, more various (with housing, for example, obtaining a slightly modified level of priority), the plan became more complex and hence more difficult to deliver.[139] At the top of the pyramid, the planning structure was made even more complicated by the establishment of Gossnab (the State Committee for Material and Equipment Supply) in 1947, creating a new triumvirate of planners with Gosplan and the Ministry of Finance.[140] The inherent qualities of overwhelming complexity, excessive speed, problematic information, formal rigidity, fractured responsibility, and de facto adaptability in the face of imminent failures made for an unstable and particularly deficient overall structure beset by chains of unpredicted consequences. Meanwhile, piecemeal and fragmentary approaches to housing policy made the task of this troubled system still more difficult.

In the housing sector, not unlike elsewhere, central planners imposed finance and output targets on ministries and municipalities, insisting on what had to be spent and what had to be produced. Even coming close to fulfilling either set of targets was often impossible, and subsequent recalibrations of the plan, while to some extent speaking of a rational flexibility, often just pushed the problem to another city or factory. Shifting one blockage in the plan tended to create a blockage elsewhere, probably a worse and unforeseeable one, while inputs leaked away, producing spurts and trickles in output, like some fiendish plumbing system that was being maintained in the dark. In Penza in November 1947, housing construction had reached 10 percent of the yearly target. But Penzastroi, the local construction trust, only had 40 percent of the required—that is, planned—workforce; it was able to make use of only 40 percent of the resources that had been distributed for the overall improvement (*blagoustroistvo*) of the city. In a letter to the republic Council of Ministers, the chairman of the Penza oblast' soviet and the secretary of the oblast' party committee argued—energetically, if implicitly—that the constraints of planning were asphyxiating their city's housing economy. After describing a housing profile characterized by dreadful problems with water supply, sanitation, and electricity, put under pressure by the growth of industry and population during the war, and shamed by its average of 3.7 square meters per person, they wrote, "A range of measures for urban improvement, accepted in 1946 . . . has not produced a noticeable effect because the city has not been seriously repaired for a full decade."[141] Indeed, the low level of facilities would act as "a major brake" on economic development (including housing construction) in the "near future."

Inputs to the reconstruction drive bore a malformed relationship to output, measured in the number of square meters of housing space constructed or reconditioned. By the end of 1948, the 1946–1950 five-year plan for housing construction in the RSFSR was fulfilled by only 33.8 percent, with local soviets at half this rate.[142] The planned housing economy could not produce efficient outcomes. This is one reason why historians, with their eyes on immediate social impact, have underestimated the structural and underlying importance of immediate postwar reconstruction. Four aspects of the planned economy of housing reconstruction changed in important ways during these years: the industrial base, the housing economy's organizational structure, labor, and finance. These changes, though, produced a mixed inheritance for the 1950s.

The war wrecked not only the housing stock but also the housing construction industry. While the population of Leningrad starved and its housing stock declined, the region's construction industry was rapidly eliminated. Before 1941 the Leningrad oblast' construction trust had 65 heavy lorries, 12 light lorries, 180 horses, and 3 timber-working plants. These all disappeared during the war. According to the responsible RSFSR People's Commissar, the whole lot "was looted by the Germans."[143] His plea for help resulted in the promise that 250 "qualified workers" and 30 drivers would be sent to the Leningrad oblast' trust for reconstruction work by January 1945. Officials insisted that priority in newly constructed housing in the area be given to these workers.[144] Failures in construction output were often blamed on an inadequate workforce or a poor industrial base, or a combination of the two.[145]

Officials in party and government recognized while the war was still in progress that they lacked the necessary industrial infrastructure for the tremendous task ahead. The State Committee of Defense (GKO) instituted a decree in May 1944, "On the creation of an industrial base for mass housing construction."[146] This concern persisted after the war, reflected in a major Council of Ministers report on this subject in 1946, and in detailed discussions in the same body in January 1948 about increasing investment in enhanced mechanization.[147] To a great extent, however, these preparations were just so much useless typescript. Lack of ambition and resources severely constrained relevant industrial expansion. No national drive developed the production of cement, timber, glass, paint, construction machinery (such as cranes), or small parts (such as nails). By December 1950 Gosplan (RSFSR) recognized the urgency of the situation and pushed for some minimum immediate targets, including 30 excavators and 115 cranes.[148] This has a modest ring, but it underscores the confidential recognition that something had gone badly wrong with the housing reconstruction effort. It points toward the slow but essential turning point that was reached in 1950–1951.

Second, in 1950 officials drew attention to serious failures in the way that the housing economy was organized. Improvements in the industrial base of the urban housing economy, however modest, required more effective administrative structures. Beneath the decision making of the top layer of dictatorship (Stalin, the politburo, and the Council of Ministers) were arrayed Gosplan, Gossnab, and the Ministry of Finance. The next level down was dominated by the housing administrations (*upravleniia*) of the republican councils of ministers, and the Ministry of Urban Construction (USSR). Subordinate agencies such as ministerial scientific research institutes were also part of the central bureaucracy. This system could generate ideas and initiatives but was less competent at following them through. It was subject to turf wars and bureaucratic infighting. The Council of Ministers (RSFSR) typically rejected a proposal by the Architectural Affairs Committee of the Council of Ministers (USSR) in 1946 that all building plans relevant to its territory should go through the committee before being granted final approval.[149] While the transaction costs of such exchanges could be higher than in less bureaucratized polities, they could also have efficient results in the context of the postwar emergency, with its novel pressure to increase the housing stock. The outcome of this dispute is an early indication that the rearguard battles of the architectural profession to defend the aesthetic content of their production were losing out to the necessary forces of standardized construction. With enhanced resources, such forms of central organization would gear up for increased construction during the launch period of 1951–1957.

As organizational units, construction trusts and their constituent enterprises were in some ways as important as the bodies of the central bureaucracy. They made up the organizational presence on the ground and undertook the actual building. Shortly after the war, measures were put in place on a case-by-case basis to merge local trusts, rationalizing construction by minimizing administrative duplication. In December 1946, Voronezhstroi merged with Voronezhgorstroi to make up a new super-Voronezhstroi.[150] Makarov, RSFSR minister of Municipal Economy, wrote in a letter of 1946, "There is nothing to say against the merger of construction trusts, because it allows the creation of stronger construction organizations and the improvement of their work."[151] Elsewhere, new construction trusts were being founded to provide organizational backbone and to channel resources to some of the areas of maximum construction need. The RSFSR Council of People's Commissars proposed a new trust for Cheliabinsk oblast' while the war was still under way.[152] Inspections of the work of trusts and local soviets and overall central oversight assumed more regularized and helpful proportions during this period. Officials in the RSFSR Council of Ministers slated the weak systems with which soviets in Kemerovo checked the local construction organizations, and they proposed additional investment for struggling trusts in Kaliningrad.[153] Central or republican officials were also anxious to foster and streamline primary-level construction organizations. The Ministry of Housing-Civil Construction (RSFSR) sponsored a conference of local building organizations, planning for 250 delegates to meet in Moscow over five days in December 1946.[154]

City housing administrations, which operated inside local soviets, worked with construction trusts in the implementation of policy. They were headed by a senior local bureaucrat who worked alongside an influential and equally well paid chief engineer.[155] The head of the administration was responsible for a multiplicity of primary-level organizational units. In 1945, for example, the Moscow Soviet's housing administration contained Mosgorzhilektro, charged with the supervision of elevators and other electrical systems; Mosremont, which oversaw repair work as well as a training unit, and an employees' newspaper; and Moszhilsnab, which coordinated supply. It was also the administrative hub of ten specialist factories, which produced items from cranes to screws, and the thirty-six district-level soviet housing administrations (*raizhilupravleniia*, or RZhU).[156] These RZhU oversaw the housing management administrations (domoupravleniia), which were reformed during this period. But reforms were matched by tensions between, on the one hand, the higher and lower levels of the bureaucracy and, on the other, the voluntary and permanent staffs of the housing management administrations.[157] Improving this system had become a priority by the end of the war, with the administrative oversight of the training of housing professionals considered one area of priority.

These various organizational improvements would be accelerated during the 1950s. Yet between 1944 and 1950, overall, they had the hesitant gait of tactical half-measures rather than any robust strategic effectiveness. More effective inspections were one thing, but in general, communications were strained between the center, the city soviets, and the construction trusts. The system militated against local initiative within the city and among the oblast' bureaucracies, while forcing local people themselves to demonstrate considerable initiative if they were personally to survive the housing crisis. But the legacy was clear.

Reforms associated with the labor force made up the third economic legacy for the 1950s. Improvements extended to enhancing skills, training, and productivity, employing more workers, and making their living conditions less dreadful. As the war came to a close, all types of construction staff were at a premium. The chairmen of the Iaroslavl' oblast' soviet and party committee noted in 1945 that their housing departments and construction enterprises were lacking in leading administrators, qualified professionals, and skilled workers. Workers' conditions were "at a low level" and their training "absent." The administrative organs themselves were in "extremely unsatisfactory" shape.[158] Central officials attempted to offer a response.[159] In some places, they tried harder to ensure that construction workers gained the first chance to occupy the new housing that they built. In November 1945, characteristically, five thousand square meters of proposed construction in Novgorod was set aside for the builders who were being drafted into the town.[160]

Despite their understanding of the problem and their attempts to rectify it, central planners could neither recruit enough skilled workers nor provide them with adequate living conditions. Lack of workers held back the capital repair of the housing stock in Kazan' in September 1946, with knock-on effects for the total housing space available for the local population.[161] Construction workers' miserable living conditions continued to inhibit their productivity and to disrupt their employers' attempts to meet plan targets through the 1940s and beyond. In Kalinin oblast' in 1948, eighty-five workers left their sites without authorization (*samovol'no*) "because of poor housing conditions."[162] Conditions were especially bad for young workers—some of whom could in practice easily move on, thus further disrupting the plan (though others were tightly tied to their workplace). In 1948, at the Krasnoiarsk construction trust, hostels for young workers were so crowded that the noise precluded any chance to obtain "proper rest," and theft was common.[163]

Such labor indiscipline and restiveness grew in the postwar period at a time of problematic "class" relations, when the gap between local bosses (*nachal'stvo*) and workers—"slave," "indentured," and "free" alike—created tension and anger.[164] Many of the most repressive of Stalinist labor mechanisms were abolished some time after Stalin's death, but even between 1944 and 1950 they were counterbalanced with gentler incentives. In Moscow in March 1944, for example, one of many competitions offered small cash prizes for the "best carpenter," "best plumber," "best yard janitor" (*dvornik*), "best cleaner," and other best employees of the Housing Administration.[165] This would stretch into a more generous system of bonuses in the 1950s, although the implementation was always very uneven, and Moscow was disproportionately privileged. Disciplinary infringements by senior employees were tackled with the big stick rather than the small carrot. Such staff were humiliated in orders of the city soviet, and the thought of the camps must have pressed on them.[166] By the mid-1950s, the worst of this had disappeared for good, and the senior management of housing administrations started to enjoy perhaps excessive working security. Failures of incentive thus persisted in a softer but still pernicious way, as an ongoing curse of the centrally planned economy.

Policies for the training of the workforce also had a repressive capacity that would mutate in the post-Stalinist period. Young "labor conscripts" who graduated from short courses at "schools of factory-plant training" (*shkoly fabrichno-zavodskogo obucheniia*, or FZOs) were directed by the Ministry of Labor Reserves to a destination about which they might have little say.[167] Other policies for training the workforce were fragmented, providing some narrowly useful precedents for the Khrushchev years as well as a foreshadowing of some of its problems. In 1947 the Moscow Soviet's housing administration was instituting a range of technical short courses for its workers.[168] This was part of a model for future development, but it was limited in scope. It added little to what would later become a long-term strength of the Soviet economy, its ability to train its workforce. But effective and lengthy training was hardly feasible during the postwar crisis, when rebuilding the construction industry and re-creating its labor cadres had to proceed simultaneously with the physical construction of housing.

Problems were equally evident in housing finance. Central planners funded reconstruction by apportioning fixed sums of rubles to city soviets, ministerial housing departments, construction trusts, and other agencies. Yet resources were limited. Heavy industry and atomic weapons were just two powerful drains on an overall budget that was still largely predicated on the sacrifice of popular living conditions. Without the exploitation of private resources made possible by the individual housing construction scheme, the funding of the housing economy would have been still more dire. Capital markets did not exist; international assistance had been rejected; war loans would not be returned to the population, but anything resembling a further "bond" issue, at this time of catastrophic poverty, was inconceivable. Within these sorry limits, expenditure on construction was higher than before the war and the dimensions of the emergency forced planners to seek additional resources and to direct them flexibly. In August 1946, Nikolai Voznesenskii, chairman of the all-union Gosplan, ordered an increase in the budget of the Ministry of Housing-Civil Construction (RSFSR) of 16,500,000 rubles, with 8,450,000 to be apportioned immediately, during the third quarter.[169] But these investment levels stood no chance of coming close to fulfilling the plan's construction targets.

The problem, moreover, lay in the plan. Experts in Gosplan laid out targets ranging from all-union construction spending on a five-year cycle to subannual apportionments for a city district's housing management administrations. Modified during these years, the Stalinist planning of housing finance would be the too rigid and wasteful framework that constricted Khrushchev's mass building program. In the immediate postwar years, low levels of investment were squandered by the clumsy mechanisms for its distribution, with a feeble mismatch between what the center thought was right and what the localities really needed. Local soviets' dependence on central and republican organs of power for finance constrained the extent of reconstruction and undermined the soviets' political and moral authority in their attempts to fulfill the plan. In November 1948, for example, following correspondence from the chairman of the Sverdlovsk obkom, the chairman of the RSFSR Council of Ministers, Mikhail Rodionov, agreed to increase the 1949 plan for spending on capital construction from 5,100,000 to 7,800,000 rubles.[170] This kind of responsive budgetary allocation is partly explained as a beneficent action. But at the same time, it was ad hoc and inefficient, ineffectively matching resources to need. And it made accountability more nebulous. People might blame local officials for their plight, but local officials could always gesture toward Moscow. Local officialdom could get away with tremendous underachievement because of the system's structural encouragement of irresponsibility.

Underachievement is the right word: they could have done better. Local soviets frequently failed to make proper use of even inadequate financial allocations. In the first quarter of 1946, only 31 percent of the planned capital had been invested in the reconstruction drives of cities from Pskov to Krasnoiarsk. This had yielded a mere 8.5 percent of the planned housing completions, as measured in square meters of housing space.[171] Local institutions wasted resources. In a 1949 drive to cut spending that did not directly fund construction, only nine of thirty-seven construction trusts of republican status in the RSFSR had made savings of the hoped-for level, while the rest had increased their costs.[172] Trusts could not fulfill their allocations if they could not find the workers, machines, or materials on which to spend them.[173] Local elites clouded the picture by siphoning off investments for their own use, while ordinary workers stole from building sites to build any kind of shelter (these were universal problems in the postwar emergency, from Germany to Japan).[174]

Proposals for dealing with the problem were drawn up by republican government in the RSFSR. They would find additional purchase in the 1950s. One report suggested that construction organizations operate "strict accounting of construction materials" at both warehouse and accounts office, and that building site accountants produce monthly sets of figures.[175] Another possibility was boosting socialist competition. This could provide incentives for individual workers, in a more systematic and realistic development of the Stakhanovite tradition. The same principle was applied to entire cities. Competitions for various aspects of urban improvement took place every quarter, with substantial cash prizes for those cities that had overfulfilled their plan by the largest margin. In the third quarter of 1946, the Podol'sk *gorispolkom* won the competition for capital and routine repair of housing, with plan fulfillment of 117 percent. The reward was 125,000 rubles.[176] Architectural competitions expanded; a Council of Ministers (RSFSR) decree of September 1947 noted increasing levels of participation.[177] But central planning struggled to calibrate appropriate awards, as incentivizing the overfulfillment of one set of categories could lead directly to the underfulfillment of others. The maldistribution of resources resulted. This problem was not unique to the Soviet economy, but the extreme power of the plan ensured that the stakes were especially high there.

The story of failure would be retold in the 1950s and 1960s, but with missing chapters and a happier ending. Thanks in part to the policy work of the immediate postwar years, finance would be manipulated at least somewhat more effectively by the Khrushchev era. Moreover, the mechanisms associated with the individual housing construction scheme of the 1940s would greatly facilitate the expansion and diversification of credit in the 1950s and after, for both individual houses and cooperatives. Such experience ensured that the planned housing economy was better run in the future, but the retention of a hardly reformed planning system meant that the lessons were only partly useful, rather like learning to drive a car without being able to change above second gear. In general, the legacy passed on by the planned housing economy was one of inefficiency. It could not be otherwise, and many officials understood this—at least through their observation of the details, if not of the broad view. Between 1944 and

1950 the housing sector performed badly, sometimes spectacularly badly, in terms of plan fulfillment. An approach to planning that was unnecessarily rigid—unnecessarily, first, because there is much evidence that people at the time understood the faults and, second, because the repeated chances for reform would in the 1950s be consistently missed—would infect the housing program for the rest of the period 1944–1964. It was a genetic fault, an unhappy inheritance, and the tragic flaw that in the next two decades would frustrate the talents, efforts, and hopes of a generation of officials, experts, workers, and urban residents.

In 1950 it might have seemed that the misery would carry on forever. A citizen of Moscow called E. G. Strel'tsova wrote to Aleksei Kosygin, her Supreme Soviet deputy, at the end of that year that "impossible housing conditions" had brought her "to complete despair." She was pregnant and had served at the front as a nurse, and now wrote, "I ask you to end my torture, suffering and purgatory. . . . I don't have any strength to cope with this impossible situation." Strel'tsova lived in a basement, sharing eight square meters with her husband, another couple, and their nine-year-old child. They were next to the central heating pipes, and the temperature rose to thirty-five degrees. There was no room for a table.[178]

The terrible failures in Soviet housing reconstruction between 1944 and 1950 were undoubtedly responsible for excessive levels of mortality and misery among the victorious population and contrast with the great achievements of the mass housing program during the 1950s. But it is important to recall the tremendous pressures under which all postwar states labored and the ineffectiveness of the immediate postwar housing reconstruction efforts elsewhere as well. West German reconstruction only became swifter after the 1949 partition: in the first few postwar years, many people were trying simply to survive, using any tactic available to them.[179] In France, there were no meaningful efforts made to rebuild until after 1950.[180] Japanese construction was also low before the 1950s.[181] In Britain, governed at the time by a Labour administration with a coherent program, a gift for rhetoric, and a thumping mandate, housing construction levels were much lower than they would be under the Conservative governments of the 1950s.[182]

It is in the light of a revised view of the period from 1944 to 1950 that the immediate origins of the housing program become explicable. During these years, Soviet housing ideology undertook a meandering and unfinished transition from being predicated on a motif of sacrifice to one of beneficence. Essential practical foundations of the housing program were thus laid. The impact on people's lives was extremely mixed during 1944–1950, and no one claimed that a mass housing program was in operation. Yet even by 1951, some voices, including Khrushchev's, were so claiming.[183] The last two years of late Stalinism and the first eighteen months after Stalin's death were crucial. During that time, the housing policy that Khrushchev later launched was fashioned out of the raw legacies of the initial reconstruction era.

The Launch of the Mass Housing Program, 1951–1957

In the rush to provide reasonably decent accommodation for the masses, it has been necessary to produce living quarters which are still somewhat below the standards of other countries and to condone the use of inferior materials and workmanship. As far as the average Russian is concerned, all he knows is that his living conditions are gradually improving. . . . By these criteria, the state must be regarded as discharging its responsibilities with reasonable credit. But if the Soviet Union is to maintain its claim to be a great and progressive nation, and its pretensions to moral and material leadership in the world, then it has failed and will continue to fail so long as it shows no signs of early and very substantial improvement.
—**The Australian chargé d'affaires in Moscow, 6 July 1951**

. . . to liquidate the workers' housing shortage in the next ten to twelve years.—**Decreed aim of the Council of Ministers (USSR) and Central Committee of the Communist Party of the Soviet Union, 31 July 1957**

"The appearance of this document," wrote the editor of the journal *Arkhitektura SSSR* in October 1957, "is the greatest event in the history of . . . construction and architecture in the USSR."[1] The document referred to was the keynote decree of July 1957 on housing construction, which declared that "the most important nationwide task" was to ensure that "in the next ten to twelve years, the housing shortage in the country will be ended."[2] What followed was the biggest year-on-year rise in the whole history of Soviet housing. Per capita construction in the Soviet Union now towered over that of its European rivals.

This was the spectacular culmination of the launch of the mass housing program between 1955 and 1957. How can this achievement be explained in the light of the housing crisis that millions such as E. G. Strel'tsova were experiencing in 1950?[3] It seems a rapid change, like many others in the postwar world. True, the suffering still went on: many people continued to endure dreadful conditions long after 1964. But even by the end of 1957, the lives of millions of families had already been transformed for the better by the activation—in two stages—of the dormant initiatives and partial policies that made up the legacies from 1944–1950. In 1950 and 1951, officials finally recognized that reconstruction, though existing, had so far been inadequate, and that the housing crisis had to be faced down. They worked with a range of experts to create the policy mechanisms, technological advances, and overall construction capacity that could generate mass housing, though their efforts were still uncoordinated by the dictatorship.[4] In the absence of political direction or large-scale investment, higher construction output did not immediately result: the actual annual rise in new square meters was not much higher in 1950–1951 than it was year on year between 1944 and 1950.

A second turning point came between 1955 and 1957 and owed much to Khrushchev himself. Taking hold of what amounted to an existing but latent policy and capacity, he launched the mass housing program between these years, with the July 1957 decree acting as the culmination. Only then did the mass building of apartments truly take off. The change after Stalin's death was associated with the new possibility of rights and respect that partly, and with numerous exceptions, marked the Soviet system after 1953. Success thus depended absolutely on late Stalinism's capacity to develop nearly all the mechanisms required for the biggest housing program of its type in world history—just as it depended on the expiration of late Stalinism for their activation and launch.

Two motifs dominated the decree of July 1957—quantity of construction and rationality of approach. Quantity was necessary to meet the twelve-year goal, while rationality would make the quantity possible. Insisting on great expansions in construction by exploiting rational mechanisms and seeking purely material outcomes was an eminently beneficent strategy: it was an increasingly serious and coordinated attempt straightforwardly to raise people's living standards. Relative rationality in housing policy was most apparent between 1951 and 1957—and especially between 1955 and 1957, at least in comparison with the next seven years of the Khrushchev era, when the urge to communism and the plan's rigid obsessions with quantity would pervert it. This rationality consisted in newly effective central control, ambition, and practices, whose aims could be defined in material, rather than consciousness-altering, terms. These years could be set up as a contrast to the rest of the Khrushchev era, which pivoted on the promises of communism made at the 1961 party congress, by which time the housing program was guided by self-consciously ideological nostrums and the aim of creating proto-communist neighborhoods. The two concepts, of "rationality" and "ideology" (broadly conceived) can thus be separated for the purpose of analysis. A phalanx of historians, however, have pointed out in one way or another that rationality was itself an ideological construct, that it was dependent on the transformative and redemptive capacities of a powerful state, capable of outstanding feats of information gathering, sifting, and cataloguing, and with a wide-ranging field of interest, vision, and capacity. Meanwhile, the Soviet bureaucracy insisted that its work was simultaneously rational and ideologically right, before, during, and after the late Stalinist and the Khrushchev eras. The communist mission of the late 1950s and early 1960s depended on statist processes that were "rational," and its rhetoric made use of the labels of rationality and communism alike. But this was not the case before 1958, and especially between 1955 and 1957, when the practice and rhetoric of rationality existed without the demands or much of the language of communist promise, and when ideological justifications were announced in a lower volume.

Facing the Crisis—The Shift of 1951–1954

Six years after the victory, D. A. Filin and V. K. Maslov of Mytishchi could not bear their housing conditions. They wrote in 1951 that the apartment they shared with their families was in a "completely wrecked condition": an external wall was "moving," the ceiling was "caving in," "the floor has rotted and given way, the window ledges and frames have given way, the roof is full of holes, water constantly stands under the floor, in the basement." Six people lived in the apartment. It was so cold in winter they had to disperse to stay with hard-pressed acquaintances. Unsurprisingly, "because of the awful conditions, many of us are often ill," and "Maslov's baby girl died in 1949." Despite the protests of the occupants, the city soviet did not undertake the necessary repairs. Only after Filin and Maslov wrote to Kosygin, and he passed on the complaint, did the soviet promise to do the work "within the shortest time [*v blizhaishie dni*]."[5]

This evidence might be loaded in favor of the correspondent, but it is an entirely plausible illustration of mass experience. Another sad story was contested by the local soviet. A. M. Kovtsurova of L'vov described her despair at the housing conditions she apparently experienced in 1951. She was a single mother who lived with her two children in a damp basement with little light, with walls pocked by holes, and no stove. "The children and I live with the rats," she protested. "I can't go on any longer like this with two children." She drew on the iconography of public culture in her petition: "Stalin talked of a happy childhood, of everything for children, but my children are hungry and cold and shoeless and undressed without an apartment, sitting in a basement with the rats." Her children deserved the fruits of Stalin's rhetoric: "Give them the chance to live and study as Stalin said it." Kovtsurova wrote all this in a letter to the Supreme Soviet. When challenged, the L'vov Soviet claimed that she had only worked for a total of one year since moving to L'vov in 1944, and that local officials had offered to help by placing her dependants in a children's home (though that kind of "help" might put the good offices of the L'vov Soviet in doubt).[6] Given that both sides had a vested interest, there is no particular reason to privilege the testimony of the soviet above that of the petitioner, and Kovtsurova's depiction of her housing resonates with that of many others. Each individual letter to the senior members of the Supreme Soviet or Council of Ministers is its own imperfect historical source; it is their cumulative testimony that presents a convincing depiction of widespread despair at housing conditions in 1951.

For all the problems of interpretation associated with this type of evidence, the weight of the postbags of the upper reaches of the leadership was figuratively commensurate with the burden of the population. The documents give historians no room to doubt the scale of suffering occasioned by the housing shortage in 1951 (as in 1945), and the political elite knew with still more precision what was going on. Their knowledge was derived not just from the scattered and impressionistic evidence of citizens' correspondence. In 1950 and 1951 the government sponsored detailed reports that checked lack of progress in reconstruction across the union. The Ministry of Construction (USSR) gathered data that became the subject of correspondence within and beyond the Council of Ministers, involving such senior figures as Nikolai Bulganin, first deputy chairman of the Council of Ministers (USSR). The information was not parked on the byways of the Central Statistical Administration; this was active information, pushed on by sectional bureaucratic interests and the ambitions of enlightened officialdom, moving through the highways of the Ministry of Construction and the Council of Ministers, and presented in the kind of reports that generated policy.[7]

There could only be one conclusion. Housing reconstruction had met with variable success whose sum was a crisis, although reports and correspondence avoided such inflammatory language. In 1950 and 1951, ministers commented with great concern on the widespread incidence of considerable failure. The data flowing across their desks included those for the ongoing catastrophe of Novgorod, which in January 1950 contained 53.5 percent of the 1940 housing fund. This meant that the average per person was 3.6 square meters, compared to 6.0 square meters in 1940.[8] Inspectors estimated that the Stalingrad state housing fund was at 67 percent of the prewar level at the start of 1950.[9] In Tallinn, 81 percent of the prewar housing fund had been rebuilt by January 1950.[10] Yet this also fell short of the plan, with the usual knock-on effects; in 1949, state bodies in Tallinn built only 57 percent of their targets for new housing, even though these various all-union, republic, and local soviet organizations had obtained 104 percent of their planned financial allocations.[11]

Faced with the evidence, some senior elements in the party-government apparently accepted the scale of the problem and the urgent need to solve it. They had to overcome past failure. The Council of Ministers (USSR) drafted a new volume of decrees whose purpose was to make local officials fulfill the specific terms of previous directives, some of which had been introduced four years or more ago.[12] Their analysis emphasized failures of "rationality" and was usually written up in measured terms. Explanations for the failures of 1944–1950 drew not on discursive categories such as "enemy" or "conspiracy" that derived from ideological excess but on such humdrum and rationally conceived factors as splintered bureaucratic structures, failures of technology, problems with labor, lack of materials, low construction quality, the uneven provision of local amenities, and the unimpeded spread of individual construction. While seeking to ameliorate the failures of reconstruction between 1944 and 1950, policy between 1951 and 1954 drew directly and quite systematically on the achievements, innovations, and lessons of the 1940s, without solving the earlier period's greatest structural problems. After 1950 housing construction capacity was outfitted in a sufficiently robust way to leave Khrushchev not only with a policy to pull together but with the technical and infrastructural means to start to implement it. The period between 1951 and 1954 was not characterized by the launch of the housing program or by striking advances in construction output; rather, during these years, officials prepared the launching ground—only sometimes realizing that they were doing it. While intense problems persisted and policy remained uncoordinated between 1951 and 1954, the volume and depth of disparate initiatives marked a step-change from the 1940s and ensured that policy contained enough functioning components that Khrushchev could bring together as a housing program from 1955.

First, a tighter administrative relationship between the center in Moscow and the localities emerged after 1950, though no one could deny it would remain a hit-and-miss affair throughout Soviet history.[13] True, old complaints persisted between 1951 and 1954. One I. S. Tarasevich of Murom asked Lavrentii Beriia, Stalin's security supremo, in a letter of January 1952, "Why is it that the party-government creates laws and a constitution but local power does not carry them out?"[14] The Council of Ministers in Moscow could introduce decrees and Gosplan could funnel out the resources, but local administrations could still fail to achieve targets for entirely avoidable reasons, including incompetence and venality. Central bodies were often enraged by the tardy submission of relevant construction paperwork by the localities, resulting in delays in the approval of new housing.[15] As a result, central officials became increasingly concerned to promote organizational reforms that could minimize the instances of such failure.

This required further rationalization of local organizational structures. A typical example shows officials' concern that the local housing economy in Tallinn was fractured into "twenty tiny organizations."[16] Such worries produced an explicit policy in October 1952, with a Council of Ministers (USSR) decree "On the strengthening of construction organizations of the Ministry of Housing-Civil Construction (RSFSR)."[17] The mergers of construction trusts accelerated.[18] Attempts were made to implement more robust inspections by central bodies of local organizations—and more fluid communications between them.[19] By the end of 1954, employees of the Administration of Architectural Affairs were traveling more frequently to the provinces, checking construction, assisting with technical documentation, and helping to increase output.[20] The growing interest by the center in the detailed operations of local housing economies was exemplified when a local production base was expanded and diversified, with more sustained attention paid to items ranging from cement to steel enamel sinks.[21]

These were significant developments, but by 1954 they had generated only an ambiguous material outcome. In assessing the program of inspections carried out by the Administration of Architectural Affairs that year, officials remarked that the gap between central and local architectural organs remained wide, and that a Central Committee demand of January 1954 to strengthen center-periphery links was being ignored.[22] Yet these reforms were a work in progress—a partly functioning model—that Khrushchev could easily exploit from 1955 onward.

Changes to housing finance also improved the organizational link between center (Gosplan, the Council of Ministers, and the Ministry of Finance) and locality (trusts and soviets), partly through the mediating influence of the Municipal Bank, though the impact of these changes would not be felt in the outcomes of lived experience until the mid-1950s. The center was now more rapid in its responses than before. In Pskov oblast' in 1952, for example, the local soviet spent its budget for housing construction so rapidly that after four months it had fulfilled the financial plan by 71.1 percent. In March, anticipating the impending shortfall, the Council of Ministers (RSFSR) responded with a substantial increase in its allocation.[23] Nervous tactical diversions of resources in response to emergencies became more frequent after 1950 and were bigger in scale. Gosplan detected in 1953 that 957 families in Voronezh were living in non-housing accommodation, that their resettlement would require new housing construction of 13,500 square meters, and thus there was needed an "urgent" allocation of 10,500,000 rubles to the city soviet.[24] But as time went on, and the more urgent aftershocks of the postwar housing crisis faded away, the role of housing finance in the center–locality relationship was at least partly regularized. Attempts were made to balance a degree of local financial flexibility with central financial discipline. In 1954 policy makers aspired to give construction trusts across the RSFSR greater financial flexibility in their month-on-month budgetary arrangements.[25]

Such measures derived from concerns about inefficiency. Minimizing waste and reducing costs required considerable technical expertise in the management of both finance and construction, qualities that were at a premium. Nevertheless, both local and central administrations paid increasing attention to such matters as regulating the accounting of district soviets and controlling the costs of even trivial items, from kitchen tables to bathroom shelves.[26] Attention to every detail of pricing required discipline. This care over pricing presaged a determination to maximize construction output within the limits of centrally planned investment; it showed how state agencies were concerned with ever finer details of a growing housing policy. Such developments would be crucial for Khrushchev, and they depended on an administrative relationship between center and locality that was less dysfunctional than before.

Less ambiguously, the shift to standardized construction became irreversible between 1951 and 1954. While significant technological advances had taken place since the war, they were applied with only mixed enthusiasm in 1951. Bureaucrats noted that construction in Tallinn still had only a "low-tech" (*kustarno*) feel, and that almost no use was being made of "rapid production line methods" or "mechanization."[27] Aleksandr Vlasov, the authoritative head of Moscow's GlavAPU and the city's chief architect, commented as early as January 1952 in a letter to the chairman of Gosstroi, "Mass housing construction, as it is being realized in suburban Moscow and Moscow oblast', demands the widespread acceptance of standardized designs of three- and four-story apartment houses." Vlasov was already an academician and would soon be the president of the Academy of Architecture. His senior and serious voice reinforced the growing consensus on industrialized construction techniques. And yet the requirements of industrial capacity and political will lagged behind technical competence and professional conviction. Vlasov went on, "The absence at the present time of approved designs that accord with the productive-technical base is slowing down the normal progress of housing construction."[28]

Such warnings had an effect. In 1952 the Academy of Architecture foresaw during the fifth five-year plan (1951–1955) "the transition from artisan or semi-artisan processes . . . to industrial processes," defined as "factory-based housing construction."[29] More new buildings directly foreshadowed what would soon become famous as the five-story khrushchevka. The June 1953 edition of the journal for housing professionals featured photographs of four-story prefabricated, mass-produced apartment blocks at Zhukovskii, which had been completed within the previous two years.[30] A Council of Ministers (RSFSR) decree of September 1954, "On the confirmation of standardized four- and five-story housing of series 1-402 and 1-408," was certainly a proto-Khrushchevian blueprint.[31] The number of projects depending on mechanization and prefabrication grew dramatically.[32] While this was still a transitional period for standardized construction, and one-off neoclassical designs remained the preferred architecture of elite apartment blocks, party or government buildings, and urban ensembles, it was also the period when the future result of the transition became unmistakable. A revealing set of architectural plans published in December 1953 defines the transition: it shows five-story apartment blocks with neoclassical façades but prefabricated parts, and apartments of as little as thirty-one square meters each, demanding single-family occupancy.[33] Elsewhere in 1954, the Administration of Tall Buildings and its construction trust Vysotstroidetal' was working on flamboyant Stalin skyscrapers as well as more modest five-story apartment blocks on Moscow's Chekhovskaia and Krasnoarmeiskaia Streets.[34] When Khrushchev condemned grandiose architectural displays in December 1954, he was announcing, almost, a fait accompli.

Almost, but not quite. During this transition, architects and engineers increasingly accepted the logic of standardization but failed to agree on what a standardized apartment block should actually look like. Professionals were starting to recognize the technical and economic desirability of apartment houses of between three and five stories, but other plans of 1951–1952 were for standardized projects of from six to seven and from eight to fourteen stories.[35] Management of the Serp i Molot factory in Moscow's Pervomaiskii raion sought to build a fourteen-story block in 1951; the same year, the construction of fifty-nine examples of one blueprint of three- and four-story blocks was completed in Moscow, with seventy-eight more planned for 1952.[36] Some standardized designs of 1954 allowed for what would soon seem lavish apartment houses of between six and eight stories, with institutions such as shops using the ground floor, while other designs of that year experimented with relatively tall blocks.[37]

Meanwhile, elite housing retained its higher style, certainly for a year after Stalin's death. Contemporary albums and journals show how widespread the construction of monumental, expensive, and individually designed apartment blocks remained. The seven Stalin skyscrapers in Moscow were only the most fantastical. A monumental new block designed by Ivan Zholtovskii was completed on Smolenskaia Square in Moscow in 1952. It had nine stories, imposing dimensions, an intricate façade, elaborate wrought-iron gates set into the yard archway, and a vestibule whose staircase recalled Florence. The average apartment had an impressive 59.6 square meters of usable space.[38] And there were numerous more examples across the union.

Yet the range of construction options was becoming smaller by 1954, as consensus slowly crystallized on what would become the Khrushchev model. The decisive shift from an ethos of architecture to one of construction took place between 1951 and 1954. Tellingly, in 1952 the Architecture Soviet of GlavAPU was renamed the Architecture-Construction Soviet and now included "experts" at its meetings, rather than just senior architects, who for all their skilled and creative professionalism had brought a kind of amateurishness to the more complex tasks of urban reconstruction.[39] The shift was decisively apparent at the full-scale all-union construction conference that was held at the Kremlin in November–December 1954.[40] Here Khrushchev formally condemned "excess" in architecture, the fatal bomb in the demise of Stalinist neoclassicism. This widely reported step was confirmed by a major decree the following year. The subsequent renaming of the Academy of Architecture as the Academy of Construction and Architecture was by then merely titular, for the academy was already working out a constructor's manifesto. This renaming was merely the culmination of many less visible changes that had taken place between 1951 and 1954—not before, when architecture had much less ambiguously retained the grandeur of individual creativity (whatever architectural critics might say of the results). By the end of 1954, the construction model associated with Khrushchev had effectively become the only show in town.

The shift to standardized construction required at least a limited improvement in construction workers' conditions, practices, and skills, as the industry expanded and became more complex and professional. Evidence shows that labor allocations were bigger in volume and more responsive to local demand than before.[41] Better training, especially in short courses, was more common.[42] Yet an array of old problems associated with the Stalinist labor code long outlasted 1954 and remained in place until 1956.[43] As long as prescriptive, repressive, and yet somewhat weakly enforced Stalinist labor policies existed, however, disciplinary infractions would be chronic. Data gathered by Moscow's big construction trust, Glavmosstroi, for the first four months of 1953 highlighted the discipline deficit, showing overall that "labor discipline continues at a low level" and specifically that 223 working days were lost to shirking (*proguly*) in this one trust alone.[44] In the first ten months of 1951, 178 of Kaliningradstroi's 307 building workers left their employer, and 33 percent of these did so without any authorization at all (samovol'no).[45] They might leave to find better work or more congenial bosses, or to return to a different part of the country; state agencies had few resources to keep them at work, and government resorted to sometimes unhelpful prescriptions.[46]

Yet a growing number of initiatives were put in place between 1951 and 1954, which aimed, more rationally and beneficently, to persuade rather than force construction workers to remain on-site. A decree of late 1950 that sought to improve the conditions of young workers resulted within a year in "well-appointed accommodation" for 1,305 of those employed in selected trusts of the Ministry of Housing-Civil Construction (RSFSR). Their access to other facilities, "the network of clubs, red corners, sports grounds, libraries and cinemas," also improved. As a consequence, only 352 spontaneously left buildings sites in the first half of 1951, compared with 616 for the same period in 1950.[47] Wage increases were approved for workers and other employees of the Ministry in March 1952.[48] Better working conditions required improved safety at building sites. In June 1953, M. S. Lomovyi, a worker in Trust 109 of the Main Administration of the Construction of Tall Buildings, was killed in an accident on a building site in Moscow. His death prompted an investigation by administration officials, who concluded that it was a consequence of "a breach in the elementary rules of technical safety." The report remarked on the lack of alarm systems, of training in safe working practices, and of "prophylactic" measures.[49] This case and its assessment were typical; the party-government was starting to place more value on its construction workers.[50] And it was doing the same for employees in the housing economy who did not work on building sites, as well. The numbers of paid professional employees of housing management administrations (domoupravleniia) increased, though not across the board.

Measures were also put in place better to regulate housing construction and the administration of local districts. Many a neighborhood remained a chaotic free-for-all where the local administration and residents alike acted to solve immediate crises with little forward planning. Soviets and commissions continued to accept as habitable new dwellings that were both incomplete and dangerous. In 1954 the Vladimir Soviet approved for settlement an unfinished and defective block of forty-two apartments owned by the local tractor factory, which had already been turned down four times by the independent approval commission.[51] Yet from 1951 onward, regulation was becoming tighter. Gosarkhstroikontrol', the checking agency in the RSFSR, was itself more closely supervised by the Administration of Architectural Affairs, which insisted that individual citizens who had built their own houses without permission or without achieving the expected norms and standards of construction should not be granted residence documents.[52] In Leningrad oblast' in 1952, E. F. Shchepaturova was ordered to vacate her individual house because it had been constructed without the use of official designs. Her action had been contrary to rules laid down in 1948. She protested. The case went through the system.[53] Regulation and systematization were thus sporadic, and successes were matched by failures, but the Khrushchevian template was becoming clearer and more operable.

Imposing more rigorous controls on individual housing construction was one means of expediting the modernization of local urban municipal economies. Another was the development of a more coherent policy for outfitting the infrastructure of local housing districts. The groundbreaking theoretical work done in 1945 on mikroraiony had straightaway fallen to the bottom of someone's filing cabinet, although Khrushchev would later dig it out (see chapter 1). In the absence of major reform to the structure of local housing districts, officials attended only to isolated aspects of the wider municipal economy. For example, housing management administrations were made more accountable for the provision of local services such as plumbing.[54] Energy was usually the priority (as it had been for Lenin, with the revolutionary talk of the electrification of the country); so called "gasification" was a major aspect of policy, expanded in places as disparate as Ufa and Stalingrad in January 1952 alone.[55] Table 2.1 shows the considerable impact on the RSFSR and the acceleration of gasification after 1950. Between January 1951 and October 1954, the number of gas-supplied apartments grew by 58.4 percent in Moscow and by 77.5 percent in Leningrad.[56] A resolution of the Moscow Soviet in March 1953 called for the complete gasification of separate apartments within the city.[57] This was a substantial state investment in one area of associated urban infrastructure.

These were strands of a housing policy, rather than a housing policy as such. Rhetoric expanded their reach, however. Hints came in the selection of words. The chairman of Gosplan (RSFSR) wrote to the chairman of the Council of Ministers (RSFSR) in 1951 about the "liquidation" of earthen shelters in Smolensk ("liquidation" would soon be Khrushchev's policy for the Soviet Union's housing crisis).[58] More significant, it was in 1951 and 1952 that people started to talk consistently about a "housing program," and occasionally about a "mass housing program." Some architects were making early reference to "mass housing construction" in October 1949; by 1951 party workers were equally prematurely (but with revealing self-consciousness) calling the process "gigantic."[59] In 1952 this phrase-making was overlaid with the rhetoric of impending communism. The Academy of Architecture anticipated a "broadening" of its work, aimed at "the construction of communism."[60] At the nineteenth party congress in December 1952, the rhetoric of communist ambition became dominant. The report on the projected fifth five-year plan (1951–1955) promised to double capital investment in housing in comparison with the previous five-year plan, to deliver corresponding increases in construction, to enhance municipal services, and "to build communist society."[61] Paradise beckoned.

This differentiation of the late Stalinist period into one in which the party-government first flailed in the postwar emergency and then started to develop policies (on paper, at least) that would shift the Soviet Union in a communist direction was not confined to housing. Historians have drawn particular attention to 1948 as a dividing line between the postwar emergency and the onset of a more ordered polity that could generate but not see through reforms.[62] The archival record suggests that the direct origins of Khrushchev's housing program lay as far back as 1944, and that 1950–1951 was the most obvious point at which early developments accelerated. In front of these hidden shifts, structural changes, and the accumulation of responses to events, however, stands a more famous causal factor of reform: Khrushchev himself.

TABLE 2.1. "GAZIFIKATSIIA" OF RSFSR TOWNS, 1940–1953

	No. of towns with gas network for use by population	Length of gas network (km)	No. of apartments supplied with gas (000s)
1940	14	630	88
1950	20	2194	417
1953	25	2893	681

Source: GARF f. A-259, op. 7, d. 6154, l. 102.

The Role of Khrushchev

The mass housing program was not created during late Stalinism. There is little reason to suppose that, had Stalin lived longer, the housing program would have taken on the enormous proportions that it did in the second half of the 1950s. Even after 1951 he did not give political leadership to housing construction. The essential ideological and moral underpinning of the mass housing program, especially its escalation of individual rights, was scarcely imaginable under Stalin. Yet even after his death, a considerable increase in housing construction was not automatic. It took determined political leadership to bring together the emerging strands of policy, and to produce from them the mass housing program. Hence Khrushchev's role was, as in some other areas of Soviet life, historic. Housing construction shot up because he decided that it should, as he also decided that maize should be grown across the Ukrainian republic. During a meeting with Khrushchev in January 1956, the British Labour politician (and later prime minister) Harold Wilson noticed corn cobs on the Soviet leader's desk. According to a Foreign Office note based on Wilson's comments, Khrushchev's "real interests [are] agriculture and [house] building, especially building, [he] spent far more time on this than on [the] H-bomb. Much more rewarding."[63] But when he turned the ignition in 1955, the housing construction engine was able to go up through the gears only because of the factors already examined here. The politics of personal contingency meshed with the imperatives of social need and enhanced state power in an upward cycle of policy effectiveness.

It seems that Khrushchev's interest in housing conditions was long held and probably genuinely felt. There is no reason to doubt his sincerity when he recalled his early years as a Soviet official, and before:

> I got married in 1914, when I was twenty years old. Because I had a highly skilled job, I got an apartment right away. The apartment had a sitting room, kitchen, bedroom, and dining room. Years later, after the Revolution, it was painful for me to remember that as a worker under capitalism I'd had much better conditions than my fellow workers now living under Soviet power. For a long time after the Revolution, we couldn't satisfy even the most elementary needs of our workers, including those who had served in the Red Army. Young couples would come to us before they got married and ask for an apartment to themselves. Not only were we unable to give them a separate apartment—we often couldn't even find a place for them in a dormitory. Isn't that awful?[64]

In his memoirs Khrushchev approached the subject as a self-justifying enthusiast, and he fancied himself an expert. He discussed the merits of different architects and building materials; he traced his fascination back to his early trade as a metalworker, and to his role in the construction of the Moscow metro in the 1930s, always emphasizing the consistency of his interest.[65] His amateur's wisdom adds to the popular image of Khrushchev as dilettante at best and bumbling interferer at worst, but this is unfair. His real contribution was not derived from his fascination with cement or his enthusiasm for talking at construction workers. Rather his political skills were crucial, and he deployed them at personal risk, and not as the indulgence of a powerful professional manqué: he was not like Hitler at the side of Albert Speer. Khrushchev seemed to believe that his place at the heart of Soviet politics was enhanced, where it fitted the imperative of ambition and lay in line with his strengths, by actively aiming to improve popular living conditions. Khrushchev might never have taken a risk with his career that he could not see to the end of, but he took risks nonetheless, and his interest in housing reconstruction from 1945 was one.[66]

Khrushchev's greatest blunder during Stalin's rule was his precipitate sponsorship of the concept of the "agro-town" (*agro-gorod*): a policy area within which housing construction was prominent.[67] Khrushchev had made housing reconstruction a rhetorical priority from 1945, when he was running the Ukrainian republic as a member of the all-union Politburo. His rhetorical stance distinguished him from many of his colleagues and to some extent exposed him unnecessarily to enhanced political risk. In a major speech shortly after the victory of 1945, he declared grandiloquently, "The most important task of party and soviet organs is the reconstruction and construction of the urban economy, construction in villages and *kolkhozy*." He acknowledged that, in cities, "many live in tremendously poor [*ochen' neblagopriiatnykh*] conditions" and that cities must be rebuilt so that they were better than before the war.[68]

Khrushchev was intrigued and stimulated by the detail of urban policy and regarded himself and his officials as responsible for its most obscure aspects. Motifs of industrialized construction and technical systems litter his speeches, motifs born of enthusiasm and hands-on participation. He insisted in a speech of 1945, "To carry out this reconstruction work successfully, to improve the cities, it's necessary deeply and systematically to study the urban economy, to study the best forms of town planning, to study and take on the positive experience of other cities." The speech centralized his own and his officials' accountability: "if there's no care being directed to the skilled running of the existing housing fund . . . then we've got to say that poor leaders are responsible." In this sphere Khrushchev demanded conviction and commitment from them as well as from himself: "In order to know the urban economy we've got to study it stubbornly, insistently. We've got to visit every alley, and not once or twice. To get to know and solve this question, it's too little just to saunter past a street. Sometimes it's necessary to see it ten times before making a decision."[69] Responsibility—a decidedly un-Stalinist attitude—was always central to Khrushchev's approach to housing questions.

In his memoirs he keenly described his unique input into policy in the Ukrainian republic before his departure from Kiev in 1949. While his comments were recorded two decades after the event, contemporary sources bear out crucial details. "All efforts were directed toward the creation of elementary humane housing conditions in cities and settlements," he claimed. "We looked for ways to build economically. . . . We undertook an investigation of the possibilities for building more housing space with fewer bricks. Such construction could not be higher than four stories and often two, and what's more, on the edge of the city."[70] His contribution expanded after his return to the capital in 1949, as party secretary once more of the Moscow oblast' and the city of Moscow too. He tied together some of the policy strands in order to make a more coherent contribution than his predecessor at the head of the Moscow party committee, Georgii Popov, had been able to achieve. Popov, meanwhile, went on to serve as Minister of Urban Construction (USSR) for the next two years, where he retained his connection to the more senior Khrushchev and was perhaps obliged to discover at least some of the enthusiasm for populist construction that had been absent from his approach before.

Of particular importance was Khrushchev's own politician's talent for selecting skilled personnel and acting as their patron, for supporting professionals who were developing innovatory techniques of industrialized construction, and for expanding the pool of knowledge and hence accelerating policy by convening conferences. Khrushchev had an intuitive grasp of the importance of nurturing skilled cadres of workers, managers, architects, engineers, and ministers. In a major speech on reconstruction, he declared his pride that in the autumn of 1945 the Architecture Administration of the Ukrainian Council of Ministers employed 1,300 people; Khrushchev was surely their effective head. Their task was to draw up serious city plans for Kiev and sixty-five other urban centers.[71] In the same speech, he made specific criticism of officials' attitude to personnel. Although such ritual humiliation of incompetent officials was a standard (and terrifying) Stalinist performance, and Khrushchev had led the Terror in Ukraine in 1938, his concern in 1945 was not to destroy his subordinates for the apparent benefit of Stalinist rule but to make them act responsibly toward the population.[72] In 1949 he brought the constructor and concrete prefabrication expert Sadovskii from Ukraine in order to bolster construction practices in Moscow. Khrushchev thought that Moscow's approach was some way behind Kiev's; for example, it was excessively reliant on individual house construction and on the old-fashioned materials of brick and wood.[73] Given the patronage networks on which cadre policy depended, such professional appointments were a matter of politics as much as administration.

Khrushchev thus invested some of his patronage and political energy in the pursuit of prefabrication and industrialization, arguing where necessary with recalcitrant architects.[74] His presence in Moscow gave him access not only to architects but to institutes and economic agencies, and he combined his status as Politburo member and city secretary into a unique political role. By 1951 no other senior politician knew more about housing policy or had the political will to put such knowledge into startling effect. Although it did not herald the start of the mass housing program, Khrushchev's convocation in January 1951 of the Conference on Civilian Housing Construction, Building Materials, and Planning-Investigative Works, held under the auspices of the Moscow Soviet between 3 and 10 January 1951 in the Stanislavskii State Musical Theatre, was crucial. Three thousand architectural and construction professionals—technicians, planners, and administrators—were present, headed by the Stalin Prize laureate Aleksandr Vlasov. Khrushchev's position was preeminent: he opened and closed the conference. Delegates were able to discuss technical practices in detail and to compare experiences from different corners of the state housing machine. Aside from its professional value, the conference ensured that the motif of industrialized housing construction was repeated in the newspapers for more than a week.[75] Perhaps now more than ever before, the future of mass housing must have been noticed (and to an extent internalized) by the news-aware public. It seems reasonable to argue that Khrushchev placed it there.

This was not the pursuit of dull detail by a man looking for a hobby; it was, rather, the most serious of politics. Khrushchev commented in his memoirs of his first expressions of interest in housing policy after moving back to Moscow in 1949: "Beriia always spoke against if any of the members of the Politburo put forward any kind of new, interesting matter: he objected, and after some time brought this [objection] to Stalin and acquired moral capital [as a result]."[76] Given the serious setback of 1949 when Khrushchev was slapped down for his proposals for agro-cities, and amid the machinations of Beriia, Khrushchev's espousal of urban housing reform must have been undertaken at some personal and political risk. It was an expression of conviction. But it must also have met with support from Stalin.[77] Khrushchev enjoyed a close if complex relationship with the *vozhd'*, evidenced, for example, by Khrushchev's enhanced role (alongside Malenkov) at the nineteenth party congress of 1952, after Stalin decided he did not wish to read out the general secretary's report himself.[78]

Khrushchev continued politically to manipulate housing policy (a policy that he simultaneously passionately supported) for his own political ends after Stalin's death. He jostled briefly and successfully with Georgii Malenkov, Chairman of the Council of Ministers and leading rival for power after Beriia's fall, for the political spoils of leading an effective housing policy. When it was more useful for Khrushchev to emphasize his interest in agriculture in September 1953, urban housing was placed on the back burner. But in February 1954 the Moscow Soviet announced yearly plans in which standardized housing was given unambiguous priority, while architects, constructors, and other city soviets showed their approval during the year.[79] The All-Union Building Conference, held at the Kremlin in November–December 1954, was of the utmost significance, for it was here that Khrushchev publicly articulated his leadership of all-union housing policy. Although all members of the Presidium sat through many of the sessions, it was Khrushchev who, in the public mind, was most associated with the conference. He staked his commitment to what was now a putative mass housing program with an extremely long speech on 7 December 1954. More than anyone else, he made the policy his own with a familiar display of rhetoric and an exhaustive grasp of detail. Listing figures for the use of space in "tall buildings," he showed how much was wasted, or "constructed." "And what is this constructed space?" he asked his audience. "It's space that is occupied by walls and other structures. And in tall buildings this space is increased against the norm in order to create the building's silhouette. So this space is only for looking at, it's not for working in or living."[80] He made his listeners laugh (nervously?) at his combination of detailed knowledge and earthy manners, tightening his grip on them.

Thus did Khrushchev attract the audience in the hall and suggest to a wider public that he was the country's construction boss. In a secret note to the Foreign Secretary, the British ambassador argued that the speech showed how Khrushchev was "extremely sure of himself, . . . capable of expressing himself forcibly and above all anxious to show off as the chief public figure of the regime."[81] The principal achievement of the conference—the formal castigation of "excess" in architecture and praise instead for simplicity and economy of form—was the universally recognized autograph of Khrushchevian construction. Later, in 1955, the Central Committee approved a decree that condemned architectural excess. In the months following the conference, architects and engineers used Khrushchev's name as the legitimating label in their discussions of the need for standardization and simplicity in housing.[82] This seems to put Khrushchev firmly at the head of the emerging program.

He fulfilled a role that Stalin could not have performed. Even if Stalin had lived a few more years, he would not have launched this program. The option of a mass housing program was surely not on Stalin's table. His general indifference to popular living conditions would scarcely have allowed him to hoard the political and economic fuel necessary to launch such a policy. The Stalinist system lacked the capacity to respect individual citizens or to act on its rhetoric of rights, so such a launch was in any case highly improbable. It is equally likely that had Malenkov or Beriia had the chance in the years following Stalin's death, they too would have laid strong emphasis on housing. But Khrushchev's interest in housing was deeper than anyone else's, and only he had a record of sustained focus on it. At the same time that he was knocking Malenkov off the apex in early 1955, Khrushchev was consolidating the existing aspects of housing policy with rising political authority. Within weeks of defeating the Anti-Party group in 1957, he introduced the most important decree on housing construction in Soviet history. In political terms, the mass housing program was substantially his. The launching ground had been prepared during the late Stalin era, but it was Khrushchev who pressed the button.

With Khrushchev in charge of policy, its scope and ambition rapidly expanded between 1955 and 1957. A Gosplan report of 1955 defined his approach, outlining coherent terms of mass industrial production.[83] Central and local organizations directed detailed attention to achieving this on a new mass scale.[84] Individual housing, both self-built and constructed in collaboration with an individual's employer, remained crucial.[85] Mechanization proceeded apace, creating a momentum of ever-faster output, and organizational and administrative mechanisms continued to evolve.[86] As a result soviets and state departments were bringing increasing numbers of people out of basements, barracks, tumbledown housing, and overcrowded communal apartments. The Moscow Soviet passed a typical resolution on 18 January 1957, which transferred citizens from 2nd Avtobaza barracks to new accommodations. The destinations of such people were the newly forming housing districts, such as the complex of neighborhoods in Moscow's Cheremushki.[87] All this was the crystallization of what had been an emerging ideological reality since 1951: housing policy as beneficence.

But this was not quite the mass construction program as the Soviet public would soon think of it. In February 1957 a Gosstroi report outlined some successes of the program but emphasized other failures. Some cities, such as Novosibirsk and Sverdlovsk, were experiencing a decelerated rate of increase in construction output. The reasons for failure included problems associated with low quality and unfinished infrastructure; the failure to keep up with repairs; and an unmodernized system of credit for individual house construction, whose loans were too small and had to be paid back too quickly.[88]

What was missing was a grand statement of political leadership, which could escalate legitimacy and boost momentum, the kind of statement that would provide not only a more sharply focused goal but also clearer instructions about how to execute detailed policy measures. In summer 1957 Khrushchev promised that the housing shortage would be ended within twelve years. He did so in a decree of 31 July that was the real manifesto of the mass housing program. It announced in permanent typescript that the core method of ending the shortage should be the construction of enclosed family living space, either in the form of separate apartments for the occupancy of one family only (the mark of the program) or by individual house construction.[89] The twelve-year promise was cavalier and overblown. Thanks to central planning, it gave rise to a chain of unintended consequences that would be partly self-defeating. Nevertheless, it was a political statement of great rhetorical force, which helped to define the Khrushchev era and to change the relationship between the party-government and the population to one that was partly based on a form of rights. It gave an immediate fillip to construction output.

The decree outlined the new policy in thirty-six points, which covered matters of organization, finance, individual- and initiative-based construction schemes, and architecture and construction techniques.[90] These made for a comprehensive consolidation of the disparate measures that had been introduced since 1944. Particularly notable was the way individual initiative and state capacity were bolted together in a more formal prescription than hitherto. The spare-time construction brigades pioneered in Gor'kii, where non-construction workers built housing in their spare time in return for the guarantee of a new home, was lauded as "high socialist consciousness" and a "remarkable initiative."[91] Individual construction and mechanisms of socialist competition were also expanded. Most essential was the great increase in investment, which was partly funded by reneging on internal public debt repayments of "bonds" taken out during the war. The decree anticipated that this would raise 62 billion rubles, and that the estimate of 78 billion rubles for housing construction contained in the current five-year plan would be revised upward. Citizens were expected to contribute through their own resources, notably by repaying their loans for individual construction, and the decree argued that rising wages (overall increases of more than 14 billion rubles were anticipated during 1958) would ease the burden. The decree proclaimed that most new urban construction would be in blocks four or five stories high, whose apartments were for the occupancy of "one family," and that life within them would be made easier by the mass production of such internal fittings as room partitions and small-scale furniture.[92] This was the khrushchevka.

Housing policy as beneficence thus reached its clearest peak. The decree was a largely pragmatic and "rational" prescription whose aim was the pursuit of a radically escalated quantity of economical housing for separate family occupancy. It did not mention the construction of communism—unlike, say, the general secretary's report at the nineteenth party congress of 1952—and in rhetorical terms can be considered a relatively unideological document. The decree's keywords were "rationality" and "quantity," defined as the promise of an unprecedented quantity of housing construction, to be realized by rational mechanisms. These prescripts gave Khrushchev the political and legal basis on which to set about fulfilling his extraordinary ambition: to solve the housing crisis in twelve years.

The Triumph of Rationality

On 28 September 1955, Vladimir Kucherenko, the leading figure in the Soviet construction bureaucracy, found himself face to face with the British prime minister, Sir Anthony Eden, in Downing Street. Eden's private secretary commented that Kucherenko was "very friendly," and that he praised "our achievements in this country in housing, particularly in the new towns." The prime minister was "favorably impressed with him."[93] During their lengthy trip around Britain, Kucherenko's delegation visited a prestressed concrete works near Glasgow, as well as other industrial sites, housing estates, and new towns. Following them round these venues, one British official was struck by their professional objectivity. "There was no criticism of our methods or way of life; indeed, in most cases there was approval," he wrote. "There was no boasting that they did things better in the Soviet Union, which in my experience had so often previously been the case, and there were several admissions that they had nothing as good at home."[94] The friendly Mr. Kucherenko, eager to learn from British capitalists and to chat with Sir Anthony (late of Eton and Oxford) about council houses, exemplified the rational core of a housing program from which the rhetoric of communism had been sucked out.

Kucherenko's career was marked by expertise and technocracy. Educated at Khar'kov's Construction Institute, he was a trained construction engineer and gifted administrator who rose easily through the professional and bureaucratic machine. He had worked in construction trusts in Ukraine and the Urals during the 1930s, taking his part in the hyper-industrialization of these strategic regions, before transferring to the reconstruction of similar projects in a number of Ukrainian cities during and after the war. Here he began his working relationship with Khrushchev, who always praised his talents.[95] In time, this relationship would become one of the most important professional axes of the mass housing program. Kucherenko followed Khrushchev to Moscow in 1950. He became the deputy head of an all-union construction ministry. It was an influential act of patronage. Kucherenko took up the position of head of Glavmosstroi, the city's big construction trust, alongside the deputy chairmanship of the Moscow Soviet in 1954.

These appointments required him to work closely in the development and implementation of aspects of housing policy. In 1955 he reached the very center of that process, when Khrushchev ensured his promotion as chairman of Gosstroi and deputy chairman of the Council of Ministers. Between then and 1961, Kucherenko was perhaps the leading figure after Khrushchev in the accelerated development of Soviet mass housing. Later, from January 1961 to his premature death in November 1963, he assumed a less hands-on though still prominent role as president of the Academy of Construction and Architecture (USSR). Reflecting his status, and by extension the prestige of the housing program, his coffin was displayed at the Columned Hall of the House of Soviets, before he was buried in Red Square.[96] The eulogies at his funeral featured the language of sacredness—he had been "a faithful son of the Communist Party and the Soviet people"—and ranged fulsomely over the trajectory of his career, but one colleague, B. G. Skramtaev, drew attention to Kucherenko's part in developing a new type of light concrete, which was playing an important part in construction across the USSR.[97] Kucherenko, like the housing program, was technocratic to the end.

He consistently acted on the careful observation of technical detail. Around the time of the 1957 decree, this approach informed the development of the urban housing program as a whole. The attitude was "rational": it had a defined material goal and was not diverted by processes or aims associated with the immediate and explicit urge to alter people's consciousness. Its aim was to build the maximum number of separate family apartments by seeking out and sticking close to the ideal intersection between cost and quality. Kucherenko and the 1957 decree were a good match for each other; he worked hard to keep housing policy in line with the decree's technocratic letter and spirit. From 1958 this became an increasingly difficult task, as the goal of housing policy became twofold: not just the straightforward measurable improvement of material conditions but also the fostering of voluntarism and the mobilization of residents. By 1961, when the third party program announced a two-decade path to impending communism, the housing program was further reconfigured as a still more explicit tool for generating a particular way of life and worldview.

In this way paradise came to replace beneficence as the guiding motif of housing policy from 1958 onward. "Rationality" and "the urge to the communist future" stand as contrasting imperatives when they are fitted respectively within the motifs of beneficence and paradise. The cult of reason that guided the launch of the housing program was different in kind from the transformative, mobilizing ideology that governed its development for half a decade or so thereafter.[98] Yet, conceptually and historically, rationality is itself an ideological approach, a core element of Enlightenment values. Taken to a logical extreme, its striving for total clarity, order, and transparency is also utopian.[99] The 1957 decree might not have talked about communism, but it symbolized an ideological change, at whose heart was an emphasis on citizens' rights. Ending the housing shortage in a dozen years and building communism by 1980 were, meanwhile, hardly antithetical goals, but ones that reinforced each other. Technocrats were indispensable to the building of communism, while the promise of communism—or at least the publication of ringing political declarations that hinted at it—gave technocrats the political and investment priorities with which they could realize industrial, construction, and technical goals.

Dry rationality and fervent voluntarism were thus two sides of the same Bolshevik coin, analytically separable but mutually dependent. The two sides can be found in the works of Marx, in the great debates of the revolution and the 1920s, and in the Stalinism of the 1930s.[100] Stalinism, violently creating Soviet modernity, always insisted on its own ruthless rationality.[101] On the party-government's terms, the mass industrialization and mass arrests of the 1930s were both determined by rational considerations. Yet ordinary people experienced the murderous caprice of political culture and the catastrophically deleterious bottlenecks of the planned economy. With regard to housing, the question remained: could there not be a policy that had rational intentions, was organized rationally, and had a rational effect on the lives of the public? Khrushchev's regional economic councils (*sovnarkhozy*) summed up his problem; they were a rationalizing measure that only compounded inefficiency, and they were abolished in 1965.[102]

Khrushchev insisted that the urban housing economy could become a rational arena only by making state agencies efficient and responsive, and by ensuring they were coherent organizations that related functionally with each other. They would marginalize unauthorized construction, make systematic the input of individual initiative, and end the fragmented tendency of policy making. But through to 1958, rationality would also, self-consciously, require flexibility; policy would reflect practical circumstances and not be constrained by dogma. During the "launch period" of 1951–1957, a plausible language of rational processes was embedded into the documents of housing policy. It grew out of the developments of 1944–1950 and to some extent of 1939–1941. Tellingly, Khrushchev's speeches on construction had elaborated the motif of rationality since 1945. Shortly after the end of the war he called for "great attention to inventiveness and rationality" in all types of construction.[103] When he looked back on the housing program as he recorded his memoirs, he repeated the word "rational."[104]

Flexibility—dispensing with dogmatic constraints—was apparent in the attempts of the Soviet architectural establishment to learn from West European best practice. Kucherenko led the way with his trip to Britain, but the process became systemic. Professional relations within the Eastern Bloc were always good; the editorial files of *Stroitel'naia gazeta* (The Building Gazette) show friendly links between professionals of the socialist countries, characterized by "*ty*" (the familiar second person pronoun) in correspondence and manifested in numerous international trips within the bloc.[105] But relations with the West were much more revealing.[106] This interaction was measured, transparent, useful, and potentially replicable; it makes little sense to compare it with earlier borrowings of Western technologies such as the fevered use and abuse of foreign specialists in the industrialization of the 1930s, or the nuclear espionage of the 1940s.[107]

In 1956–1957 the Ministry of Foreign Affairs and Gosstroi set about the process of inviting foreign architects to the USSR to help with housing construction. These agencies wrote jointly to the Soviet Embassy in London, "The Ministry of Foreign Affairs (USSR) and Gosstroi (USSR) request you to establish which of the most qualified progressive architects of Great Britain can commission designs for the planning and construction of a [Moscow] housing district, [plus its] apartment houses and public buildings." Gosstroi had in fact already started some "preliminary negotiations" with Frederick G. Osborne, the eminent urban planner. Those architectural firms that seemed most likely to obtain the commission would first be inspected by "three or four specialists" sent to Britain specially, with the successful firm flying its representatives to Moscow "at the start of November 1958" to sign the contract.[108] Gosstroi and the Foreign Ministry sent similar letters to their ambassadors in Sweden and Finland.[109] They were prepared to work with whichever foreign specialists were deemed best, provided they seemed (notionally) "progressive" and their terms were reasonable. The determination explicitly to learn from foreign examples was great and demanded that Soviet experts go abroad and foreign experts come to the USSR.

Individual housing in Moscow before the launch of the housing program: a tumbledown style that remained a late Stalinist construction solution. (L. Kovalev, *Moskva* [Moscow: Rabochaia Moskva], 1935, p. 216)

New housing for the late
Stalinist elite: Smolensk Square,
Moscow. (*Sovetskaia arkhitektura,
ezhegodnik*, 1953, p. 67)

Grand living under the red star of late Stalinism: Smolensk Square, Moscow. (*Sovetskaia arkhitektura, ezhegodnik*, 1953, p. 69)

Another late Stalinist solution: new housing in Pushkin, Leningrad Region. (*Sovetskaia arkhitektura, ezhegodnik*, 1953, p. 109)

Мо

НОВОЕ СТРОИТЕЛЬСТВО

Ви

В жилищном строительстве нашей страны наиболее широкое распространение получили типовые проекты крупнопанельных жилых домов серии 1-464.

Для выпуска домов этой серии построено более 200 домостроительных предприятий.

Многие из них уже выпускают
дома для застройки новых
микрорайонов Москвы, Ново-
сибирска, Минска, Вильнюса,
Риги и многих других городов
страны.

На снимках — новые комп-
лексы крупнопанельных жи-
лых домов серии 1-464.

НОВОЕ СТРОИТЕЛЬСТВО

Across the union (Mogilev, Riga, Vilnius, Minsk): the wide geographical scope of the Khrushchev-era program. (*Arkhitektura SSSR*, February 1963, pp. 30–31: with permission of the Library of the School of Slavonic & East European Studies, University College London)

Row after row of Khrushchev-era apartment houses (the famous *khrushchevki*) in Khar'kov. (*Arkhitektura SSSR*, January 1963, p. 29: with permission of the Library of the School of Slavonic & East European Studies, University College London)

Khrushchev-era housing in contemporary Moscow (photograph by Anna Solov'eva).

Kucherenko started preparations in 1956 for possible trips by Soviet construction professionals to the United States and Western Europe, whose aim should be to isolate techniques for the reduction of costs and the improvement of quality.[110] At a time of superpower rivalry, this was a pragmatic expression of the rational imperative.[111] Kucherenko scheduled trips to Scandinavia and the Federal Republic of Germany for October 1957.[112] The specialists' findings would not question the broad path of Soviet policy, but they were supposed to challenge its technical details, by providing examples of technologies that worked better. The report on Scandinavia stated that the trip had confirmed Soviet policy of "recent years" with regard to standardized construction and prefabrication, single family occupancy, reductions in ceiling height, the choice of four or five stories as optimal, and the general removal of architectural excess. It proposed modifications whose content was explicitly or implicitly "rational": the "necessity" of developing new parts from plastics; the need for "rational volume-planning and construction decisions"; a Household Economy (*Domovodstvo*) Institute within the Academy of Construction and Architecture for "working out questions of the rational organization of the household's economy, the improvement of domestic facilities and of the economic means of those who run the household [*domashnye khoziaiki*]."[113] These notions were pulled together in a long report on "The Study of Foreign Science and Technology in the Area of Construction in 1957."[114] Such materials were available for perusal by the Central Committee, emphasizing the role of these trips not only in the improvement of narrow policy detail and its implementation but also in the wider political and strategic context.

While the encounter with the West facilitated a more rational housing policy, it did not act as a clear filter for the importation of improvements. The language of reports and correspondence reflects how decisive policy developments were taking place in a society that was pierced by ambiguity. Stalin's death had caused a decisive change in housing policy, but rhetorical and substantive features of his system remained in place. Much of the reports' content was straightforward and technocratic, explicitly and repeatedly emphasizing the concept of "rationality" in the discussion of how foreign examples could be exploited. But even Kucherenko was liable to a Stalinist turn of phrase. Official language was not just routine; it had demonstrable consequences. It could destabilize, however briefly, the rational basis of policy.

In a report of December 1957 to the Central Committee, Kucherenko expressed his suspicions about the West Berlin exhibition "Interbau," and about a conference that had been organized by the West German Ministry of Housing Construction earlier in the year.[115] Kucherenko acknowledged Western successes in housing construction (he had, after all, just sent delegations to learn from them), but the mentalities of Cold War and even Stalinist suspicion persisted. He wrote that the conference was a forum in which "successful examples of such construction by capitalist countries is widely used as bourgeois propaganda in the ideological struggle with the countries of socialism." So he proposed a rival conference for 1960, which would showcase socialist achievement.[116] True, Kucherenko's was a required response in a Cold War ritual: the Interbau event and the housing development in the Hansa district of West Berlin that it showcased was itself conceived in answer to the new Stalinallee in East Berlin.[117] As long as Kucherenko's aggressively ideological coda was confined to language alone, it was harmlessly ritualistic: a stylized evaluation of technical information. But Kucherenko's proposal of a conference was not just cheap words; it implied both expense and wasted time. Cold War tensions (keeping up with the other bloc) and ideological requirements (grand public promises) could boost production, but they could also create wasteful, irrational diversions.

When Kucherenko's experts visited Sweden, they must have been struck by the wide range of financial instruments and tenures that underpinned construction there. These mechanisms produced effective and highly layered partnerships among individuals, businesses, local authorities, and the state, thus facilitating mass construction. They fitted within a quite distinctive social democracy that was particular to Sweden, but their flexibility and variety derived from a generally rational, even pragmatic, approach that could be applied elsewhere.[118] Observing such transferable examples influenced Soviet policy but also confirmed Soviet officials in their existing path. Pragmatism had been built into housing policy since the 1920s, producing a certain variety and complexity in the financial and tenurial arrangements that underpinned the housing stock; the responses to wartime destruction had added further flexibility and pragmatism to this process. The expanded state capacity that was the mark of the housing program from the mid-1950s required, moreover, additional flexibility if it were to function properly. Flexibility was written into the introduction or extension of such schemes as cooperatives and exchanges. Earlier, when the state was weaker, outcomes were more random and arbitrary, qualities not associated with rational flexibility. Yet the increase in state capacity and the call of the communist future soon caused Khrushchev to reduce the extent of individual construction and personal property in the housing economy, a development in financial and tenurial structures that seemed neither rational nor flexible.

Individual construction (and thus the tenure of personal property) had helped to save the country from the complete collapse of its housing capacity in the immediate postwar years, and it remained of crucial importance after the emergency had passed. This pragmatic approach persisted until Khrushchev's deliberate decision—based on a reckless celebration of ideology—to minimize its contribution in the 1960s. The ongoing development of individual housing in the 1950s was explicit policy, the subject of hundreds of resolutions and decrees. It was not without problems. For example, in the city of Kalinin, 62 percent of new construction in 1950 was in the individual sector, but inspectors deplored the "rural aspect" of the peripheral districts where such houses were located.[119]

Yet a persistent and even growing emphasis on individual housing was central to policy throughout the 1950s. This applied across the union, and not just in those areas worst damaged during the war or those with a recent tradition of family-style urban houses such as the Baltic republics. In May 1955 the Council of Ministers (USSR) called for 10,210 houses to be built in 1955–1956 in Primorskii krai in the Far East, following disappointing individual construction levels in the early

1950s in the region.[120] Central administrators in Moscow knew that access to credit should be enhanced if such levels of individual construction were to be replicated elsewhere, as they had to be if the plan were to be fulfilled. A major Gosstroi report of 1956 argued that the limit of loans should be increased from seven thousand rubles to between ten and fifteen thousand rubles, and the length of repayment prolonged to fifteen years.[121] This required more substantial relationships between the Ministry of Finance, local soviets, and regional ministries, enterprises, and individuals, expressed in rational and flexible forms. Such flexible responses to problems resistant to conventional solutions extended also to a form of trade. In the Far East, in order to achieve the necessary construction level of individual houses in 1955–1956, a Council of Ministers (RSFSR) resolution of August 1955 demanded the sale of such houses "through a trade network" that was administered by state agencies.[122] Once again, individual initiative and state capacity were yoked together in a policy mechanism that reached a high level of flexibility and effectiveness between about 1955 and 1958.

The tenurial balance—the proportion of housing owned by soviets, state departments, and by individuals as personal property—varied from town to town. These differences reflected local conditions, and the persistence of variety throughout the 1950s is further evidence of a flexible and pragmatic attitude to the housing program. Table 2.2 shows that the share of personal property in the total housing fund hardly changed in eight out of seventeen cities between 1937 and 1960. In five it fell by more than 10 percent, and in four it rose by more than 10 percent. This flexibility allowed specific ministries or departments and geographical localities to develop the individual housing sector, often with the help of additional credit from the Ministry of Finance, if this was perceived as the most useful route to maximize construction. For example, the Ministry of Power Stations planned to increase the proportion of individual housing in its construction program during 1955.[123] It seems that, while the housing economy required a broadly consistent approach to tenure, it was capable of generating variable emphases in different cities in order to improve construction output. The level of flexibility was most marked in Orel, where early postwar reconstruction seems to have been very heavily dominated by individual housing, only for the state fund to catch up and reach its prewar level by 1960.

Similarly, the shares of the state housing fund owned by city soviets or state departments varied in a way that looks powerfully pragmatic. The engine of the mass housing program was departmental tenure. Tables 2.3 and 2.4 show that cities across the RSFSR and other republics experienced year-on-year falls in the share owned by soviets. This shift to departmental ownership reinforced existing structures of the economy; ministries and the industrial enterprises under their purview had been responsible for a range of "welfare" duties, headlined by housing, since the Stalinist command economy had been set up. So it was a rationally conceived, workable shift. But the balance between soviet and departmental tenures was also sensitive to marginal variations and exceptions, which in turn speaks of rational

TABLE 2.2. PERCENTAGE OF TOTAL CITY HOUSING FUNDS HELD
AS PERSONAL PROPERTY IN FIVE REPUBLICAN CAPITALS
AND TWELVE RSFSR CITIES, 1940–1960

		1 9 4 0	1 9 4 5	1 9 5 0	1 9 6 0
Cities with	Smolensk	17.3	30.0	31.4	27.8
10 percent or	Voronezh	37.4	52.2	48.4	41.7
more increase	Leningrad	0.8	0.5	0.6	3.6
in personal	Tashkent		56.2	60.1	64.8
property share					
Cities with	Omsk	58.6	46.0	47.8	47.1
10 percent or	Vladimir	39.4	35.4	31.8	32.2
more decrease	Cheliabinsk	28.1	25.1	26.4	24.5
in personal	Novosibirsk	48.7	40.6	41.8	42.4
property share	Moscow	2.5		2.5	0.2
Cities with	Vladivostok	25.3	22.9	20.3	26.3
approximately	Pskov	30.6		31.6	33.2
constant (less than	Penza	42.1	39.8	41.0	42.9
10 percent change)	Orel	47.0	57.8	53.9	47.7
share of personal	Gor'kii	20.2	21.1	20.8	22.2
property in total	Riga		11.3	11.0	10.9
housing fund	Tbilisi			37.8	41.3
	Minsk	27.8	28.2	29.0	26.1

Note: Pskov 1940 entry is actually 1937 data. Some statistics, including missing years, are apparently not kept in the TsSU archive fund at RGAE: this also applies to tables 2.3 and 2.4.

Sources: Calculations based on RGAE f. 1562, op. 14, d. 1212, ll. 1, 6; d. 1424, l. 9; d. 2767; d. 2771, l. 2; d. 2767; d. 2771, l. 2; d. 2785, l. 2; 2031, ll. 7, 11, 15, 19, 23, 25, 45, 77, 141, 157; d. 2027, ll. 74, 79, 88, 94; d. 2032, ll. 53, 61, 67, 109; d. 2686, l. 2; d. 2693; d. 2695, l. 2; d. 2696, l. 2; d. 2707, l. 2; d. 2710, l. 2; d. 2712, l. 2; d. 2717, l. 128; d. 2718, ll. 2, 74; d. 2719, ll. 2, 146; d. 2726, l. 2; d. 2731; d. 2767; d. 2771, l. 2; d. 2785, l. 2; d. 3002, ll. 19, 26, 32, 34, 35, 37, 39.

flexibility. Where the demands of reconstruction were especially enormous, as in Minsk and Smolensk, the engine of "departmental" housing worked particularly furiously; but where the administrative burden of recent requisition was particularly high, notably in the Baltic republics, the share of soviet tenure remained high and hardly fell. In areas of particular complexity, like the Far East, the share fluctuated in line with the specific responses of local organizations.

Anchoring the poles of this tenurial balancing act were newly rationalized processes of distribution. Regardless of the formal owner, soviets rather than departmental administrations were now more often the distributors of housing. The aim was equality. One of the most distinguishing marks of Soviet housing from the 1950s was its relatively equitable attitude to distribution: for all recent historiography's focus on the rapaciousness of elites, the really interesting historical point about Soviet housing distribution was its exceptionally equal outcomes. It is true that the government did not live up to the purity of its rhetoric, but Soviet distribution of housing was nevertheless considerably more equal than at any other period of Russian—or European—history.

TABLE 2.3. PERCENTAGE OF STATE HOUSING FUND OWNED BY SOVIETS IN FIVE REPUBLICS AND THEIR CAPITALS, 1937–1960

	RSFSR	Moscow	Belorussia	Minsk	Georgia	Tbilisi	Uzbekistan	Tashkent	Latvia	Riga
1937		76.22		77.17				58.76		
1940		70.72		71.78				52.56		
1943	49.50	70.68			68.94		48.90	96.54		
1945	47.82	68.81	67.94	61.92	68.46	81.90	46.14	54.22	93.36	93.05
1947	44.37	66.98	52.86	42.91	62.84	79.03	43.53	50.27	85.57	87.87
1948	43.06	66.18	50.57	38.77	62.15		41.88	48.38	84.40	86.77
1949	41.56	65.60	48.38	35.28	61.44	78.70	41.33	47.37	85.22	87.30
1950	40.59	64.75	47.43	33.15	59.68		40.47	46.73	84.25	86.40
1951	38.91	63.94	44.99	29.84		76.33	39.83	45.89	83.72	86.15
1952	37.50	62.92	43.70	30.07	55.65	75.75	38.80	46.28	83.53	85.88
1953	36.15	61.56	42.45	27.15	53.52	72.31	37.83	45.34	84.31	87.48
1954	34.59	60.33	40.84	25.52	51.83	71.19	36.93	45.35	83.41	87.05
1956	32.16	58.86	38.03	22.72	48.39	70.30	35.55	44.08	81.53	85.61
1960	32.36		36.51		48.24		34.50	83.52		

Source: Calculations based on data derived from archival references listed for table 2.2.

TABLE 2.4. PERCENTAGE OF STATE HOUSING FUND OWNED
BY SOVIETS IN FOURTEEN RSFSR CITIES, 1937–1956

	Moscow	Leningrad	Gor'kii	Novosibirsk	Cheliabinsk	Vladimir	Voronezh	Omsk	Orel	Penza	Pskov	Smolensk	Vladivostok	Molotov
1937	76.22	87.27	47.83	26.62	17.89	60.59	47.29	41.11	72.53	70.75	81.27	71.37	38.11	48.87
1940	70.72	83.91	43.25	20.90	16.43	62.09	45.85	39.72	70.25	67.98	75.36	64.58	39.86	38.98
1943	70.68	87.93	43.39	17.87	13.60			35.34		64.55				34.36
1945	68.81	85.27	41.22	15.55	12.60	56.98	25.83	27.15	81.20	60.14	83.12	52.59	36.02	29.78
1947	66.98	81.44	40.29	15.10	10.92	50.00	24.49	26.22	74.56	58.82	51.13	35.26	30.56	29.00
1948	66.18	80.62	40.62	14.47	10.43	49.06	23.65	25.91	70.98	57.65	49.05	32.21	28.97	27.90
1949	65.60	79.14	39.12	14.40	10.18	46.66	21.99	24.78	71.07	57.01	50.17	28.00	28.27	27.80
1950	64.75	78.52	38.78	14.50	10.01	45.03	22.53	25.39	67.64	56.31	51.28	29.72	27.95	27.17
1951	63.94	77.52	37.60	14.17	9.84	41.31	21.27	24.91	64.97	54.94	50.34	31.22	27.68	26.51
1952	62.92	76.60	36.98	12.46	9.35	39.90	20.92	24.45	61.60	52.67	50.59	32.20	28.34	25.32
1953	61.56	76.12	36.35	11.93	8.56	40.23	21.05	22.47	58.25	52.00	50.85	30.53	28.92	24.30
1954	60.33	75.18	35.76	12.18	8.01	39.53	21.01	19.71	55.75	49.16	49.84	33.23	29.71	22.66
1956	58.86	71.26	34.24	10.96	7.08	36.86	20.53	17.22	51.19	46.42	48.45	33.36	28.98	19.27

Source: Calculations based on data derived from archival references listed for table 2.2.

Equality was an aspiration born of proto-communist ideology, but it depended on rational systems. These were not properly in place by 1957, though the trend toward them can be traced to 1954. It required the greater idealistic pull of the post-1958 period for a more rigorous and regularized distribution system to emerge, an example of the imperative of paradise driving a "rational" policy development.

As long as a majority of people obtained housing from the enterprises for which they worked, or owned their house thanks to state credits, various housing queues would remain in every town. As yet, no substantial central queue in a given town existed, and rigorously enforced appeal procedures were lacking. Multiple queues, most of which were governed by workplaces, increased the possibility that people in need might not be noticed or might be deliberately ignored. By allowing a given enterprise to distribute its own housing, the queuing system privileged the requirements of a workplace over those of citizens and facilitated corruption based on local patronage. From 1954 onward, officials sought to remedy these failures of efficiency and equity by basing distribution in each town on more universal norms. In July 1955 the Leningrad city soviet was required to distribute all the new housing built by the construction trust Glavleningradstroi.[124] An additional measure of June 1957 allowed city soviets to distribute any excess housing, regardless of its tenure.[125] This did not yet make for a systematic approach. All housing administrations, in soviets, enterprises, or other departments, still lacked a proper sense of accountability through responsible structures of appeal and complaint. But the path of policy had become clear. The attractiveness of the single queue was acknowledged by all apart from vested departmental interests, including trade unions and institutions' housing management administrations. As a rationalizing measure, the single queue acted to limit waste and save resources.

Economy was the stark centerpiece of the rationalizing agenda. Calls for cost reductions became an increasingly persistent chorus, which sounded loud in Gosstroi in 1957. A report Kucherenko signed off on in January that year used precise evidence to build the argument that the optimum number of floors for an apartment house (four or five) was "the most economical option."[126] The same month, Gosstroi sent out letters to various ministries and other administrative bodies (such as the Ministry of Transport Construction and Central Statistical Administration), asking them for estimates of the cost of building one square meter of new housing.[127] In the spring of 1957 Kucherenko completed another report entitled "Ways to reduce the cost of housing construction."[128] That October he was responsible for a twenty-five-page booklet called "Regulation of planning and construction of cities—an important factor in the reduction of costs of housing construction."[129]

One of the most favored strategies for the rational minimization of costs and improvement of technology was socialist competition. This was a means to reduce failures of incentive and resource allocation and was a Stalinist approach to the management of the economy.[130] Competitions designed to increase the performance of employees or to find the best technical solutions to construction problems were completely institutionalized and extremely widespread by this time.[131] The Presidium of the Moscow oblast' trade union of municipal economy employees noted all-round improvements as a consequence of socialist competition in October 1954.[132] In an all-union competition of 1956 for the best prefabricated housing construction designs, V. P. Popov, candidate of technical sciences, won 5,500 rubles.[133] These sought-after prizes could be much bigger, with research institutes and other design agencies competing in 1956 for a cash prize of 40,000 rubles for the best design for standardized factory-produced wooden houses.[134] The prestige and significance of such competition was evident not only in the size of the rewards but also in the promised location of the best new designs; in a competition for the most effective four-story housing in 1957, the winning entry was destined for a flagship site in Moscow's Novye Cheremushki.[135]

Yet the most visible mark of the rational by 1957—its unforgettable monument—was the near absolute commitment to standardized projects of the four- or five-story model. A Gosstroi report of March 1956 on housing construction in Novosibirsk emphasized above all the advantages of four- and five-story standardized housing blocks.[136] Other reports on Kareliia, Voroshilovgrad, and Magnitogorsk showed that these places were still using a variety of standardized designs and were moving rapidly toward more universal use of the standard medium-rise model.[137] Thus did rational modernity, in the guise of the khrushchevka, change the face of Soviet cities.

The Limits of Rationality

Rationality might be triumphing in some areas, but it was held back by the structural deficiencies of the Soviet system. Even the positive results of a rational approach, like the investigation of foreign best practice, could be reduced by the linguistic and political conventions of administration. The most serious structural deficiency was central planning (see chapter 3). Two other inbuilt brakes on rationality might be explored first: the patronage system and the challenge of Gulag releases. These show that the malfunctioning of rationality was intrinsic to the system. Rationality and irrationality were crucial and inseparable components of the Soviet housing economy during 1951–1957. The point was that rationality and order were starting to overshadow irrationality and arbitrariness in the Soviet Union's confused and painful emergence from full Stalinism.

With regard to the 1930s, Sheila Fitzpatrick has written of "patronage acting as a nonmarket mechanism for the distribution of scarce goods, above all housing."[138] Numerous categories of ties bound patrons and clients, and multifarious types of network, structured horizontally or vertically, existed. Patronage transactions were rational responses by citizens and institutions to given situations, though their sum total produced irrational effects in the system as a whole. Members of the academic and creative intelligentsias formed one of the categories that were entitled to extra housing space, on the grounds that they had to do a proportion of their work at home. In order to exercise (or make a case for exceeding) their rights, they used vigorous professional organizations and networks of peers or they appealed to patrons.[139] An academic, Aleksei Mandryka, relied on patronage-based petitioning to try to bring forward future additional housing entitlements (dependent on, for example, his own academic advance) in order to offset the loss of space that would formally come with the impending death of his mother-in-law.[140] His aim was to ensure that his family kept their large apartment. Another type of client enjoyed old family connections. For instance, one Comrade Kataiama, who had lived in a single hotel room with her husband since the war, wrote to Kliment Voroshilov, the nominal head of state, in April 1953, "Dear Kliment Efremovich, this year is the twentieth anniversary of the death of my father, San Kataiama, who was well-known to you, and I ask you to help me obtain an apartment." She elaborated: people back in Japan, and especially the "bourgeois press," knew how badly she lived.[141] Such attempts to invoke national prestige were no guarantee of success. Kataiama's application was approved, however, and it seems she owed it to Voroshilov's memory of her father.

Patronage most distorted the urban housing economy when it influenced whole organizations and building projects rather than the distribution of individual apartments; the quick-fix lubricants of many of these large-scale separate transactions actually threatened to glue up the system as a whole. Prestigious institutions had an unfair advantage in catching the ear of officials. In January 1953, the Malyi Theater in Moscow was looking forward to the construction of a new block for its employees, at 33 First Brestskaia Street, but work was held up by concerns about fire safety, to the frustration of the theater. An extensive correspondence between the director of the theater and senior officials in the Council of Ministers and Moscow's GlavAPU demonstrated that such a petitioner could get about the higher reaches of the housing economy with ease and influence.[142] In 1954 the director of the *Pravda* publishing house, Comrade Feldman, wrote to the chairman of Gosstroi, Konstantin Sokolov, expressing concern about the public institutions that might be constructed on the ground floor of *Pravda*'s uncompleted new apartment block.[143] The airy tone of the correspondence suggested that Feldman was hardwired into the right connections in the housing economy, and that he and Sokolov were men of the world who should resolve this minor matter easily. Feldman's objection was on the characteristic, revealing, but in this case specious grounds of "rationality." An interest that could hardly be more vested was Gosstroi itself. In March 1956 the deputy chairman made an appeal to the Council of Ministers claiming that "a significant number of highly qualified employees" were "in extreme need" of housing.[144]

The Soviet system institutionalized the notion of special pleading, by encouraging letters of appeal and complaint and by granting limited formal privileges to certain categories of citizen. Academics made up just one profession with exaggerated status; writers were another. In late 1954 the Central Committee and the Presidium discussed the construction of houses for "superannuated writers" in "beneficent climatic conditions."[145] But despite the existence of relative privilege, rule-based distribution did exist, and officials observed and maintained it—though somewhat sporadically, and sometimes for their own reasons. Thus in 1952, when a long-lost relative of Lenin wrote to Kosygin with a story about the promise of an apartment on Moscow's imposing Gor'kii Street, Kosygin requested that the correspondent be placed in the right queue.[146] He did not, apparently, shunt her to the front of it (though officials might thus have interpreted his request). At other times patrons rejected overtures, or informal networks were snapped. On the day before Khrushchev delivered the Secret Speech, N. Tikhonov, the chairman of the Soviet Committee for the Defense of Peace, wrote to Mikhail Suslov at the secretariat of the Central Committee, describing the inadequate housing conditions of the illustrious writer Il'ia Erenburg. Although his apartment was on Gor'kii Street, Erenburg shared it with his wife and two sisters, which made the space too "tight" for entertaining foreign visitors on behalf of the committee. Three months later Tikhonov sent a letter to Khrushchev, pressing the same case. As the Moscow Soviet investigated the substance of the appeal, it emerged that Erenburg and his three family members shared sixty-one square meters in three rooms—in two apartments. They rejected the appeal.[147]

Petitioning by different interests in the urban housing economy was not of itself an irrational process. The problem consisted in the inability to balance different interests transparently and systematically; it was exacerbated by the presence of powerful special pleading alongside the absence (until the end of the decade) of the basically competent regulation of mass distribution. True, by the end of the launch period in 1957, individuals had more hope than ever before of obtaining new housing space without the intervention of a patron. It would not, however, be until the late 1950s and early 1960s that rational and fair arrangements for distribution and appeal, underpinned by a concept of rights, were instituted. Even then, murky patronage infiltrated the Weberian rationality of the housing economy, weighing it down.

Threats to rationality did not come just from patronage and special pleading. A country that between 1951 and 1957 suffered the distortions of Stalinism and then its aftershock could hardly generate a housing policy that was consistently rational in its approach and effect. The distribution of housing to the victims of Stalinism shows that rationality had clear limits. Returnees from Gulag and exile made demands on the housing stock that the government did not understand how to handle. The desperate, bemused, or unrealistic reactions of former prisoners showed something of the tragic impossibility of a situation that defied reasonable settlement. Many who complained with a particularly ostentatious sense of unreality were former members of the elite. Some had enjoyed extraordinarily favorable conditions before their arrest; despite their ordeal they could often barely understand why they could not return to something similar. In letters to the Supreme Soviet asking for help with their personal housing crises, some of them wrote that their years of suffering in the camps, the injustice of their arrest, and their long service to the cause warranted extra help now—which might be at the expense of others, who had not served time, in the sometimes zero-sum game of a housing economy skewered by acute deficit.[148]

At the time of her arrest in December 1937, for example, Anna Osipovna Zelenina was living in an apartment that belonged to the Commissariat of Defense, thanks to her marriage, which had been dissolved in 1935. After her arrest the apartment was awarded to one L. V. Frunze, and Zelenina's son went to live with her mother, who also had her own separate apartment. In addition, there was a dacha in the ex-husband's name. During the war the son was called up, the grandmother's "good" apartment was bombed, and she was rehoused in much less desirable conditions. After Zelenina's release in 1953, she returned to Moscow and joined her eighty-three-year-old mother, her son, daughter-in-law, and grandson in a room of 18.5 square meters. Zelenina's life had already been ruined by nearly sixteen years' of captivity; she now faced a catastrophic reduction in the elite housing conditions that she and her family had enjoyed before her arrest. "I do not have my own corner," she wrote. "After so many years of undeserved suffering and homelessness [*skitanie*] I think that I have the right to an apartment." Zelenina wanted a home where she could pursue her work of editing and translating in relative calm, where she could "live in cultured conditions together with my mother, for whom I must care because of her age." She added, "I think it would also be just to return my dacha to me, on which I spent so much money and labor."[149] But to grant her an apartment would have been to lift her in the queue, above someone else; and the return of the dacha would have meant the eviction of the present occupier. The government to some extent operated inside a discourse of "deserving" and "justice" but applied it to the ideology of revolutionary beneficence and to the consequences of the war, not to making a settlement with its own victims, despite official policy claims.

It made no difference if the victim was an Old Bolshevik. The case of N. A. Emelianov, who had joined the party in 1904 and sheltered Lenin in Razliv when he was on the run in 1917, underlines the sense of arbitrariness and cruelty in the process of distribution. In 1928 he was awarded a three-room apartment of fifty-four square meters in Moscow, and in 1935 he was arrested. Nineteen years later he was fully rehabilitated. In 1943 his younger son, daughter-in-law, and two teenage grandsons were removed from the apartment and reassigned a room of seventeen square meters. Emelianov himself returned from captivity to an individual house in Razliv, where he lived with his wife, older son, daughter-in-law, and three grandchildren. The conditions in winter were desperate for an elderly couple, and Emelianov appealed to the Supreme Soviet to grant his younger son extra space, perhaps a separate apartment, so that he and his wife could stay with him in Moscow. He appealed on twin personal grounds—of tragedy borne and long-standing contribution given. Extra housing space was due to his family "thanks to the fact that I so guiltlessly suffered." He went on, with the breathlessness of desperation, that he had to live in Razliv in the summer to help at the neighboring Lenin house museum. Many visitors came to see him, "comrades" and "foreign delegations" alike, because he was "the only witness to Il'ich's last hideout." He wrote, "I give my all for the construction of communism. In winter I want to live with my son, in Moscow."[150] His request was refused. Letters like Zelenina's and Emelianov's are complex examples of that type of correspondence noted by Sheila Fitzpatrick for the 1930s as charged by "the trope of past oppression."[151] Here the letter writer was seeking sympathy and redress not for suffering endured under tsarism but for Stalin-era tragedies.

Within a few years, appeals cast as emotional entreaties would have a passé feel about them: people would claim housing space above all because it was their due as citizens. The norm was taken more seriously, implying universal rights, rationally exercised. But this was not achieved in the first few years after 1953. Confusion filled the gap. Ex-prisoners' requests and declarations revealed a universe of incomprehension. Such a sense of fantasy infests the case of Boris Zbarskii, the illustrious biochemist who had embalmed Lenin.[152] He was arrested in March 1952, his wife a few months later, and they were released at the end of December 1953. Meanwhile, they lost their palatial apartment of six rooms and 175 square meters, granted to them in 1931. After their release they were assigned two rooms in a communal apartment. The unreality of Zbarskii's sense of grievance was a function of his sad failure to recognize his lack of a bargaining position, and his refusal to equate his own conditions with his fellow-countrymen's misery—in a society that had talked of communism at the recent 1952 party congress. "At the present time," he wrote to Kliment Voroshilov, "I and my family find ourselves in a calamitous situation and have effectively been deprived of housing." Life in a communal apartment "of course deprives me of the possibility of continuing my scientific work. . . . I earnestly request you now, dear Kliment Efrimovich, not to delay in helping me and my family (six people) receive an apartment of four or five rooms."[153]

As time went on, a more coherent approach apparently emerged. A Council of Ministers decree of September 1955 accorded special favor in housing distribution to former prisoners, and to those who had been denounced or had suffered by association with someone labeled an enemy of the people.[154] But it seems unlikely that this was of much force.[155] Solzhenitsyn exposed the "vicious circle" whose linked poles were legal housing and official employment, which squeezed the spirit out of many ex-*zeks*:

> they won't give you a job if you don't have a propiska, and you can't get a propiska if you don't have a job. And no job means no bread card. Former zeks didn't know the rule that the Interior Ministry must fix up work for them. And those who knew were afraid that they would be sent back to the camps.
>
> You're free—weep freely.[156]

Between 1951 and 1957 the Soviet leadership set about rationalizing housing policy and then launching a housing program, defined by rational imperatives and by material results. Yet any notion of rationality could only be extremely relative in a society that was malformed by recent atrocities and disoriented by the shadow of Stalinism. The fingerprints of Stalinism were everywhere—the persistence of personnel, the confusion of party members, the persistent motifs of popular language.[157] Still more pervasively, the attempt by the party and government to deploy rational means to improve living conditions—even in the terms of beneficent improvement—was so all-embracing of society that it logically prefigured Khrushchev's impending proto-communism. The keynote housing decree of 1957 expressed this systemic paradox. Its terms were rational and technocratic, yet it contained a promise to end the housing shortage within at most twelve years. For all the political value of such a promise, it encapsulated the Stalinist giantism that foreshadowed failure. It ensured an enormous volume of construction, just as it produced distorted and irrational results. From 1958, the bolting-on of proto-communism would magnify the paradox and exacerbate the program's major flaw.

To the Communist Future, 1958–1964

With every passing year, Moscow is more visibly assuming the

features of a city of the communist tomorrow.

—Vasilii Promyslov, chairman of the Moscow Soviet, April 1964

Aleksandr Iakovlev, who would find fame as one of Gorbachev's reformers, worked in the Central Committee for much of the 1950s and 1960s. "As a very harmful utopian, a Soviet high priest [*zhrets*] of universal happiness, Khrushchev strode without hesitation towards communism," Iakovlev wrote, decades later. "He strove for the horizon, but the closer he tried to approach it, the further it receded. As the ancients used to say, a man goes on and on when he doesn't know where he's going."[1] Iakovlev's critique might apply not only to Khrushchev the leader but also to his housing program. Between 1958 and 1964, housing construction was so great that at times it did indeed seem to bring the communist future within reach. Yet, paradoxically, the more its output accelerated, the more disoriented the housing economy became, and the more paradise became a mere figment of the future.

The housing decree of 1957 was one of the great signals of the Khrushchev era. Between 1958 and 1964 it acted as the green light for unparalleled construction, by far the highest per capita construction in Europe, which greatly improved the lives of tens of millions of Soviet citizens. Yet this drive was no longer just a matter of improving living standards in easily measurable material terms. The ideological atmosphere of 1958–1964, though never constant, was substantially different from what had gone before: the third party program, approved at the twenty-second party congress in 1961, was the route map to communism. As the guiding motif of housing policy morphed from beneficence to paradise, the housing program was made self-consciously, explicitly, and even aggressively ideological. Its goal was no longer simply to benefit as many people as possible but to transform their consciousness in the context of proto-communism.

Unintended consequences quickly emerged. By setting a target of twelve years for the eradication of the housing shortage, the 1957 decree forced all the relevant state agencies to focus on the output of physical square meters of housing space, to such an extent that they severely neglected wider municipal construction and other considerations of general sustainability. This single-dimensional target was a reductive consequence of central planning. The twelve-year promise's political and ideological significance was thus challenged by its economic and administrative effects. Despite the systemic shortcomings, the volume of new construction was remarkable: it was a historic achievement. Between 1958 and 1964, it transformed the Soviet cityscape. This transformation of physical space helped to modify residents' ideological consciousness within the new microdistricts. The apparently ideological crucible of the microdistrict is a distinguishing mark that separates the period 1958–1964 from what had gone before, although its impact on people's consciousness was inevitably mixed and difficult to calibrate systematically. More dramatic was the effect on living standards. Improvements were both greater and more equally distributed than historians have usually been willing to acknowledge.

Much of the historiography has judged the urban housing program of this period by implicitly comparing it to some abstract standard to which no national housing drive could ever have measured up, or to Khrushchev's wilder flights of rhetoric, or to the disappointed expectations of those who moved in to the new housing.[2] Such analyses draw attention to the shortcomings of the housing program. But the most interesting historical point about the mass housing program is not so much its relative failure as its relative success. Perhaps the most useful way to illustrate this success is also a means to explain the program's relative failure: by exploring the definable gap between planned targets and their realization. The plan's targets were so ambitious that narrow shortfalls implied real achievement because so much housing was actually constructed. Yet the problem with the promise—and with the planning targets it generated—was actually insuperable. True, the promise was the political signal that made the grand scale of the housing program possible, and such unlikely declarations were part of the Soviet way of doing politics. But the planned economy did not only render Khrushchev incapable of keeping the promise, it also ensured that his attempts to do so were counterproductive. Regardless of the value or morality of his quest, Khrushchev made bad judgments. He established policy mechanisms that delivered undesired results. Specialists could sometimes foresee such outcomes but could not prevent them. Seeking paradise, Khrushchev marched with unfailing confidence in the wrong direction. Soviet society was obliged to follow. The horizon never contained even a glimpse of the destination the leader had in mind. He could not find the right path. It was as if his compass was broken, and his officials could not or were not allowed to repair it.

The Obsession with Square Meters

The decree of 1957 set an unambiguously material benchmark: the housing program should be judged by the number of square meters it could turn out each year. In 1959 the seven-year plan, approved at the twenty-first party congress, repeated the commitment.[3] Superficially, this was the apotheosis of rationality in the housing economy; the aim was simply to rehouse as many families as possible in their own separate dwellings, not to use their new apartments to reengineer their souls. The commitments of 1957 and 1959 produced impressive achievements in terms of construction output, which accorded with the party-government's professed "rational" objectives. At the plenum of the Central Committee in November 1962, Khrushchev stated that 50 million citizens had improved their housing conditions in the last four years, with 9 million new apartments, making up 325,000,000 square meters, constructed in cities alone.[4] A year later, at the December 1963 plenum of the Central Committee, he claimed that in the ten years from 1954, 108,000,000 people (half the population) had been rehoused in better conditions.[5] Khrushchev was casting the housing program as his own epochal achievement. Cities were transformed. Harrison Salisbury, the veteran American journalist and Russia watcher, came back to the Soviet Union in 1962. He landed in Uzbekistan and wrote, "I had visited Tashkent twice previously, most recently only seven or eight years ago. But there were great patches of the city which I did not recognize, transformed as they were from ancient Asian mud hovels to areas of apartment houses."[6] A range of statistical sources can test such assertions and impressions and provide answers to two core questions. How powerful was the impact of the 1957 decree? And how much housing was constructed during the high noon of the program, between 1958 and 1964?

CHART 3.1. THE IMPACT OF THE 1957 DECREE:

ANNUAL CONSTRUCTION RISES (URBAN AND RURAL)

IN THE USSR, 1955–1960

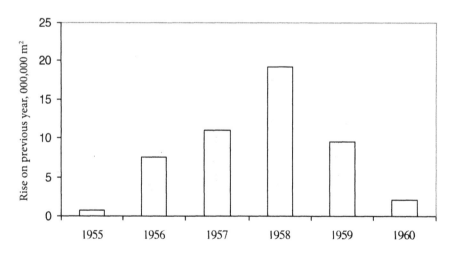

Source: Tsentral'noe Statisticheskoe Upravlenie, *Narodnoe khoziaistvo SSSR v 1958 godu: Statisticheskii ezhegodnik*, 636; ibid. *1960*, 611.

CHART 3.2. THE EXTENT OF THE POST-1957

KHRUSHCHEV-ERA HOUSING PROGRAM: NEW HOUSING

CONSTRUCTION IN THE USSR (URBAN AND RURAL),

1951–1964

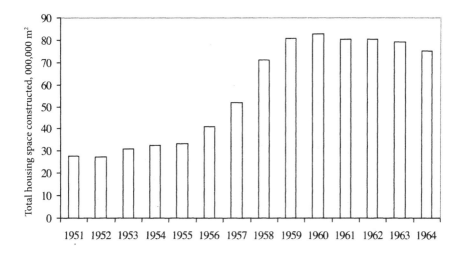

Source: Tsentral'noe Statisticheskoe Upravlenie, *Narodnoe khoziaistvo SSSR v 1958 godu: Statisticheskii ezhegodnik,* 636; ibid., *1960,* 611; Ibid., *1964,* 605–6.

Charts 3.1, 3.2, and 3.3, based on published data, illustrate generally plausible, though measurably inflated, answers to these questions. In chart 3.1, each column represents the difference between construction for the given year and the year immediately preceding it. The rise for 1956 on 1955 reflects the start of the Khrushchev-era program, while the still greater rise for 1958 on 1957 illustrates the impact of the keynote housing decree. This was the largest year-on-year rise in Soviet history. Thereafter, rises were much smaller. Chart 3.2 shows that, though construction output soon leveled off after 1958, it did so at very high total levels. The Khrushchev-era housing program at its greatest extent was a phenomenon that followed the introduction of the 1957 decree.[7]

This is still more obvious when viewed from comparative perspectives. Chart 3.3 shows the per capita construction output of fifteen European countries (urban and rural, all tenures) between 1953 and 1970. The data, which were gathered by the United Nations, all come from official government sources. They show that per capita housing construction in the USSR towered above European competition between 1957 and 1963. The most serious rival was Sweden, but much of that new housing was clustered near Stockholm, whereas in the Soviet Union new construction was

CHART 3.3. HOUSING CONSTRUCTION PER ONE THOUSAND
RESIDENTS IN TWELVE EUROPEAN COUNTRIES, 1953-1970

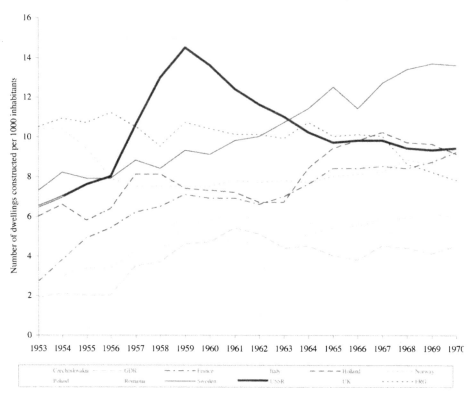

Source: Economic Commission for Europe, *Annual Bulletin of Housing and Building Statistics for Europe, 1957*, 14–15; *1964*, 10–11; *1967*, 12–19; *1970*, 13–32.

dispersed across the geographical and climatic range of the biggest country in the world. The sense of spectacular achievement conjured by these graphs recalls the industrial leaps of the 1930s. Khrushchev, who retained an unreconstructed view of Stalin's industrialization, must have found in such numbers the heady neo-Stalinist gulp after which he so thirsted. The Soviet program also outstripped the two most usefully comparable non-European housing programs of the period: those of Israel and Hong Kong.[8]

Only a major comparative project could challenge the findings of chart 3.3. The Soviet data are sometimes difficult to interpret, partly because of discrepancies between archival and published statistics. If the archival collection of the Central Statistical Administration (TsSU) is more reliable than its publications, then published data seem to have been inflated by around one-fifth.[9] This is an important difference, but when the all-union data are disaggregated into republican and city shares, and when TsSU data are compared with archival data from other sources (in the RSFSR government, the Construction Committee of the Council of Ministers (USSR), city soviets, and other bodies), the general picture of great increases, especially after 1957, is sustained.[10] Chart 3.4 uses data from the TsSU archival collection to illustrate the rises in the RSFSR (not USSR) urban housing fund for all tenures, comparing 1950 and 1960.[11]

Another way to measure the impact of the 1957 decree is to set it against the level of immediate postwar reconstruction. The Belorussian republic provides a tough evidential control, as wartime destruction was particularly severe and the response to it comparatively daunting. Archival data show that the state urban housing fund increased by 88.3 percent between 1945 and 1949.[12] In Minsk, by the end of 1949, the fund had returned to its 1940 level.[13] Although these raw figures do not show that standards of building and reconditioning were often poor and that living standards could remain very low, they still reveal an exceptionally focused reconstruction drive, whose extraordinary scope was repeated at the end of the 1950s. Following a relative lull in the first half of the 1950s, a second leap took place between 1956 and 1960, during which 1.7 million square meters were constructed: substantially more than the total fund in 1945, and double the rise for 1952–1956.[14] The second acceleration cannot be explained by a forceful push for reconstruction

CHART 3.4. INCREASE IN THE RSFSR URBAN HOUSING FUND,
1950–1960

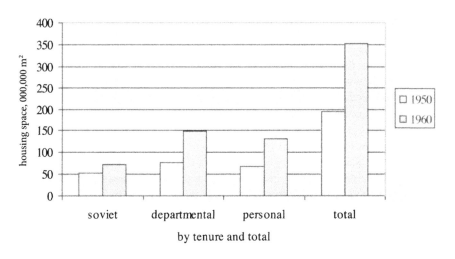

Source: RGAE f. 1562, op. 14, d. 2027, l. 1; d. 2031, l. 1; d. 3004, l. 5.

but, rather, by an especially determined application of the 1957 decree. Whichever illustration is deployed, it is certain that from the second half of the 1950s the party-government sponsored an all-out push for square meter after square meter, counted in hundreds of millions, and that a considerable surge in output resulted.[15]

All this was underwritten by a major spending commitment, whose uncertain origins during late Stalinism reflected an emerging shift from an ethic of sacrifice to one of beneficence, but whose fundamental expansion after 1957 was soon determined by the aspiration of paradise. Such spending increases on housing construction were by then affordable because of economic growth, changes in investment priorities, the cancellation of obligations arising from the wartime bond issue, and the efficient mobilization of citizens' own resources. Yet the push to paradise necessitated considerable expenditure in other areas of the economy, including the space program. CIA sources wrote of Khrushchev's "excessive optimism" in 1957 and 1958, "as a result [of which] the USSR will face accumulating difficulties in its efforts to raise living standards, and perhaps a further slowdown in the tempo of general economic advance."[16] Despite this competitive budgetary environment, spending on the housing program was maintained throughout the Khrushchev era. The promise of 1957 had a powerful impact on expenditure priorities.

Yet published data for all-union budget expenditures are opaque and unreliable. Using them to calculate patterns of spending on housing construction (which is anyway not listed as a separate category) is fruitless, when they show that defense spending hovered around 15 percent of total expenditure between 1958 and 1964, a willful misrepresentation.[17] "Headline" archival data, which might show a more reliable and detailed picture, remain elusive. It is possible, though, to deduce spending increases from reports rather than from budgets, and from local examples. In a major report of March 1958, for example, the Ministry of Finance (USSR) proposed substantial increases for 1958 compared with 1957; the provision of extra credits; and incentives for local soviets and enterprises to spend 100 percent of their allocations.[18] In 1958 Gosplan committed 19,700,000,000 rubles for housing construction in the RSFSR. When the republican Council of Ministers asked for an extra 600,000,000 rubles, it was granted, though at this stage budgetary allocations were increasing faster than construction capacity could absorb them.[19] For Vladivostok, planners projected an extraordinary fivefold rise in investment between 1959 and 1965 (see table 3.1).

Such investment required the retention and the expensive refinement of a range of associated "rational" mechanisms between 1958 and 1964. Technological infrastructure continued to improve, with the rationalization of the relevant research institutes, the promotion of new technical journals, and several major conferences.[20] Officials planned further efficiency-driven organizational innovations.[21] Competitions provided further incentives for better technical and architectural solutions.[22] Construction personnel were being better trained, better rewarded, and better protected on building sites.[23]

These "rational" processes were a precondition for building paradise, but an insufficient one. The program was structurally flawed, and the makers of policy

TABLE 3.1. PROJECTIONS IN 1959 OF SPENDING ON HOUSING AND
MUNICIPAL INFRASTRUCTURE IN VLADIVOSTOK, 1959–1965

	Millions of rubles
1959	250
1960	300
1961	500
1962	700
1963	850
1964	1050
1965	1150

Source: RGAE f. 339, op. 3, d. 780, l. 44.

could not escape its self-limiting characteristics. Khrushchev's promise (it sounded like a personal commitment) to end the housing shortage within a dozen years embedded within the program an infection of failure. Soviet urban housing became the victim of the optimism of the age. The problem was the promise. Its malign effects slowed down the housing program's rational processes.

The twelve-year deadline forced central planners to impose extremely high annual construction targets. Some specialists appreciated how improbable these targets were. The difficulty of fulfilling construction plans was evident even in the first year after the 1957 decree. Despite the astonishing rises in construction output that followed July 1957, the decree did not achieve all the immediate goals demanded by the plan. Officials in Gosplan (RSFSR) showed that construction in the Russian republic during the first nine months of 1958 was 20 percent up on the same period for 1957, but that the plan had still only been fulfilled by 86 percent.[24] True, even the enormous housing economy, which had grown so quickly, was capable of recalibrating itself: the same report revised downward some of the construction targets for the subsequent three years.[25] But as the housing economy grew bigger, the capacity for effective and consistent recalibration grew more difficult. Between January and October 1962, the all-union construction target was fulfilled by 91 percent.[26] The dynamics of planning ensured that even minor shortfalls in plan fulfillment could be magnified beyond the confines of their apparently marginal size or their geographical location. Meanwhile, hidden by the republican averages, some areas performed catastrophically badly: Vologograd oblast' was at 22 percent, for example.[27]

It would have been almost impossible to meet the planners' targets everywhere, but the only way that local administrations could come close—as they so frequently did— was by directing toward housing much of the investment that the plan had dedicated to other areas of municipal construction, and by racing to build apartment houses too quickly. Khrushchevian housing policy generated an obsession throughout the housing economy with the construction of the maximum number of square meters of housing space at the maximum speed. In 1959 constructors used applications of the new architecture to assemble a five-story, eighty-apartment house in Leningrad in thirty-three days.[28] The paradoxical consequence was a brake on output. Neglect of wider municipal services contained within it a slow-burning fuse, because sooner or later, some resources would have to be switched to the construction of kindergartens, shops—even water pipes. Meanwhile, spending too little on local infrastructure that was essential not simply for residents' quality of life but for the ongoing process of housing construction itself—things such as roads—could reduce output not in the medium but in the short term. Very high housing construction targets also forced builders to work with undue haste. Results could be shoddy. Resources had quickly to be diverted toward repair and were effectively lost.

Many professionals understood these self-defeating structural dynamics better than Khrushchev. Kucherenko, the chairman of Gosstroi, was convinced that the only possible way to end the housing shortage in the promised twelve years was to continue with the large-scale construction of individual houses alongside the building en masse of khrushchevki. Individual construction remained crucial to the housing economy in the late 1950s and made a disproportionate contribution to total output. But at the same time, Khrushchev was looking toward the marginalization and ultimate disappearance of such old-fashioned houses in his proto-communist cities. In July 1958, an *ukaz* of the Presidium of the Supreme Soviet for the first time limited the size of individual houses in terms of square meters; the limit before had only been in rooms (five) and stories (two). It was now illegal to construct an individual house of more than sixty square meters, a more aggressive limit.[29] The knell was sounded in 1963, when construction was banned in cities of more than 100,000 people. Now the dozens of towns whose soviets would not grant plots of land or within which the Municipal Bank would not offer credits for individual construction included Vladivostok, Volgograd, and Voronezh—and that was just some of the "V"s.[30]

At the same time cooperative housing was reintroduced as a major lever of policy in decrees of 1958 and 1962.[31] Although cooperatives would make a considerable contribution to the expansion of the urban housing fund during the Brezhnev era, they were subject in the short term to multiple practical problems and were still numerically few by 1964. Problems included the disproportionately large number of cooperatives whose members came from elite groups such as ministerial officials or cultural professionals; disconnections between the trade unions that often organized new cooperatives and the local soviets that were responsible for granting land and providing municipal services;[32] insufficient shareholder investment;[33] failure to build the types of apartments that were most in demand, thus reducing participation;[34] and incomplete administrative infrastructure, especially of banking and credit.[35] These were early days, and the policy was already becoming more effective by 1964.[36]

But by switching funding away from a relatively successful policy—individual construction—and toward an effectively untried one, Khrushchev was taking a major risk with the viability of his great promise.[37] In a letter of 28 November 1958 to the deputy chairman of Gosplan, G. V. Perov, Kucherenko seemed implicitly to doubt the wisdom of a recent speech by Khrushchev at the all-union construction conference in which he reduced the twelve-year promise to nine or ten, a seemingly arbitrary redefinition with considerable consequences; Kucherenko also emphasized the crucial significance of individual housing to fulfilling either the old or the new target.[38] This letter's argument is coded, but it can be read as a manifestation of the gap between the cool professional construction elite and the gigantomania of Khrushchev, or between a rationally judged beneficence and a hot-headed call to paradise. Despite the culture of professionalism in the Soviet bureaucracy in which qualified experts held positions that in the British civil service remained the preserve of sometimes clever amateurs, the top decision makers in the Presidium were, by definition, nonspecialists. Lacking professional expertise, they were not immunized against particular forms of the big-number bug that infected the centrally planned economy. But they were also beholden to Khrushchev, and the big picture of housing policy was his production. The twelve-year promise sounds like Khrushchev talking; it has the merit of his enthusiasm and determination, but the demerit of his lack of realism. Kucherenko understood this. Some of his professional colleagues spoke more openly about the problem with the promise.

Such discontented colleagues applauded the level of investment in construction but deplored the way in which they were forced to spend it. At the All-Union Urban Construction Conference of June 1960, the minister of the Local Economy of Estonia argued that while apportionments for municipal construction (on associated infrastructure and services) were increasing every year, the results lagged far behind those of housing construction. According to "generally accepted" norms, the minister maintained, municipal construction should obtain 25–30 percent of the capital investment devoted to housing, but in Estonia it had run at only 15–16 percent. He insisted that this "has caused a sharp holding back of the development of municipal enterprises and communications in many towns of the [Estonian] republic. It is necessary to correct this abnormal situation and allot the required resources to municipal construction."[39] An official in the Council of Ministers (USSR) stated in the professional press in 1962 that, in a given budget, 50–55 percent of capital investment should be directed toward housing, with 20–23 percent in "social and cultural" (*kul'turno-bytovye*) facilities, and 23–25 percent in "municipal" works. In practice, he argued, housing was excessively favored; in Volgograd, for example, 82.5 percent of the relevant part of the 1959 budget was spent on housing.[40] According to unpublished information gathered by Gosstroi, local services in many RSFSR cities were in a parlous condition in 1958. Only 25–30 percent of housing space was equipped with adequate access to water supply and sewerage.

Gosstroi highlighted the danger for housing construction: "The further falling behind in the construction of water supply and sewerage facilities and networks can act as a serious brake on the realization of housing construction plans."[41] At the 1960 construction conference, the director of the Academy of the Municipal Economy of the RSFSR argued that this investment lag "substantively complicates and in many cases can slow down the further development of housing construction." He insisted, "It is completely clear that during 1960–1965 we must eliminate this gap and supply all branches of the urban economy proportionately, in scale and speed."[42] Government in Moscow listened to these voices, recognized the seriousness of the problem, and attempted to make improvements. The Council of Ministers (RSFSR) introduced measures in July 1959 on urban water supply that were the subject of checks and follow-ups by the Council of Ministers (USSR) five years later.[43] But the broad thrust of policy remained the same. It could not do otherwise, thanks both to Khrushchev's misguided enthusiasms and their systemic match in overcentralized planning.

The poor quality of the new buildings also threatened the success of the housing program. In its review of the first year's progress since the 1957 decree, Gosstroi officials noted "widespread defects" in numerous aspects of construction (such as the laying of timber in floors and the installation of bathrooms) and that the "majority" of new apartment houses were approved for occupancy merely as "satisfactory," with "extremely few" (only 4 of 276 in the city of Khar'kov, for example) considered "excellent." Gosstroi recognized that this caused higher expenses associated with catch-up, especially repairs.[44] Yet local bodies failed to make use of the resources allocated to them for repairs.[45] The Housing Administration of the Moscow Soviet noted in June 1964 that only 61.4 percent of budgetary allocations for housing repairs for the first quarter of the year had been spent, and in the second quarter spending was only 36.9 percent.[46] Not only did this affect people's living standards, it further unbalanced municipal budgeting.

Incentives to complete buildings quickly were factored into the documentation of the housing economy; if the papers were not submitted on time, the building would not count toward that year's plan.[47] This placed officials and professionals under tremendous pressure and even created moral discomfort. Evgenii Samokhin, the hero of Vladimir Voinovich's 1963 novella *I Want to Be Honest*, cannot fulfill his duties as a supervisor in a housing construction trust with honorable reasonableness.[48] Senior managers of the trust order him to complete an apartment block for the Komsomol in time for the holiday on 7 November, a showy and irresponsible deadline. At the end of an inspection, which passes the block for habitation even though the members of the commission are aware of its faults, Samokhin refuses to append his signature. If this were a socialist realist novel, this apparent epiphany would derive from Samokhin's concern for the Komsomol, and a rebuilt apartment block might be a symbol of the durability of the communist future. Yet it is no epiphany, as Samokhin already has a sporadic record of rebellion, and his motives are private and personal, not social and political, so the structure of the socialist realist aesthetic is denied. Like Voinovich's novella, the housing economy itself no longer made sense on approved, official terms.

Voinovich showed that central planning placed local officials in professional dilemmas that made honesty a luxury; archival records reveal beyond doubt that another consequence of central planning was to make that corner of the communist future dedicated to housing supply objectively unrealizable. Nevertheless, by the end of the Khrushchev era, the obsession with square meters had changed the Soviet Union in both major and minor ways—and frequently for the better. The cityscape was dramatically transformed. For a brief period popular idealism could sometimes mesh with state power—visibly, as student "volunteers" went to the Virgin Lands to help with housing construction (as in the case of a major Belorussian contingent in 1963).[49] A new stripe of ideology seemed to govern the urban way of life. Popular living standards had risen significantly. This was, after all, one of the biggest social reforms of postwar European history. The extraordinary successes and inherent failures of the urban construction program helped to define the Khrushchev era. New apartment houses were even called khrushchevki. (The wittier *khrushchoby*, or Khrushchev slums, beloved of external observers, seems to have been a less common formulation.) Their sudden ubiquity created a new, defining Soviet cityscape. The potential of the technological and architectural advances of the 1940s and 1950s was now being released on more than the most feasible scale. For all the flaws of the economic system that underpinned it, this looked like a new kind of Soviet city.[50]

The Mass Production of the Cityscape of Communism

In 1964 Laurens van der Post published an account of his recent journey across the USSR. Recording Tashkent, he described the stupendous volume of housing construction. Could he see inside one of the new apartments? No, said his guide, softening the refusal:

> "You'll have plenty of time to see new apartments in other cities later on."
> "But they will not be the same," I protested.
> "Don't worry," she urged me gravely, "they are all the same wherever you go in the Soviet Union."[51]

From Minsk to Magadan and from Alma Ata to Archangel, Khrushchev's urban planners constructed a strikingly uniform cityscape. The new cityscape looked the same because it was composed of the same units: similar apartment blocks, standardized housing districts, and a public architecture and overall urban layout whose shape conformed to central directives. Most characteristic among the generic apartment blocks was the prefabricated, five-story, standardized khrushchevka. Clusters and rows of these famous buildings were located in the new microdistricts. The mikroraiony were designed to conform to proto-communist norms. Their layouts reflected local conditions (apartment blocks set at the correct angle to maximize environmental advantage, and the inclusion of more or less green space, for instance), but in general they followed similar plans. Long rows of typically five-story apartment blocks were separated by "yards," containing playgrounds and, increasingly, garages. Schools and low-rise buildings for communal and public services, all constructed to a limited range of blueprints, were nearby.

When all this was new, it was a physical imprint of communist possibility; precisely its mass replication, under construction, reinforced the sense of an impending communist future across the union, at least before the haphazard construction of too many garages encroached on the yards, or before gatherings of elderly women near the staircase entryways added too much of a timeless rural sense to the surroundings. Elsewhere in Soviet cities, grander architecture also pointed the way to the communist future for a time. Neo-modernism juxtaposed glass, steel, and concrete in such buildings as the Palace of Congresses in the Kremlin (designed by Mikhail Posokhin et al., 1961) or the Palace of Arts in Tashkent (Vladimir Berezin et al., 1964).[52] This was an architecture that evoked transparency, accessibility, participation, and the transition to a new life, in contradistinction to the heavy closed façades of Stalin-era neoclassicism.

Perhaps briefly, this cityscape seemed to capture the future. At the reception to mark the opening of the Palace of Congresses, the living symbol of the Soviet space age, Iurii Gagarin, stole the show.[53] The young characters in the 1963 movie *I Walk around Moscow* are at ease in a gleaming cityscape, complete with self-service shops, cafés, and the expanding metro.[54] Tarkovskii's short color production of 1960, *The Steamroller and the Violin*, shows a brilliant, resurrecting Moscow, in blues and reds, where a worker and a small boy befriend each other in the shadow of some building works.[55] Yet this cityscape's intensive replication, in the different districts of each city and across the union, struck outsiders as producing the opposite effect: oppressiveness.

For most foreign visitors, this new urban arena was the concrete manifestation of totalitarian sameness, perhaps distinguished only by shades of unattractiveness. In 1960, when many of the buildings were still brand new, Stephen Spender visited Guy Burgess in Moscow; Burgess's apartment block was "one of the ugliest."[56] Soviet citizens responded in a more varied way. At its most stylized, this was a matter of "speaking Bolshevik." Van der Post said to his Tashkent guide:

> "But don't you find it depressing to have the same apartments for everyone everywhere?"
> She bristled at that and reproved me: "Why should I want anything any different from any of my fellow citizens? What is good for one is good for all. We are all equal in the Soviet Union."[57]

But citizens' responses were also informed by more down-to-earth considerations. People were as likely to be disoriented by urban transformation as to discern its implications for equality. Indeed, physical confusion was sometimes an unavoidable side effect of urban improvement. After all, within a few years, the appearance of people's urban space and their means of occupying it had been transformed. One citizen expressed bewilderment in 1960, writing to architects about the stresses of living in an environment where every block looked the same. She highlighted in particular the practical difficulties this caused for children, who would get lost and not find their own apartment block and staircase entry.[58] But such comments were no more frequent than the contrasting response of wryly affectionate jokes—or so the loaded historical record might suggest.[59]

Wry affection rather than the sensation of urban oppression was possible because this cityscape—faulty and unsightly to some—was explicitly designed to improve the living standards of ordinary citizens. For all its flaws, it might even be capable of dealing with citizens as individuals rather than indistinguishable population units. The principles that guided the work of architects took into account, at the formalized level of design, that families varied in size and composition and had different needs accordingly.[60] A more flexible range of apartments was available in an experimental microdistrict in Cheliabinsk in 1959, for example.[61] In Marlen Khutsiev's 1964 film *Il'ich's Gate*, where the city is so thickly and variously presented that it effectively becomes a character, images of thawing and demolition alternate with representations of urbanites experiencing the interior and exterior of their city as individuals, families, and groups of friends.[62] Similarly, a thick urban description realistically portrays varied family life, individuality, and generational difference, all ultimately focused on a family apartment, in Vasilii Pronin's film of 1965, *Our House*.[63]

Perhaps paradoxically, this differentiation of the urban population and the incipient possibility of limited individual rights in the housing economy coincided with the newly uniform and undifferentiated Soviet cityscape.[64] It was mass-produced similitude that gave more and more families the right to a reasonable home. To some extent, this was the end of architecture in terms of housing, and the final takeover of the profession by construction experts.[65] By 1962 GlavAPU in Moscow had become the City Planning Soviet, losing its architectural title, and its meetings gathered more non-architectural experts than before.[66] By contrast, the documentary record of analogous bodies during the closing stages of the war conjures an atmosphere of gentlemen-amateurs, notwithstanding both their qualifications and the horrific demands of reconstruction that they faced.

Meanwhile, the enhanced status of construction workers and professionals was ritualized in public culture with the celebration of a Builders' Day. On 31 July 1956 (precisely one year before the keynote housing decree), Khrushchev buoyed up the crowd at the opening of the Central Lenin Stadium in Moscow: "I want to wish you all the best, comrade builders—workers, technicians, engineers, architects—for your [determined] attention, energy and effort not just in fulfilling but overfulfilling this year's housing construction program. And this is no small program."[67] In 1957 the day was set for 2 August. Gosstroi officials discussed ways of propagandizing the builders' contribution, to provide them with additional incentives to outstrip targets, and to publicize the spirit of the age. Appropriate celebrations were lined up in different republics.[68] Stylized pictures of building workers in the early 1960s conformed to the socialist realist aesthetic—the worker-hero, surrounded by the tools of his trade, new cityscape to his back, head tilted upward, smile on his face, staring into the communist future.[69]

Prefabrication, the most crucial technology for building the future, now became increasingly ubiquitous. In April 1959 the Council of Ministers planned a twenty-five-fold growth in the volume of large panel housing construction (then the advanced form of prefabrication) through to 1964.[70] Gosstroi organized conferences and seminars about this emerging technology for specialists in Minsk, Leningrad, and Baku in 1961.[71] In the town of Cherepovets within Vologda sovnarkhoz, whose housing construction was dominated by the local metalworks, serious industrialized construction using prefabrication dated from 1955; by 1959 output was more than three times higher. Large-panel construction there dated from 1957, accounting for 37.5 percent of total output in the period through to 1960.[72]

According to data gathered in the Council of Ministers (RSFSR), advances in prefabrication technology generated major cost savings between 1957 and 1960. In Cheliabinsk, the saving was 10.1 percent, but in many other cities it was higher: in Orel it was 19.8 percent, for example; in Leningrad, 22.3 percent; in Tashkent, 23.3; in Riga, 38.2.[73] These efficiency savings were backed up with economies of scale, in a dynamic that spread and intensified urban uniformity. Pressure, sometimes exerted through the banking system, fell on enterprises to cut costs. Prefabrication, the dynamo of urban uniformity, was the mechanism by which the bank encouraged enterprises to make their economies. In correspondence of 1960 with the Council of Ministers (RSFSR), officials of the republican Construction Bank (Stroibank) emphasized that the cost of large block construction was 5.2 percent lower than construction in brick, while the cost of large panel construction was 14.9 percent lower still.[74] Costs per square meter continued to fall through to 1964, or sometimes remained level.[75] This made possible the mass production of the cityscape of communism—mass replication might have looked like communist uniformity, but it was driven by the intense systemic pressure of cost reduction.

On a less spectacular level, the same drivers of cost reduction created sameness inside people's apartments.[76] If prefabrication built the Khrushchev-era cityscape, then analogous processes of standardized production furnished what van der Post's tour guide promised was its counterpart, a uniform domestic interior across the Soviet Union. Estimates of 1959 suggested that the equipping of new apartments with newly designed furniture would for 1960–1965 cost 68.4 percent of the total costs of older furniture designs, which in turn fed through to a degree of sameness of domestic space.[77]

The constant replication of identical correspondence from Gosstroi to republican state bodies—the same signed letters to multiple addressees—is a documentary mirror of the massive geographical scope of the construction of uniform urban proto-communism.[78] Creating such similitude required a considerable variety of engineering solutions: the Soviet Union contained earthquake zones, areas of extreme heat, areas of extreme cold, areas of both, and some that would regularly experience extremely high winds. Housing construction inside the Arctic Circle posed particular technical challenges.[79] Some places had to be rebuilt after extreme climatic events. In 1962 the Council of Ministers discussed the reconstruction of parts of Archangel oblast' following severe storms: housing was a particular priority.[80] In the freezing Far North, construction was "extremely expensive," but it was even costlier in the still less hospitable Kolyma. Each square meter in Magadan cost 39 percent more than in Noril'sk.[81] In 1961 the costs of construction in Vorkuta were 88 percent higher than in Tula.[82] Engineers, architects, and other "scientific-technical" personnel made tremendous efforts to adapt prefabricated designs to the Soviet Union's geographical and climatic range, so as to deliver the Khrushchevian city at affordable rates to the most unlikely places.[83] Constructing the proto-communist cityscape in such a wide variety of settings while sustaining very high levels of square meter output inside the confines of a centrally planned economy was a remarkable achievement. Without it, the program could not have been one of the major European social reforms of its time.

Throughout the Soviet Union, the physical epitome of the new Soviet cityscape and its most vivid cultural construct was Cheremushki. The old village of that name to the southwest of Moscow was overrun with building sites in the late 1950s, in a network of khrushchevki that was near simultaneously pioneering and archetypal.[84] Particularly influential was the well-known ninth experimental district, which worked out in physical form some of the principles of mikroraion development that would find ready echoes across the Soviet Union.[85] From 1959, when Novye Cheremushki's ninth experimental district was showcased, the architectural press featured self-consciously similar developments of clustered khrushchevki, laid out according to architecturally rational and ideologically proto-communist principles, in city after city across the Soviet Union. In principle, these districts were supposed to foster the highest possible standard of living for the lowest possible cost. Environmental considerations (light, noise, air quality) were paramount. Facilities for communal life, neighborhood interaction, and domestic mobilization—from clubs to sports facilities to red corners—were all tilted toward paradise.

Rappaport's popular 1962 operetta-film *Cheremushki*, which was scored by Shostakovich, tells the story of the colonization, not of southwest Moscow, but of a housing district that might be anywhere; as a narrator declares at the start, "Cheremushkis" are springing up across the Union.[86] In the film, Cheremushki is a universal new neighborhood of magical potential and actual achievement, the object of great affection. Characters express warmth for this universally located place, which offers so many citizens a better life, and they show their vituperation when a corrupt official threatens their access to it. Their singing is joyful, and images such as magic carpets make obvious the sense of impending paradise. Drawing more soberly on the same trope in 1962, a trade journalist allowed readers to form an instant mental picture of Ryshkanorka, a housing district in Kishinev, by writing that it looked like Novye Cheremushki.[87] "Cheremushki" was a shorthand for the urban housing program, and its rhetorical ubiquity suggests it was one of the codes by which Soviet citizens could make sense of the changes to their cityscape, and even to identify themselves within it.

Cheremushki was not just a physical reality located in real time but an early sign of future paradise: in this abstract sense, it was the ultimate example of socialist realist architecture. Moreover, the general fact of all-union uniformity was a major ideological statement. It implied a "totalitarian" reach, though this seems an unfruitful form of explanation. A more helpful viewpoint comes from the discourse of the time. The mass production of this cityscape was an emphatic statement of communist possibility. And inside its housing microdistricts, communism was to be built.

Building Communism in the Mikroraion

The promise of 1957 to end the housing shortage within a dozen years implied the transition to the next stage of the Marxist-Leninist scheme, because Khrushchev partly defined communism in terms of its capacity to provide material plenty. This filled out the empty talk of communist possibility at the nineteenth party congress in 1952. In the third party program, published in 1961, the 1970s were foreseen as a decade during which material abundance would become the norm, allowing genuine "distribution according to needs."[88] The party program described the implications for housing, which was considered "the most acute problem in the improvement of the well-being of the Soviet people." Most crucially, the program insisted that "[i]n the course of the first decade an end will be put to the housing shortage in the country." In the first instance, those families in "overcrowded and substandard dwellings" would get "new apartments." Housing for peasants would be modernized in the same way as for urbanites. Within twenty years, "every family, including newlyweds, will have a comfortable apartment conforming to the requirements of hygiene and cultured living," and this would "gradually become rent free."[89] This was a vision of paradise that deliberately echoed Lenin's seminal text of 1917, *The State and Revolution*, and its concrete proposals had effectively been prefigured in the 1957 decree, but in itself it announced a major ideological advance.

Housing would be abundant—but for its users it would also be free. Moreover, payment-free abundance should exist in a new setting of communality, cooperation, the scaling back of the state—in short, mass democratic mobilization. The program called for the "All-round extension and perfection of socialist democracy, active participation of all citizens in the administration of the state, in the management of economic and cultural development . . . the maximum encouragement of local initiative."[90] Signs of what this meant started to emerge from the late 1950s inside the newly conceptualized and constituted microdistricts. The microdistrict was the distinctively new urban arena in which the epochal project of building communism would take place. Unlike the separate apartment, and despite very rudimentary origins in late Stalinism, it really was an invention of the Khrushchev years.

At first glance, it was a housing district of between five and twenty thousand residents, living in new, state-owned, mass-produced apartment houses, supported by a carefully calculated level of public services, and fitting into a wider network of urban provision. While the myriad housing districts that sprang up during this period might have created a new cityscape of forbidding uniformity, were they not simply a particularly compelling example of the world's new urban modernity? Those skeptical of Soviet uniqueness might argue that there were similarities between the Soviet urban housing district and the housing estates of other European countries, or the "projects" of the United States. Typically, a professional correspondent wrote to *Arkhitektura SSSR* in 1955, raising practical concerns about the arrangement of housing blocks. His comments might just as easily have been found in the professional journals of Britain, Sweden, West Germany—or East Germany. "Housing," he maintained, "demands the maximum of clean air, greenery, separateness from noise and dust. All this is more easily and better achieved not by building apartment blocks facing the street, but in the interior of the housing district [kvartal]."[91]

Both *kvartal* and *mikroraion* might be translated as "neighborhood housing district," but the terms derive from different ideological presuppositions. The transition from one to the other represented both a narrowly architectural and broadly ideological shift from one stage of the Soviet project to another. In essence, the kvartal was a Stalinist and neo-Stalinist arena of conventional new construction, whose layout and function were not necessarily very different from districts in the capitalist West, whereas the mikroraion was part of the Khrushchevian route to the communist future. The Stalinist kvartal did not contain or aim to provide, on a mass scale and with a fierce ideological charge, communal living structures alongside separate dwellings, but this was the principal goal of the Khrushchevian microdistrict. Yet in the first instance, the microdistrict was indeed a universal modern form. The practical and universal aspect was confirmed at the fifth congress of the International Union of Architects, held in Moscow in 1958, at which delegates approved a resolution that "The planning and construction of housing must be based on the principle of the microdistrict," whose size "depends on realistic economic, geographical, and social conditions."[92] In exclusively Soviet discussions, however, its ideological potential was prominent, as architects and government approached the issue from different sides. And it was replicated under similar conditions in other parts of Eastern Europe, notably in such troubled model settlements as Nowa Huta in Poland.[93]

The first official discussions about microdistricts probably took place in 1945. Planners defined the concept foremost as an extended, rationally organized neighborhood unit and to a lesser extent described it as a living environment with proto-communist implications. The word *mikroraion* did not, however, emerge in public discussions with any regularity until 1957, and by 1958 it had assumed a thickish ideological color.[94] It soon became apparent that the microdistrict was something other than the kvartal, and hence different in kind from its Western analogues; even in 1958 more farsighted architects and planners were coming to understand it as the basic urban communist arena whose purpose was to enhance people's socialist and proto-communist consciousness. In February 1958 the original and provocative architectural writer S. Khan-Magomedov claimed that in the preceding ten years architects had hardly considered the problem of "the restructuring of daily life [*perestroika byta*]." But now things were changing; he compared the new type of housing district to the house-communes of the 1920s.[95] In other words, what was once gathered in (a very small number) of ideal-type apartment houses should now be applied to housing districts as a whole, and en masse: communal structures providing cooking, laundry, and other services, which should especially reduce women's burdens, as well as other cultural and educational facilities. All this should foster a community-minded local population (obshchestvennost'), raising the proto-communist consciousness of residents.

In 1962 the housing professionals' journal claimed that a mikroraion in Moscow's Kuibyshevskii raion contained "a people's university of culture with two faculties: music and health." It declared, "And often in the evenings, residents hurry to the club '*Na ogonek*,' in order to listen to an interesting lecture on medicine, talk to a doctor, or get acquainted with new productions of musical art." This represented part of a substantial communist project: "If two or three years ago you could count on your fingers the number of apartments in the capital into which a communist way of everyday life [*byt*] had entered, then now hundreds of houses, whole apartments struggle for the right to call themselves communist."[96] New ideological pressures were also exerted in housing beyond the microdistrict. Hostels (*obshchezhitiia*), which were constructed with some frequency during the 1950s and 1960s, were a particularly likely arena.[97] There were 887 hostels in Karaganda in 1960, and fifty-two thousand people, many of them students or young workers, lived in them. Conditions must often have been difficult, but in one hostel two brothers campaigned for an appropriate room of "communist daily life [*byt*]," an analogue of the red corners.[98] The imperative thus existed even in remote hostels, but this last, single example underlines how difficult are the evidential problems in assessing its relative extent.

Yet the microdistrict was the future. Even though the language of idealism might only have reflected small scraps of reality, some true believers (or rhetorically minded pragmatists) were convinced that the networks of local facilities emerging in some microdistricts were a basis not only of full communist consciousness but also of individual comfort and enjoyment. An architect, V. A. Samarov, wrote to the Moscow construction conference of June 1960 on the subject of houses of culture, in which "a visitor spends the whole of his evening relaxing, watching films or stage productions, using the library or the restaurant, or visiting an exhibition."[99] Another letter to the same conference, from one A. S. Poletaiev, was couched in an optimistic Khrushchevian idiom: "We live in a happy time," he claimed. "The day of communism is near, and very much depends on you, the constructors of new cities, for bringing this day close." Yet making communism real was about activating everyday functions: public canteens and laundries should be in large apartment houses "to bring relief to the separate household economy of every family, and, more importantly, liberate the women of the house." He wanted red corners, but as a place to "read a paper, magazine or book, and watch a film on television," activities that were hardly inspiring of collective enterprise.[100] Another citizen, N. I. Lebanova, wanted more red (or Lenin) corners, as the location "where a residents' meeting can be conducted, residents can listen to talks and lectures, play chess or draughts, read a magazine or newspaper, and share opinions with comrades." Such a format was not formally influenced by the Party. She also understood the difference between official rhetoric and practical delivery and called for the latter to live up to the former: "Public dining is so widely propagandized, it's necessary as well to have space for a buffet in every apartment house in which one can have breakfast and an evening meal—tea, coffee, hot dishes."[101]

The red corners in a microdistrict might mean some set-aside space, either in what would otherwise have been a ground-floor apartment or in a separate building such as a club. Notwithstanding their functions in entertainment and relaxation, red corners were an obvious gathering place for Khrushchev-era obshchestvennost' and were accordingly the focus of much rhetoric. Local government also encouraged them in very practical ways. For instance, the Moscow Soviet Housing Administration committed 22 million rubles in 1958 for the provision of furniture in housing administration offices (domoupravleniia) generally and red corners specifically in Kalininskii raion.[102] Party-government agencies were required to boost and channel the popular enthusiasm that existed. It is an enormous methodological challenge to measure citizens' spontaneous voluntarism; the statist traces of the archival documents instead show the influence of local housing administrations and the deliberate fostering by local decree of an idealized obshchestvennost'.[103]

Reform now came to the Stalin-era housing management administrations (or domoupravleniia), partly so that they could fulfill this function better. They were now recharacterized as "housing operation bureaus" (or ZhEKi), and their professional work was supplemented by a revitalized neo-Leninist approach to apartment house committees (*domkomy*). The new ZhEKi were arranged as streamlined administrations, so the demands of paradise and bureaucratic rationalization complemented each other. In 1958 the reform had reduced the number of separate bureaucratic units in Gor'kii, for example, so that the city's 3 raiony were administered by 29 ZhEKi instead of 225 housing administrations.[104] A correspondent to the leading professional journal commented that the savings in Rostov-on-Don were worth tens of thousands of rubles.[105] As the early 1960s progressed, more and more ZhEKi were created, increasingly dominating local housing administrations.[106]

Yet these new units were designed not only for rationalizing purposes but for deeply ideological ones, too; they were supposed to be infused with a proto-communist charge capable of mobilizing local communities. One means to do this was through the establishment of social commissions (*obshchestvennye komissii*).[107] The tasks of these commissions included "the utmost development of the initiative and autonomous activity [*samodeiatel'nost'*] of residents, with the aim of improving the operation of the housing fund" and "public supervision [*obshchestvennaia kontrol'*]" to make residents observe the rules of apartment use.[108] The invasiveness of institutionalized resident-on-resident observation will be addressed in due course, but in organizational terms these commissions were part of a ground-level infrastructure with a proto-communist agenda, whose existence alone fundamentally distinguished the microdistrict from the housing estates of the West.

This infrastructure was also marked by the return of the revolution-era house committees (*domkomy*), in which residents had briefly helped to run housing space after 1917 (a collectivism that had taken place in the absence of effective state structures). Published data suggested that 33,000 volunteer activists (*aktivisty*) were operating in 1,425 house committees in Moscow and Moscow Region in 1960, under the general auspices of ZhEKi.[109] House committees were run by enthusiastic volunteers—or busybodies—and they organized repairs, sanitary campaigns, and ideological instruction. These activists did much of the work in red corners. Other volunteers worked outside the remit of the house committees.[110] A 1958 resolution of Moscow's city soviet made an award to activist-medics.[111] In 1964 the multifarious welfare role of ZhEKi extended in Moscow's Sverdlovskii raion to pioneer camps.[112]

Within the borders of the microdistrict, to very variable but nevertheless real levels, there existed between 1958 and 1964 a mix of professional and voluntary activity that redefined obshchestvennost'. An obshchestvennitsa would no longer be stereotyped as a lofty bureaucrat's wife, as she might have been during the 1930s, but was now likely to be a factory worker, or a retired cleaner, who spent her spare time working on a voluntary basis in the microdistrict.[113] The practical results were mixed, at best. In Moscow's Kalininskii raion, the soviet housing administration noted in 1963 that the number and value of red corners had generally increased. The administration praised ZhEKi 6, 8, 9, and 11 in particular for their operation of red corners in an appropriately ideological and "systematic" way. It criticized ZhEKi 1, 3, 5, and 10 for the red corners' poor management, their location in basements, their lack of furniture and equipment, and the low level of ideological instruction they offered.[114]

The mobilization of obshchestvennost' in the microdistrict during the Soviet Union's high noon was doubtless disappointing, but it was rhetorically prominent in public culture. "Mass educational [*massovo-vospitatel'naia*] work among residents is very effective," declared a typical article. "The overwhelming majority of residents . . . work together to repair apartments, pursue cleanliness and order not only in their own rooms but also in areas of common use."[115] According to such rhetoric, local mobilization was personally and communally advantageous. This rallying and mustering continued the tradition of the *subbotnik* or *voskresnik* and repeated those wartime and immediate postwar calls for citizens to look after the housing stock: the call to communism and the reaction to catastrophe produced similar imperatives.[116] Public culture continued to assume that citizens had a competent level of domestic and technical skills and should use them in checking windows, keeping stairwells tidy, maintaining heating systems, and making repairs. In this way, obshchestvennost' carried out self-interested activity in a communal context. Proto-communism in the microdistrict deployed the language of idealism but had the practical effect of everyday usefulness, as celebration merged with the mundane. An order of the Housing Administration of Moscow's Sverdlovskii raion soviet of April 1959 required "simultaneously providing for the [1 May] festival, and also strengthening the preservation of houses." In the run-up to the holiday, ZhEK employees had to deck out the housing districts of the raion with the appropriate flags, banners, and posters, and to run checks on water pipes, elevators, and other municipal services.[117] Volunteers also worked on professional maintenance crews, described (like the better-known local citizen patrols) as *druzhiny*.[118] Publications claimed that such voluntary activity was essential for the practical maintenance of the microdistrict.[119]

Although public culture had promoted such voluntary maintenance work during the late Stalinist era, the work assumed a much more credible form in the early 1960s. Before, citizens did such work in order to survive, and with very limited support from agencies of the state; now, a plausible and even proto-communist template existed for combining voluntarism, non-state communality, and the organizational backbone of local state bodies. The existence of idealism, difficult to gauge but risky to dismiss, is perhaps not the main point. A revealing hint of cynicism comes in a short story by Andrei Bitov, in which the main character, an "idler," talks of the local beer stall having its own mikroraion, of its drinkers forming a kind of collective.[120] Residents of microdistricts no doubt thought and expressed a range of opinions about the proto-communist quest, but its viability was extended as significant numbers of them participated, for their own practical and personal benefit, in this institutionalization of voluntarism.

The Soviet program was unique not because of the enormity of the construction project or because of the ideology and practices of the microdistrict but because of its effect on everyone's lives, not just the poorest. This separates it fundamentally from the welfare states of Western Europe and the United States. Unlike the increasingly troubled council estates of Britain or the housing projects of the United States, all kinds of people lived in Soviet microdistricts, bringing traditional family and neighborhood rhythms to complement and clash with those of proto-communist organization.[121] Iulii Raizman's 1961 film *But What If It's Love?* carefully re-creates this authentic-seeming living environment, with its connected sense of safety and exciting potential, and its depiction of traditional and modern forms of community surveillance, as the setting for its story of youthful love.[122] This story in turn combined themes of personal fulfillment and collective endeavor. One way or another, and increasingly as the Khrushchev era gave way to the next two decades, very large sections of the population, including parts of the top elite, spent a part of their lives in these places. Their experience between 1958 and 1964 was often rough-edged but contained enticing glimpses of the starry transition to communism, which party-government rhetoric had given them grounds to expect.

Toward Communist Living Standards?

High levels of poverty existed in towns and villages during the late Stalinist and Khrushchev eras alike.[123] At certain times and places it gave rise to great anger and unrest; in Novocherkassk in 1962, when people rioted in response to rising food prices and the sneers of the local elite, they met with a violent crackdown. The size of the urban housing program, which seems indisputable, surely made for the progressive alleviation of this poverty over time. Yet historians have questioned the extent to which people enjoyed higher standards of living as a result. By focusing on the rich archival source of citizens' letters of complaint to the authorities, scholars have examined trends of ongoing deprivation and new kinds of relative poverty, which include persistent overcrowding, isolation in areas ill-served by social infrastructure, and the intense stress arising from poor sound-proofing.[124] Khrushchev himself acknowledged problems associated with hasty building but emphasized, imprecisely, that 75 million people enjoyed improved housing conditions as a result of his reforms.

Khrushchev's varying claims about the scope of his own achievements should not detract from the genuineness of the attempt to establish communist living standards during this period. The government failed not on the basis of comparative historical example or reasonable historical expectation but, rather, on its own exceptionally ambitious terms. Qualified failure was something more like relative success.[125] True, considerable deprivation continued, and the new housing contained many faults. Yet the tens of millions who moved in to new apartments did enjoy a rise in living standards, and their complaints, which in any case describe only a trace of lived experience, sometimes (but not always) reflected a radical reorientation of expectations. But the question remains: how communist were these living standards?

Khrushchev packed three main elements into his definition of proto-communist living standards. The most important was material plenty, as he announced in Moscow during his famous 1959 public argument with Richard Nixon about Soviet and American consumption.[126] In terms of housing, the goal was an adequately sized separate apartment for every family; during this transitional period, however, living standards could more meaningfully be measured with reference to the number of square meters occupied on average by each individual, the amenities their apartment offered, and their access to adequate municipal facilities. Khrushchev also emphasized the importance of high standards of construction. Unbridled material plenty was a defined ambition throughout the first and second worlds of the 1950s and 1960s; the Khrushchevian understanding of communist living standards, though, differed from affluence on the Western model.[127]

Two additional elements, particularly Soviet and particularly Khrushchevian, were packed into the baggy understanding of communist living standards. First was the difficult-to-quantify molding of consciousness inside the microdistrict. Second was the push to equality, a force that was quantifiably different to the social differentiation of Stalinism and the more gentle redistributions of Western welfare states. Applying both elements on a mass scale, however imperfectly, was a novel experiment. They were linked tropes of Khrushchevian rhetoric; proto-communist consciousness could exist only if access to improving living standards was at least reasonably equal. Although both controversial and partial, quantifiable evidence is available to illustrate a rough index of equality. Material plenty is easier to measure.

Measured in square meters, the urban housing program was plenteous, and this alone provides evidence of enhanced standards of living. For all the constraining pressure of central planning on the sustainability of increasing output, hundreds of millions of square meters were constructed before Khrushchev was ousted from power, and tens of millions of people obtained new homes. Khrushchev's son remembered, defensively, fifty years on: "If today we say that the five-story apartment blocks [*piatietazhniki*] are not of the right standard, at that time they were the only means of quickly giving people housing." While he spoke in guardianship of his father's reputation, his call to avoid anachronism is right. "People lived in places swarming with bugs, in basements, attics, and overcrowded communal apartments, where there was no real standard of living," he went on. "But thanks to these khrushchevki, the majority of people could move to an apartment. The WC might have been in the bathroom, but it was a separate apartment."[128] Many people moved out of basements, barracks, wretched shacks, and worse.

The form of the new housing, the separate apartment, meant that new residents had the chance to pursue an enclosed family life, and to have exclusive family access to a kitchen and bathroom. A private way of life that revolved around kitchen table conversations unrestrained by thoughts of surveillance—though a cliché—was certainly more real in the new housing than in the old. Yet families might find that their new apartment, though private, was not much bigger than their old room, or it was located a couple of hours on two or three buses from their workplace, or it was plagued by serious construction faults. Sometimes larger families found the new housing space intolerably small. Still, it is doubtful that many of those who complained to the authorities would have swapped their new apartment for their former housing; the typical expression of disappointment was that the acknowledged improvement should have been greater. And the sound of satisfaction in the archives is usually inaudible: the vast majority even in this culture of letters of complaint never complained about their housing conditions, and historians should at least entertain the possibility that people who did not write were generally satisfied.

Data for average housing conditions in 1960 show a decisive improvement in people's standards of living, which was by Khrushchev's definition a clear step in the direction of the communist future. Most notable, average housing space in the big cities (see table 3.2) was a significant improvement on wartime and immediate postwar experience, even if it still did not match the sanitary norm. In comparison with the recent past, the average dwelling was not overcrowded. But by 1960 the typical Muscovite or Leningrader was still some way from a new apartment. The high average of residents per household there suggests the persistence on a large scale of communal living arrangements; the task confronting the housing program remained formidable in 1960.[129] Basic facilities, meanwhile, were still hit-and-miss; few Tashkent dwellings had running water, for example, and hot water was scarce in homes in Minsk.

TABLE 3.2. AVERAGE HOUSING CONDITIONS
IN SIX SOVIET CITIES, 1960

	Average housing space (m²)	Average number of people per apartment	Average number of people per room
Moscow	6.1	8.0	2.5
Leningrad	6.6	8.1	2.5
Minsk	5.4	5.8	2.5
Tashkent	6.0	4.2	2.3
Tbilisi	6.4	6.3	2.6
Riga	8.2	4.3	2.0

Note: These data include all tenures.

Source: RGAE f. 1562, op. 14, d. 3002, ll. 24–25.

TABLE 3.3. PROVISION OF AMENITIES IN APARTMENTS
IN SEVEN SOVIET CITIES, 1960 (PERCENTAGES)

	Running water	Sanitation	Central heating	Hot water	Gas	Bath / shower
Moscow	91.22	89.70	79.50	24.21	96.80	54.70
Minsk	55.15	51.57	50.23	15.72	13.53	38.03
Tashkent	14.42	9.99	8.30	0.83	5.67	7.60
Tbilisi	57.48	58.37	15.62	1.77	5.35	15.10
Riga	88.53	84.18	28.15	4.64	34.58	44.30
Vladimir	68.57	61.06	50.66	7.12	37.25	34.48
Pskov	58.47	56.33	29.13	0.37	13.70	24.15

Note: These data are for soviet and departmental tenures only.

Source: Calculations based on data in RGAE f. 1562, op. 14, d. 3002, ll. 26, 132, 139.

For all their mixed story of disappointments and achievements, the aggregate of these statistics shows that standards of living had risen to the highest level yet for Soviet citizens. The standards might be compared with the situation in France—where, in 1954, 76 percent of urban households had no hot water; in 1958, 30 percent of four-member families lived in one- or two-room dwellings, 90 percent of homes in Paris had no shower or bath, and 73 percent no WC.[130] At the same time, the Soviet figures mask the variation that constituted people's experiences and the ongoing existence of considerable poverty. In Moscow, by 1963, the city soviet calculated that 1,100,000 of the city's population enjoyed satisfactory housing conditions, assessed both in terms of square meters and quality, while the standard for 2,300,000 was unsatisfactory. Of these, 835,000 lived in houses in need of heavy repair (*vetkhie doma*) or in barracks; 176,000 lived in basements, or sub-basements; 23,000 lived in accommodation not designed as housing; 450,000 had less than three square meters; and a further 800,000 had between three and five square meters.[131] Yet the top one-third were now living better than the top one-third had ever lived before; and given the extent of construction and the possibility of accountable distribution based on the principle of need, the bottom two-thirds had the reasonable expectation that they would also, soon enough, enjoy better conditions.

In the meantime, examples of particularly terrible deprivation persisted. The direc- tor of the Ordzhonikidze Machine Construction Plant in Podol'sk in Moscow oblast' complained in September 1960 that his housing stock was occupied on the basis of 1.39 square meters per family member. Among the least lucky, forty-five families lived two families to a room, and thirty-eight families subsisted in basements, boiler rooms, huts, and worse.[132] Within the boundaries of Khabarovsk sovnarkhoz in 1961, 2,940 families lived with less than three square meters space per family member.[133] Conditions were especially poor in those areas that the government was seeking to open up for economic development. Here, industrialization took place according to renewed Stalinist dynamics of sacrifice. Nursultan Nazarbaev, who worked in Termitau in the early 1960s and was later first secretary of the Kazakh republic, and its president after independence, made the connection explicitly in his memoirs:

> Our own living conditions were particularly intolerable: after a short time in damp and dirty basement accommodation, we were moved to an unheated dormitory where we kept warm by sleeping in twos on iron cots covered with mattresses. There was no place even to hang out our clothes to dry. We left our canvas work-clothes out in the frost because it was easier to put them on when they were frozen than when they were wet and heavy. There were no recreational facilities—the only entertainment that people had was big fights. Murders and other serious crimes were rife. We survived because we were young and strong, yet there is no justifying the hardships that we all suffered. Such a justification might have existed in the 1930s, when the Soviet Union knew that its very survival depended on industrialization, but this was now the late 1950s and 1960s, and still the Soviet system remained indifferent to the people in whose name it was supposedly ruling.[134]

Like Novocherkassk, Termitau had an especially acute housing shortage and was the site of a violently suppressed protest. It is hardly surprising that instances of particularly poor conditions prompted disturbances against local elites.[135]

Even the tens of millions across the Union who were more fortunate—those who obtained a new apartment—did not always experience their anticipated rise in standard of living, though in objective terms the improvement for new residents was, on average, considerable. The greatest problem was the small dimensions of the new apartments. The race for square meters was constrained by the commitment that the resulting apartments should be for single-family occupancy. As a result, apartments were small. Daily indignities—or more serious suffering when overcrowding was especially acute—resulted. One of the characteristic strategies for maximizing the efficient use of space was to build apartments of walk-through (*prokhodnye*) rooms. In a typical example, doors to the bathroom and the first room led out of the hallway (*koridor*); doors to the kitchen and a second room led out of the first room. Such an arrangement could be intolerable if even three related adults shared the space. One A. F. Timofeeva had lived for a year with her husband and two daughters, who were sixteen and twenty-two, in an apartment of two interconnected rooms. When her elder daughter got married, the son-in-law moved in. "There was a question," wrote Timofeeva, "who should live in the walk-through room? The young ones, who saw it as their right, asked for the separate room. . . . We were so glad to have new housing. But I honestly say to you that I am not happy. I want peace and quiet in my old age."[136] Her younger daughter was also approaching marriageable age: a hellish prospect. Timofeeva suggested that families with daughters who were older than fifteen be granted additional housing space.

Overcrowding thus damaged family relationships and individuals' well-being, while apartment design could compromise health and hygiene.[137] Another consequence of apartments that were too small was the accretion of petty inconveniences, which played on nerves and eroded dignity. The citizen S. N. Rezimov commented on the sixty-centimeter width of his corridor at its narrowest point, the impossibility of bringing furniture into the apartment through the front door, the narrow one-meter doors, and the store cupboard that encroached into the room; he also commented that two people could not pass each other on the apartment block staircase, and that occupiers of corner one-room apartments, which had two windows, had great trouble arranging their furniture.[138] Rezimov referred to the space-saving practice of locating the WC and the bath in a single bathroom. This was a source of intense unpopularity among residents who frequently shared the living space with a number of family members. When space-saving measures meant that a coffin could not be carried out of the apartment but had to be lowered from a window, wounded dignity viciously exacerbated frustration.[139] Another despised trait was low ceilings. One E. Lanuberg wrote from Baku that low ceilings of 2.5 meters were inconsistent with the demands of hygiene, that they recalled conditions for low-paid groups in bourgeois states such as Britain and Sweden.[140]

Other sources of complaint related to the quality of construction. N. Vorob'ev, a metalworker, compiled a list of his apartment's various flaws, which included doors and windows that would not close properly, and the lack of sound insulation, so that he could hear his neighbors talking in the next apartment.[141] I. Z. Fedorov complained that he and fellow residents had moved into their new apartment block while it still lacked a roof, that running water was practically unavailable on the fourth and fifth floors in summer, and that the surrounding concentration of apartment houses was so great that peace and quiet were unattainable. Citizens were aware of the obsession with economy and sometimes deplored it, interpreting problems of quality in its light. Fedorov summarized his plight simply: "I understand that everything is for the sake of economy."[142] One of the most hated consequences of strict attention to spending was the absence of elevators in five-story blocks. As many citizens commented, this condemned the elderly and infirm to extraordinary and pointless hardship (see the case of Mal'tinksii of Minsk described in chapter 5).[143]

These living standards were supposed to be communist, and citizens frequently expressed themselves accordingly, using the language of socialist achievement or disappointed socialist expectation. Thus an engineer called Ivanov castigated the especially small *malometrazhnye* apartments as "shaming our state, our socialist state."[144] In a waspish and witty letter, he compared the "narrow and very low rooms" to "prison cells," an implicit reference to, or at least an unintended evocation of, the retrogression to an apparently expired Stalinist past, not the advance to the socialist-communist-Khrushchevian future. One anonymous correspondent from Gatchina in Leningrad oblast' wrote in a more ingenuous tone, but within essentially the same frame of reference: "People of communist society will indisputably live in the [apartment] houses and apartments that are being built today. . . . [But] Our planners resolve only one construction question—the question of today—how to supply apartments quickly to those that do not have them, forgetting other tasks." The devil was in the details: in some apartments, "the height from floor to ceiling is two meters forty centimeters."[145] I. A. Dobzhinskii expressed a familiar complaint about the WC/bathroom in communist terms, which would sound inflated and easy to mock were it not for the substantial effect that this particular problem had on people's lives. He wrote: "It is completely impossible in essence to justify . . . the arrangement of the WC next to the bath without a partition in new apartments, [both] for Soviet citizens and for the future high communist society."[146] A second common frame of reference by which even true-believing citizens assessed their new housing was not socialism-communism but humanity, the appeal to humane treatment. This might or might not be expressed in the idiom of socialism (it certainly lies inside the tradition of Russian socialism). M. D. Kondrat'ev of Moscow wrote, "Of course it's necessary to build cheaply, but also not to forget about the living person who will live in the completed housing space. Listen to his voice."[147] The call to common humanity—to be treated "like a human being"—was a powerful trope.[148]

Such voices frequently expressed frustration about shortages of furniture that resulted from the structural inefficiencies of the planned economy. One wrote in 1960, "It's well-known that in the new apartments, which millions of our families are moving into, there is nowhere to keep your perishable foods even in winter, not to speak of summer." She called for tenants to make extra payments so that they could have fridges, and for sufficient availability of cupboards with sealable doors.[149] Kucherenko wrote to Kosygin at Gosplan in April 1960, arguing that "an extremely difficult situation" existed with regard to furniture provision, and called for detailed planning to assess demand for the next five years.[150] Symptomatically, Glavmosstroi was obliged to speed up the construction of a new furniture factory in 1961.[151] In 1962 central government officials discussed the need for properly centralized direction of furniture production.[152] But a serious problem continued, the result of too many resources being focused on output of square meters of housing, so that apartments were completed but were difficult to furnish. Dissatisfaction was widely felt.[153] These complaints reflected real problems, some of which drove people beyond frustration to fury, or knocked them back to bitter impotence. The complaints represent a compelling cross section of the archival trace of lived experience, though their actual social representativeness is much less clear, allowing the drawing of only tentative conclusions.

Yet the substance of people's complaints was no longer a matter of life and death. Poor sound insulation, though certainly not trivial, was a different order of problem than surviving in a shelter hacked out of the ground. Much scholarship underestimates this epochal shift.[154] Material plenty, even should it be attainable, was only one thing, however. Khrushchev himself recognized that capitalism was good at creating that. For him, the success of consumerism in the West rested on the unequal division of its fruits, a process that in turn flowed from class-based repression. Proto-communism, by contrast, required equality. Historians have been skeptical about the results. Donald Filtzer explains inequality and ineffectiveness in terms of the repressive capacity of policy; turning Khrushchev's explanation for inequality in the West inside out, he explains inequality in the Soviet Union with reference to a neo-Stalinist elite repressing the working classes by keeping hold of an unfair proportion of the "surplus."[155] Others, while eschewing the Marxist paradigm, emphasize the privileges of local elites and the relative poverty of most of the population during the Khrushchev era.[156]

The Stalin-era background supports their arguments. At least until 1952, equality was not even part of the rhetoric of Stalinism. A Soviet propaganda publication written for a British audience and published in London in 1946 declared that "All citizens of the Soviet Union have an equal right to a life of well-being. This does not mean, of course, that the standard of living of all is the same, that wealth is divided among them equally. Living standards largely depend upon the amount and skill of labor performed, the size of the family, and so on."[157] Under Khrushchev, the increased level of security that party and government officials enjoyed throughout the union allowed them to consolidate a level of privilege. This was deliberate policy, derived from the perceived need to shore up the whole structure of rule and to strengthen Khrushchev's own networks of support. The anger of the crowd in Novocherkassk in 1962 was only the most famous popular rejoinder.[158] By the 1980s the specific nature of *nomenklatura* privileges contributed to the collapse of the system, and especially to the form that the collapse eventually took.[159]

By reading too much back from the 1980s and too much forward from the 1930s, the picture of the late 1950s and early 1960s loses focus. The weaker historiography for the post-Stalin period, as well as the challenge of teleology, artificially load the prescription of the lenses. However, evidence suggests that much more remarkable than the consolidation of elite privilege was the housing program's delivery of relative equality during the high Khrushchev era.[160]

A week before the Central Committee and Council of Ministers approved the major housing decree of 31 July 1957, the head of the Central Statistical Administration (USSR), V. Starovskii, signed off on a long and influential report on housing conditions. Based on data collected during the first quarter of 1957, the report surveyed 64,100 people from the families of workers, engineering-technical staff, white-collar industrial employees, teachers, doctors, and other medical personnel.[161] It revealed a historically exceptional level of equality during the early stages

TABLE 3.4. HOUSING CONDITIONS OF FAMILIES OF
DIFFERENT PROFESSIONAL STATUS, 1957 (1)

Professional status of family	Average space per family member (m²)	Percentage within status group living in		
		separate apartment or house	1 room in communal housing	basement or attic
industrial worker	4.8	28	47	2.1
engineering-technical	5.9	40	42	1.1
other white-collar industrial	5.8	30	49	1.7
teacher	6.5	34	47	1.6
doctor	8.0	34	41	1.2
mid-level medical personnel	6.1	32	50	1.7

Note: "Average space" excludes data for people living alone.

Source: RGANI f. 5, op. 30, d. 222, ll. 168, 170.

TABLE 3.5. HOUSING CONDITIONS OF FAMILIES OF
DIFFERENT PROFESSIONAL STATUS, 1957 (2)

Standard of living indicator	Percentage within status group enjoying indicator					
	industrial worker	engineering technical	other white collar	teacher	doctor	mid-level medical
running water	44	60	48	52	72	45
sanitation	40	54	45	44	66	40
central heating*	35	47	38	34	45	25
bath or shower	15	30	16	21	42	13
gas	16	20	16	24	33	23
electric light	99	99	99	100	99	99
direct radio feed	51	46	58	58	65	56
independent radio aerial	44	61	42	42	48	39
television	6	12	7	7	13	10
telephone	1	12	5	10	24	5

or equivalent

Source: RGANI f. 5, op. 30, d. 222, ll. 172, 176.

of the program's launch. The families of higher-status employees enjoyed higher standards of living—but only by small margins. On the eve of the housing decree of 1957, the gap in housing conditions between a factory worker, a clerk, and a doctor was significantly lower than in any Western polity.

If these data are representative, then they imply that the vast majority of the population—corresponding to the highly stratified working and middle classes of Britain of that time, whose dwellings ranged from council houses to big suburban villas—enjoyed relatively equal access to housing. True, the tables exclude the core privileged groups: senior officials in city soviets, sovnarkhozy, ministries, and the local party apparatus; the bosses of enterprises and institutions; senior military officers; some artists, academicians, and writers; as well as the top layer of the governing machine. Yet this was a very small group—an upper, not a middle, "class." Members of this group had disproportionate access to a comfortable life, even a good life. The enjoyment of large state dachas was just one example. In July 1960 the Astrakhan' sovnarkhoz successfully applied for permission to build twenty-two new dachas during the forthcoming year for some of their "senior employees [*otvetstvennye rabotniki*]."[162]

Through privileged access to information, not to mention personal contacts, such elites were better able to access goods that were only formally available to all. The new housing cooperatives of this period tended to be made up of employees of elite institutions. Professional and administrative elites, which had been granted the best housing under Stalin, did not lose it under Khrushchev—and through a form of inheritance a level of housing privilege flowed down to the next generation. Such people made robust attempts to maintain all aspects of their standards of living. In late 1958, when the president of the Academy of Medical Sciences was unhappy about the car parking arrangements at his "tall building" in Moscow, he did not contact the local housing administration but wrote instead to E. A. Furtseva, a senior figure in the Central Committee.[163] Yet the "housing gap" between such groups and the mass of the population was certainly smaller than it had been under Stalin, because the standards of living of ordinary people were generally better, elites were no longer favored to the same degree (and in some contexts their privileges were even attacked), and new structures of accountability made the system of distribution fairer. Khrushchev's desire to hold in check elite privileges was manifested in a range of measures. Proposed changes to education seemed transiently to threaten the advantages of the children of better-off groups,[164] while the nomenklatura recoiled in horror from Khrushchev's plans to devolve some economic and administrative functions (and thus senior appointments) to the regions. His rule was least effective when he lost sight of the different interests upon which he ultimately relied, and which would in time combine to force his ouster. Such ambiguities were visible in reforms to the system of housing distribution.

Many citizens considered that the acid test of communism in the housing economy was fair and equal distribution, thanks not least to their bitter experience of greedy local leaders and to the pressures of public culture.[165] The distribution system was bedeviled by failures, and demands for reform resulted from practical necessity as well as from the general context of the push to paradise.[166] In Rostov-on-Don in 1962, for example, the distribution system was spectacularly ineffective.[167] The want of "slack" in capacity meant that the presence of 2,200 families of military officers, who had been discharged or put on the reserve following Khrushchev's reductions in armed forces personnel, threw distribution mechanisms off balance. Such families' housing conditions were specifically protected by law, but the Rostov authorities conspicuously failed to fulfill the duty. Another typical problem arose when apartments were mistakenly released for the use of families who already owned an individual house, or who did not really need substantial improvement in their conditions. Comrade Serefimovich, the head doctor at polyclinic number 4 in the city's Proletarskii raion, was allocated an apartment of fifty-two square meters for his family of four by the district soviet housing administration, giving each family member more than double the local norm of 6.4 square meters; previously, they had lived in a more-than-adequate apartment of forty-three square meters.

The housing authorities in Rostov also failed to meet their obligations to those who had been rehabilitated of Stalin-era political crimes.[168] In 1961, there were 249 victims of repression queuing for housing in Rostov; only 42 obtained it, frequently from the city's "old housing fund." One such, A. M. Usova, worked at a pharmacy and lived in private accommodation; her income was fifty rubles a month, and her rent more than twenty. Before the catastrophe had fallen on her family, they had lived in a separate apartment, also in Rostov; now they languished in the queue. So-called isolated apartments, which were usually required by those suffering from contagious diseases (often tuberculosis), were also wrongly distributed. Decrees of September 1960 required that housing administrations use their powers to help with the struggle against such diseases. In 1962, 265 people were waiting for an "isolated" apartment, although there were 374 TB sufferers in the city. In a particularly extreme example of suffering that the housing authorities allowed to exist, A. Z. Polianov, a TB sufferer who had been invalided out of his work as a metalworker at the Krasnyi Aksai factory, lived in an apartment of twenty square meters with his family of eight persons, including three children younger than fourteen.

Corruption in housing distribution was widespread. In 1959 the chairman of Moscow's Tushino district soviet, N. T. Madzhugin, was accused of illegally obtaining for himself a large three-room apartment on Leningradskii prospekt during the previous February. Such corruption seemed egregious; preparations for his arraignment before a court were in hand.[169] During the early stages of 1963 the head of the Pskov housing administration, Comrade Drozdov, was responsible for the distribution of 249 apartments out of a total of 355 without formal approval by the city soviet; of the remaining 106, a further 12 were distributed without the proper documentation. Drozdov faced the legal consequences.[170] Yet these consequences also pointed to the possibility of rooting out corruption and making distribution fairer.

Reforming this creaking system was difficult. It required a series of sturdy and transparent bureaucratic mechanisms, among which the concept of the single city queue was of emerging appeal. Each city had several housing queues, and each queue was separately administered: by the housing offices of every district (raion) soviet and by every enterprise and organization that had a housing portfolio. A typical example of the failings that reform should remedy was recorded in Rostov in 1961, when one O. N. Abramova obtained a separate apartment for her family of four via the Leninskii raion soviet queue; ten days later, her husband obtained a similar allocation of departmental housing space.[171]

The ideal solution was to have single queues in every city. This single-queue system was a major breakthrough, simultaneously "rational" and fair: it was a true marker on the path to the communist future. Leningrad was one of the first cities to introduce the system, in 1961.[172] The 69,413 families who were in the queues of the city's district soviets were joined by 178,192 families waiting on the numerous queues of enterprises and other departmental institutions, to form a single queue. An official in the All-Union Central Union of Trade Unions (VTsSPS), V. Tel'nov, elucidated the advantages, which came down to "strict verification [*chetkii kontrol'*]," efficiency, and flexibility, all of which should allow the queue to move more quickly and fairly. Having a central queue in a city such as Leningrad allowed more efficient matching of family size with apartment size. Tel'nov showed that housing construction had a stubborn default setting of the two-room apartment, even though families of four, who would be expected to settle such apartments, made up only 22 percent of the queue. One-room apartments, though only 20 percent of new stock, were the most likely destination for the 43 percent of queuing families that consisted of two or three persons. But the single queue should make it easier to reconcile such disparities. Families would be more quickly housed; fewer vacant apartments, administered by separate enterprises, would await suitable families. The system should also clarify demand, allowing officials to recalibrate the plan. In December 1961 the Moscow City Soviet resolved to construct more apartment houses for small families of two persons, and for single people; it approved a further resolution the following June on the same subject.[173] Citizens, in turn, should have greater confidence that they would obtain their new housing quickly and fairly. Single-queue systems, however, only existed in some places. Elsewhere, trade unions retained their role; in Moscow, for example, the union for employees of electrical industries continued to argue vigorously over detailed cases of housing distribution in the early 1960s.[174] Patronage networks associated with this model of distribution would not disappear during the Brezhnev and Gorbachev periods. In the 1960s, moreover, technical and administrative inadequacies persisted. A step had been taken toward the communist future—but not everywhere.

This step was matched by a new system of appeal, making the distribution and construction authorities more accountable to new residents, and making more than a token shift toward the obtaining of housing on the basis of rights rather than gratitude. Decrees of 1957 and 1958 insisted that soviets quickly resolved citizens' letters of complaint.[175] This was essential for the regularization of the distribution system. Of the letters that citizens sent to the Rostov city soviet in 1961, 45 percent concerned housing; over 50 percent of these had to be sent to higher authorities because they were complaints about the way the district soviets were managing distribution.[176]

Despite greater regularity and accountability, considerable imperfections persisted in the distribution system. The theory of central planning had come to acknowledge different types of family unit, and architectural practice had acted on it to create a slightly more diverse range of apartment designs, but planning's chronic lack of subtlety remained. Less usual family arrangements were badly served by the reductive logic of the sanitary norm. The single-queue system retained inflexible characteristics. Single people were typical victims. Even when the queue diverted from its mechanistic tendency to focus its resources on family groups of four and above, its administrators self-consciously insisted that this was the result of an exception. One female worker, who was born in 1917 and had worked in Leningrad's Egorov carriage-repair factory for twenty-seven years, had consistently been refused access to better housing. She subsisted in a hostel. In March 1962 she was at last allowed to enter Leningrad's central city queue, albeit as an "exception." She wrote, "It's terrible even to think that such an inhumane law exists. How cruel to punish an honest worker."[177] Given the demographic catastrophes that had unfolded since before this woman's birth, her generation contained huge numbers of women who in gentler times would have expected to be married. The system's inability to provide for them adequately and coherently during this period was a primary, not secondary, failure of the means for delivering the communist future.

Such noisy cases of scandal or failure rather than quieter ones of satisfaction or achievement emerge from the workings of the historical record. The system of distribution was always infested with informal practices, but it was still the subject of a partially successful reform that created more equal access than hitherto to an adequate standard of living. It was a historically exceptional experiment. Officials in Khrushchev's Soviet Union undertook a serious and not unsuccessful attempt to create equal access to equal housing. This was self-consciously the opposite of what had always happened before, and of what continued to happen in the capitalist West. Indeed, the comparison with the West defined communist living standards. These were often identified as communist because they were not Western. For Khrushchev, communism meant nothing if it did not provide a better life than capitalism. That was the substance of his commitment to overtake the United States. Even under Stalin, the Soviet cityscape had been appropriated as evidence in Cold War competition. But this had been a matter of prestige projects, not the mass improvement of living standards.

At the end of the 1950s and early 1960s, the Cold War comparisons were made more systematically and less aggressively (excepting Khrushchev's colorful rhetoric). In a candidate's dissertation of 1959, A. A. Tomsen compared housing construction under the two systems; according to his science, Soviet socialism was better. "Under socialism," he wrote, "the housing question is not only posed in a new way as a matter of principle, but for the first time in history, the social preconditions for its resolution have been created." In other words, a renewed ideological imperative latched onto the preexisting absence of capitalist restraints on the use of land and the exercise of property to make possible "the conditions for the radical improvement of the housing conditions of workers in line with the general tasks of the construction of communism."[178] B. E. Svetlichnyi, the head of urban development at the State Science-Economic Council of the Council of Ministers (USSR), commented in an interview published in 1962, "It's well known that already the Soviet Union stands in first place in the world in the quantity of apartments constructed per thousand residents, and the general number of apartments that are put up every year in our country are more than are built in the United States, England, France, Belgium, West Germany, Sweden, Switzerland, and Holland taken together."[179] In a book of 1964 entitled *The Housing Question under Capitalism and Socialism*, M. A. Shipilov hammered home his points: "In the resolution of the housing question, the socialist system secures one victory after another." The impressiveness of these victories was made apparent through "comparison with the difficult conditions in which workers and peasants lived in pre-Revolutionary Russia and in which hundreds of millions of workers in capitalist countries live now."[180]

Shipilov dramatically overplayed his argument, yet behind his rhetoric lay a valuable point. Although the urban housing program had many inherent flaws, it enhanced people's lives considerably; both the good and the bad were entirely wrapped up in the ideological system of which the housing program was a part.

One of Vasilii Aksenov's "youth" novels, *The Colleagues* (1959), follows the lives of three young medical graduates of varying levels of idealism as they embark on their careers. Aleksandr, the most ideologically convinced, goes to the Far North, where he meets the chairman of the township's soviet. They discuss their idealism, and the chairman says:

> a few people imagine communism as some kind of Arcadian idyll, and a few mouth the words, not thinking about their significance. . . . Perhaps I imagine it too earthily, but I transfer the dream [of communism] to local reality. Here was the village Kruglogor'e . . . it became the township Kruglogor'e. . . . This will become a city, Kruglogorsk. And our children will unleash atomic energy. This unbroken chain is going out into the future, and I see bright, futuristic houses reflected in warm waters, palm trees shaking, glass cars flying along concrete highways. Kruglogor'e! And what do you think? It's going to happen.[181]

Such wild optimism, expressed without irony, was an essential component of the public culture of the Khrushchev era. During moments of great collective joy or satisfaction such as Iurii Gagarin's return from space, this hopeful enthusiasm was perhaps broadly evident among the population. In more sober moments, people needed to anchor future possibility in present realities. Even Aksenov's soviet chairman expressed a sense of the present and the palpable on which he could base his notion of paradise. In the housing economy more generally, the motif of paradise was bolted into the practical organization of the new building block of urban life, the microdistrict. Proto-communism in the microdistrict made no sense as a purely idealistic or abstract force. By tying it to the fulfillment of practical tasks that raised standards of living, it became, briefly, a vehicle for paradise. Together with the unprecedented level of mass construction and the institutionalization of certain rights, it provides the evidence for housing's contribution to the communist future.

Yet the rises in standard of living brought about by new housing construction were uneven, and the proto-communist structure of life in the microdistrict was very imperfect and in some places derisory. The plans that derived from the great promise of 1957 were so flawed that eradicating the housing shortage ultimately became progressively harder. Rights, though robust in the housing economy, were rendered ultimately vulnerable by their absence in some other parts of Soviet life. Huge amounts of housing were built and millions of lives were improved, however. Such was the program's epochal character, through its transformative impact and capacity to deliver relative equality, that it amounted to one of the great social reforms in postwar Europe.

No one thought this was communism, though, and as a model of proto-communism it was obviously malformed. Soviet society was marooned outside communism, which stubbornly remained somewhere out of view. Iakovlev wrote that Khrushchev was lost, that the further and faster he marched toward the communist future, the less sure he became of where he was and of how to recover his path. Historians have a better view. For them, the coordinates of the urban housing economy might not be so elusive. They might be conceptualized in a new way, as a historically unique crossing point of property relations and welfare. That nexus is the subject of part 2.

PART TWO

The Nexus of Property and Welfare

Possibilities and Paradoxes of Ownership

> Though the earth and all inferior creatures be common to all
> men, yet every man has a property in his own person; this
> nobody has any right to but himself. The labour of his body and
> the work of his hands we may say are properly his. Whatsoever,
> then, he removes out of the state that nature hath provided
> and left it in, he hath mixed his labour with, and joined to it
> something that is his own, and thereby makes it his property.
>
> —John Locke, *Second Treatise of Government*

> The distinguishing feature of Communism is not the abolition
> of property generally, but the abolition of bourgeois property.
>
> —Karl Marx and Frederick Engels, *The Communist Manifesto*

Individuals won the war, and individuals would build the communist future. In his Kremlin toast of June 1945 to participants in the victory parade, Stalin very famously raised his glass "To the people who are counted as the cogs [*vintiki*] of the great state machine, but without whom all of us marshals and commanders of fleets and armies, to put it crudely, couldn't stand up."[1] Sixteen years later, in his speech introducing the new party program at the twenty-second party congress, Khrushchev proclaimed, "All Soviet people must work so well as to be able to say, when the bright edifice of communism is built: I have done my bit for it as well."[2] Although the motives behind the speeches were different (the first was Stalin's cynical salute to ordinary citizens, the second showed Khrushchev's wide-eyed desire for a better life for everyone), they shared the sense that citizens, working together in their tens of millions, composed the destiny of the Soviet Union.

Stalin and Khrushchev recognized that citizens had the capacity, duty, and right to contribute to victory in the war and to the collective shaping of the communist future. What the leaders did not acknowledge was that citizens could make viable differences to their own separate and individual destinies. And yet, urban housing policy throughout this period was deliberately designed in such a way as to incorporate a high level of citizen autonomy: both law and its local interpretations specifically allowed individuals to improve their own conditions. The principle of ownership was written into the process.

Officially sanctioned individual initiative was more various and substantial during late Stalinism than under Khrushchev. This was most especially so during the peak of the postwar emergency, when state organs could retrospectively legitimate the illegal activities that citizens had undertaken to ameliorate or rectify their personal housing catastrophes. Some scholars have placed workers' autonomous efforts to improve their general living conditions in effective opposition to the prescriptions of the authorities. The tactics that people adopted in order to acquire basic goods thus became gestures of resistance, which the "regime" was effectively obliged to tolerate. In the case of housing, however, individuals' autonomous contributions were not really acts of resistance but, instead, represented positive interactions with policy and with the practices of officials. It is not entirely helpful, therefore, to place an entity such as the "state," and another that might be the "people," in conceptual opposition. Such entities as "state," "economy," "society," or "citizen" are not discrete and will always overlap. The state-society binary is a commonplace, however, and of all historiographical territories, Russia's has been particularly subject to a reductive analysis via sets of crude binaries. One of the most prominent of these is the common distinction between "official" and "second" economies. Yet in the urban housing economy, the "official" economy formally accepted elements of the "second" in order to function, while aspects generally considered "second" were actually "official."[3] Political scientists and historians have isolated general instances of the "symbiosis" between these categories, in such contexts as the trade of the 1930s and the consumption of the Brezhnev era.[4] Their insights deserve a wider application.

In the urban housing economy, citizen autonomy and state planning did not just operate in symbiosis as useful parasite and host, they were to some extent made of the same stuff. Planners continued to calculate construction targets that factored in the results of citizens' autonomous responses. Individual construction outlasted late Stalinism, while a mix of individual construction and participation in cooperatives persisted beyond the end of the Khrushchev era. These various types of permitted autonomy created a specific form of property relations, which contained a substantial element of individual ownership.[5] In turn, these forms of individual ownership were expressive not just of property rights but of welfare rights. This nexus between property and welfare became increasingly secure as the 1950s and 1960s progressed and was the defining conceptual feature—the unique watermark—of Soviet urban housing from the closing stages of the Great Fatherland War through to the end of the Khrushchev era.

Most scholars have long misunderstood or ignored the problem of property relations in the Soviet Union.[6] By tending to take at face value the most general statements made by leading Bolsheviks about the abolition of private property, scholars have usually not taken into account the more difficult, meandering reality of specific legal texts, or the surviving evidence of how ordinary people really related to their housing. All European postwar urban housing programs magnified the role of the state, changed balances of ownership, and invented tenures. The Soviet Union's urban housing program was no exception; it was also characterized by complexities of ownership, for the system was so constituted never to be able to achieve—or never really to desire—anything approaching monolithic state ownership. Individual ownership of urban housing had always existed in the Soviet Union, however. Soviet citizens exercised a type of individual ownership—not only over housing they formally owned according to the unique tenure of personal property but also over housing they rented from agencies of the state. In both cases, these forms of ownership fit within the European history of property and were never invalidated by some general failure of Russian culture to comprehend the dynamics of individual ownership. The Great Fatherland War and then the ending of full Stalinism enlarged the possibility of individual ownership and founded it on a mutually enhancing relationship between property rights and welfare provision. Yet this seems provocative. What could individual ownership possibly mean in a country that apparently had a weak tradition of property rights, and where private property had certainly been abolished between 1917 and 1922?

Property lacks fixed definitions and is always contentious, in theory and in practice. All items are owned by somebody, but as property laws distinguish between the movable and the immovable (and take for their subject the latter), land and housing become the focus of any definition. An item of property might be owned by a legal personality because (i) its physical boundaries are definable; (ii) within these, it is his and not somebody else's; but (iii) while he alone has rights over it, which society might or might not consider to have an explicitly moral character, these rights are subject to limitations and duties, defined by contract, tradition, or legislation.[7] According to such a working definition, the legal personality that holds the property can be anyone—individual citizen, company, trade union, city government, federal state, the Crown. It is the *citizen's* possibilities of ownership, in an economy apparently dominated by state-held property, that particularly illuminate the Soviet urban housing program. While private property did indeed cease to exist in the cities of Russia and the Soviet Union between 1917 and 1922, individual ownership of housing space did not.

Historians have paid little detailed attention to the ownership of Soviet urban property and have usually been satisfied that the revolution demolished the status of the individual as an owner. Richard Pipes has argued this point with most vigor, explicitness, and consistency over several decades, firmly rooting it in the historical long term. He makes the case that an apparently weak conception of individual property was intimately related to the sad course of Russian history, and notably its lack of freedom. The core of Pipes's argument is that the Muscovite and post-Muscovite polities—until at least 1785—were "patrimonial" in form. The tsar to all intents and purposes owned his subjects, and they in turn had no right to private property in the sense that such property was demonstrably theirs and not his, in theory and practice, as "freeborn" Englishmen by contrast had been able to claim continuously since the thirteenth century.[8] During the nineteenth century, and especially in the decade that preceded 1917, a sense of private property developed, Pipes maintains, as patrimonialism gave way to a system of more regularized property norms, under the influence of tsarist concessions, bureaucratic normalization, advancing industry and business, and legal modernization.[9] For Pipes, however, this was private property on shaky foundations, hardly to be compared with the example he places at the other end of the scale, England.[10] Then came the deluge.

Other scholars have unpicked the Pipes schema. Geoffrey Hosking argues that a system of patron-client relations of balance and nuance existed throughout Russian history, which made property rights more complex and real than Pipes allows for: they existed but were "diffuse."[11] Edward Keenan posits that "clans" in the late Muscovite period displayed a sense of ownership, and that the forms of absolutism they observed in their relationship to the tsar were primarily symbolic rather than practically operable; their purpose was to sustain the stability of their own property. In the village, he argues, mutual responsibility and the separate autonomy of individual households were interwoven, but both existed; at village meetings, the elders (bol'shaki) had great status but still conformed to the village consensus, the combined product of the individual households.[12] In his analysis of the principal sources of Kievan and Muscovite law, including the early medieval Russkaia pravda, the Pskov and Novgorod charters, and the codes of 1550 (sudebnik) and 1649 (ulozhenie), George Weickhardt concludes that "Russia gradually developed a concept of private property for land which more or less approached that of the English 'fee simple' and that the only significant limitations on individual private property in Russia were in favor of clans rather than the state."[13] For Pipes, medieval Russia lacked a concept of "property" beyond "patrimony" (votchina), but Weickhardt isolates reference to "property" (imenie) in Russkaia pravda.[14]

Inheritance laws and their social application provide further evidence of an imperfect but existing tradition of individual property. Richard Hellie summarized this heritage of "relatively elaborate" (though very far from robust) inheritance procedures from the eleventh to the seventeenth centuries.[15] Nancy Shields Kollmann shows that, by the seventeenth century, forms of tenure and inheritance "converged in law and practice," making them stronger.[16] Other scholars have emphasized that the property rights of Russian noblewomen were especially robust in comparative European terms following the reforms of Peter the Great, and that greater (though qualified) regularity in the legal conception of property, from the perspective of civil law relating to the family, followed the judicial reform of the 1860s.[17] At the very least, this brief foray into the historiography shows that enough evidence exists to render invalid the broad-brush assertion that weak recognition of individual forms of ownership is part of Russian history's DNA.

Yet property relations changed fundamentally between 1917 and 1922, in a transformative sweep that set the Soviet Union's course, and that heady transformation has formed subsequent perceptions of the whole Soviet period. It has provided the conceptual start and end point of most general historical study that has mentioned urban property, though decades of legal scholarship and more recent historiography have added subtlety to the picture.[18] The Soviet urban housing economy was marked by complexity, and four tenures governed the ownership of urban housing for most of Soviet history: the "socialist property" of soviets, "departments" (vedomstva), and cooperatives, and the "personal property" (lichnaia sobstvennost') of individual citizens.[19] During the revolutionary period and the 1920s, the "municipalization" of much housing and the policy of *uplotnenie* (the redistribution and the "packing in" of new residents) produced the formal ownership of housing by local soviets. As Stalinist urbanization and industrialization proceeded, more workers lived in housing owned by such departments as industrial enterprises. Cooperatives were usually a spin-off from departmental housing—in which the state owner ceded some of the formal rights of ownership to the occupier in return for the occupier paying off a "mortgage" at a predictable interest rate of under 1 percent over a period of up to fifteen years.[20]

The ownership rights of a cooperative shareholder and of a holder of "personal property" were quite distinct. Personal property was not private property. It retained some of the characteristics of private property, though even these had been sifted, filtered, and modified by Soviet law. Various pieces of legislation that were introduced between 1917 and 1922 and consolidated by article 10 of the 1936 constitution allowed citizens to own their house as personal property if it was small enough to be a one-family home and if they undertook its maintenance.[21] As owners, they had multiple rights of transfer: by sale, gift, rental, or legacy. These rights were exercised as socialist transactions, which could not produce financial profit or accumulate unearned resources.[22] The tenure of personal property and the practices that surrounded it derived from a practical revolutionary compromise. Agencies of the revolutionary state lacked the resources and expertise to manage the whole of the housing fund and had to leave much of it as citizens' personal property. The theoretical justification for this ambiguous tenure rested on compromise; in arguing that it was both practically operable and morally socialist, legal scholars of the 1960s continued to deploy the justifications of the legislators of 1921.[23] They still insisted, above all, that personal property was explicitly not private property, because it ultimately derived from labor not profit and was only for personal use (like a toothbrush and, later, a television). On both these counts, a citizen who owned a dwelling as personal property could not use it to exploit another citizen.[24]

Some scholars even argued that personal property should retain a role during communism. L. S. Pavlov maintained that the essence of communism—"Everything in the name of the person, for the good of the person"—was closely related to "the supply of a high standard of living for members of communist society, of the creation of abundance of wellbeing for everyone and all." Personal property would still be an important component of this material plenty and abundant consumption. Under communism, the moral basis of personal property would shift. Its defining principle would no longer be the direct relationship between the owner and his work but between the owner and every member of society: "Personal property can and must be fully subordinate to the construction of communism, satisfying the reasonable needs of the fully sided development of the builder of communism, correctly connecting personal and social interests." In this new scheme, the nature of individual ownership would transmute and become still less absolute; the external boundaries of items of property would become permeable.[25] Thus at the peak of the Khrushchev era, a scholar construed the moral arguments for ownership during communism on the basis of existing legal categories of property.

Pipes is right when he states that "the abolition of private property was completed" by the end of the 1920s, with the nationalization of "productive assets" and "national income." This was the task the Bolsheviks set about and successfully fulfilled. But he is in error when he states baldly and unambiguously that "urban real estate was nationalized."[26] True, the Bolsheviks abolished private property in housing in both cities and countryside, with serious legal reductions in the status of ownership. Most notably, they removed the owner's legal right to extract profit from housing. This transformed the economic relationship between individuals—and between individuals and their housing. Dwellings now became, in legal terms, items only of consumption, with no revenue-raising implications. Yet individuals could still own urban housing, and they retained limited possibilities for renting parts of it out. The consequences of this underpinned the whole housing economy. About one-third of the urban housing stock was consistently held as personal property until the 1960s.[27] Private property had certainly gone, but individual ownership on a major scale remained, even in formal legal terms.

Furthermore, state tenants and cooperative shareholders also possessed forms of individual ownership, even though they did not control the title deeds. The absoluteness of property is always subject to constraints, which might be imposed by tradition, by the state, or by contract, and the ownership of any item must be divided into constituent and complementary parts. Even in the United States, perhaps the most trenchant historic upholder of private property and where the understanding of property rights is the most sharp and least diffuse, property has never been anything like an absolute entity. The legal scholar A. M. Honoré influentially argued that "ownership has never been absolute. Even in the most individualistic ages of Rome and the United States, it has had a social aspect."[28] Honoré showed that it was divided into "incidents of ownership," including such things as rights of possession, use, and management, as well as the right to control the income and capital it could generate. For any given item, these incidents could be split up in various ways and enjoyed by different parties. In the Soviet Union a form of individual ownership became possible when the occupier of a dwelling enjoyed enough of these "incidents" (or "elements," to use a less technical word), no matter if that occupier was its formal owner in law or not.[29]

Some of the principles that governed these elements of ownership lay squarely inside the framework of European history. Although the Soviet housing experiment overall was sui generis and gave rise to unique forms of individual ownership, aspects of these forms and components of their theoretical foundations fitted inside a non-Marxist European tradition. Soviet justifications of individual ownership bear initial comparison with those of Aristotle and St. Thomas Aquinas. Aristotle has been one of the most enduring proponents of the need for property to be owned by individuals. In *The Politics*, he argued that, "while property should up to a point be held in common, the general principle should be that of private ownership." Common ownership created "mutual recriminations," but "with every man busy with his own, there will be increased effort all round."[30] Aquinas extended the same point: "human affairs are conducted in a more orderly manner if each man is responsible for the care of something which is his own, whereas there would be confusion if everyone were responsible for everything in general."[31]

For all their focus on the individual rather than the collective, Aristotle's "general principle" and Aquinas's view of the best operation of "human affairs" had vital traction in Soviet cities. The urban housing fund was a precious commodity in the Soviet Union, its upkeep always a priority for every municipality and department. Ever since the civil war, officials emphasized that the quality of the housing stock deteriorated if residents were not given incentives to maintain it.[32] In the closing stages of the Great Fatherland War, as well as during its immediate aftermath, authorities appealed to citizens to collaborate with housing administrations in the maintenance of housing, especially during the run-up to winter. Newspapers represented citizen initiative as an idealistic force, benefiting a local community. In August 1945, six houses of the fifteenth house administration (*domoupravlenie*) of Moscow's Krasnogvardeiskii raion were already being repaired and fixed up for winter, and residents themselves were preparing fifteen rooms for returning veterans.[33]

Idealism could only go so far, however, and was at its most effective in the immediate glow of victory. By contrast, during the apparent transition to communism at the start of the 1960s, the Moscow Soviet drew attention to some of the ways in which citizens should have a stake in the whole of their mikroraion. Drawing on the paradoxes of ownership, officials in the Moscow Soviet manipulated ideology, law, and customary understandings of ownership to persuade citizens to look after their own dwellings and the common areas of apartment blocks and microdistricts. "The housing fund is state socialist property [*sobstvennost'*], all-people's property [*dostoianie*]," they wrote, and "citizens are obliged carefully and caringly to relate to their housing and to places of general use."[34] Incentives were sometimes modulated through the honor and material rewards of socialist competition.[35] But idealism, common ownership by citizens, and material inducement were not enough; agencies of the state had to cede enough of the elements of ownership to individuals in order to give them sufficient incentives to keep the housing stock, that precious deficit commodity, well maintained. As a result, however, citizens ultimately obtained greater incentives to maintain their own housing space rather than the common areas.

Ceding need not imply reluctance; one of the reasons that historians have not much noticed this process of transferring ownership rights to individual citizens is that it was organic and not troublesome. It was a natural part of the Soviet moral system in the system's late Stalinist and post-Stalinist incarnations alike. And it drew ultimately on a justification that had been most famously elaborated on the other side of Europe in the seventeenth century: that an individual was entitled to own things because he had earned them through his labor. For Locke, certain goods (including "the earth") were the property of all, and the local economy must support everyone. Within these constraints, a man had the right to own the product of his work.

In the Soviet Union, public culture both insisted that people were working together on a communal cause and also described a direct, unmediated relationship between the allocation of resources and an individual's work. No contradiction existed between the great communal project and the possibility of individual ownership. This was the workers' state, where jurisprudence and practice alike defined labor as the great justification. People were allocated housing as workers, and very often by their workplace; petitioners supported their cases for extra housing, or the return of a previous home, with reference to their work record; and perhaps most explicit of all, the tenure of personal property was explained and justified in almost precisely Lockean terms. Lenin wrote, in the tradition of Proudhon, that private property was theft. But he deemed it acceptable that a citizen owned a house as personal property because that citizen's ownership was the consequence of his income from work. In the socialist economy, work could not by definition exploit the worker, and a worker-citizen's rights of ownership only extended to personal use, so he could not legally accumulate property and use it to exploit others in the capitalist fashion. A. Ia. Koshelev explained, "There is a direct connection between personal property as a form of personal consumption, and personal income that has been earned by workers according to the socialist principle of distribution based on work."[36]

Arguing about the origins of property in explicitly moral terms was in any case easier and superficially more probable in the Soviet Union than in Western countries, given that it was a new polity, whose foundation remained in sharp view. Elsewhere in Europe and the United States, the justification of individual ownership tended to be based on its pragmatic effect: it was the most stable and prosperous way to organize a society and to defend the interests of that society's dominant groups. Such a justification had been prominent during the founding of the modern era in the eighteenth century, though after 1945 it could not but be held in check by the mass demands of welfare. In Western countries, welfare rights tended to reduce property rights because of the implications of taxation, whereas in the Soviet Union they complemented each other. Especially before the advent of mass welfare, though since then too, a case was made that the differential between state and civil society and the existence of numerous interests within civil society were the basis of stability, prosperity, even democracy. Adam Smith explained that "Wherever there is great property there is great inequality. . . . The acquisition of valuable and extensive property, therefore, necessarily requires the establishment of civil government."[37] Engels developed a similar interpretation of the purpose of the state, which flowed into his justification and operational plan for the proletariat's requisition of housing space in the cities of nineteenth-century Europe. For him, the state represented violence and used this violence to protect the property interests of a minority.

Adam Smith's is a case against which it is possible to define the core of the Soviet attitude to individual ownership. Government for him should defend the property rights of unequal and various interests. James Madison argued that a society could only be free and properly governed when the plurality of different groups that constituted it had the right to follow their own interests (and a wise central body would ultimately be able to act as their umpire); property rights derived from this regulation of the conflicts between "different interests and parties."[38] This is the opposite of the Soviet Union's conception of the purpose of individual ownership, which was to enhance the unity of society, not to protect the diversity of multiple and competing interests. Party, government, and social organizations all seamlessly connected with the people, and in the absence of conflicts in civil society an umpire was not required.

Madison's vision was also the near opposite of the schematic organization of Soviet property relations. During the late Stalinist and Khrushchev eras, as well as before and since, no true division between state and society existed. Citizen autonomy was an organic condition, required by the state to make the urban housing economy function, but which agencies of the state could regulate and change at will. State, society, and individual were wrapped together far more closely than could be possible in a polity that was institutionally democratic or that contained private property.

Three related examples show what this partial conflation between state, society, and individual meant in the urban housing economy. First, individual citizens possessed important elements of ownership over socialist property (dwellings that were formally owned by agencies of the state). Second, separately definable legal personalities or corporate interests such as cooperatives or trade unions were really parts of the state. Third, individuals could only obtain housing, and hence elements of ownership, through their direct relationship with agencies of the state (broadly conceived), such as soviets, departments, trade unions, and the Municipal Bank. This was about as far as a functioning system of ownership could get from the overall scheme of property relations as it has generally existed in the United States since its foundation.

Nevertheless, the underlying principles of Soviet property relations bear comparison with those of the European tradition and its descendants. In the light of this tradition, the forms of individual ownership that existed in the Soviet Union were objectively legitimate and comprehensible. Similarly, some of the most important specific practical operations of Soviet property had crucial Western analogues and precedents, including the difference between possession and ownership, state interference in inheritance, and the pattern of tenure.

Roman law demonstrated the practical difference between possession and ownership. Ownership meant holding the formal right to a particular immovable item.
Law in the later Roman Republic and early Roman Empire established the category
of *dominium*, ultimate or absolute ownership. Possession meant the legal or de facto
occupancy of an item of property and was not necessarily identical to ownership. He
who possessed and he who owned could have different identities. But in Roman law,
the frequent absence of title deeds meant that those who possessed a property might
be able to claim that they owned it.[39] Milovan Djilas noted in his polemic about the
Stalin-era nomenklatura: "As defined by Roman law, property constitutes the use,
enjoyment and disposition of material goods. The Communist political bureaucracy
uses, enjoys and disposes of nationalized property."[40] His conceptual point is sure,
but empirical research shows that the division of property rights favored ordinary
citizens as well as—though of course less than—the political elite.

A comparison with England is illuminating. English common law held a category
that was similar to *dominium*: fee simple. In formal terms this was also absolute
ownership. Yet a leading scholar argues that English property law is "remarkable
for the absence of remedies based upon proof of ownership. . . . [O]ur remedies are
usually based upon possession."[41] Such a disputatious space was directly paralleled
in the Soviet urban housing economy, with citizens using their rights of possession
to accrue something not dissimilar from effective ownership. The most important
ultimate owner in Soviet property law was the people, who had owned all the land
since 1917. Yet the sociolegal reality was more various and controversial. Resolving
personal property disputes in urban housing usually meant confirming the owner,
whose identity might be in doubt if the dwelling had been left vacant for some time
or if inheritance was contested. More frequently, however, disputes tested who
(resident or formal owner) had the greater rights over a dwelling: for example, the
evacuated family who had been living there or a veteran who was returning home.
This required, effectively, measuring how the elements of ownership were dispersed
and on whom the greatest number rested. During the Khrushchev era, the increasingly secure nature of possession became an element of ownership of particular
clarity and force.

Moreover, changes to the laws of inheritance in Western Europe during the
nineteenth and twentieth centuries made the nature of ownership still more relative
and diffuse. In the many national legal systems that derived from the influential
Code Napoléon (the French civil code that dated from 1804), the state effectively
held major powers over how individuals arranged their property for inheritance.[42]
Elsewhere, in the run-up to the First World War, Asquith's radical Liberal government introduced "death duties" in Britain, raising the curtain on the spectacle of
advancing inheritance taxes in the twentieth century. This troubled relationship
between inheritance and the state was partly replicated and partly resolved in the
practical operations of the Soviet urban housing economy.

The difference between medieval fee simple and modern property categories in
England suggests an evolution of tenure. Absolute ownership has perhaps always been

an improbable concept, squeezed by the Crown and then the modern state in ways ranging from requisition to taxation and compulsory purchase. Centuries of development have created a nuanced range of tenures, which contract, equity, and legal instruments such as trusts have further spliced and repackaged. A range of different types of property owner has thus emerged, some more secure than others and some with more rights than others, but all could make a claim to be owners. The simplest division still exists, between freeholders and leaseholders. Freehold and leasehold properties trade for roughly equal values (assuming the length of the lease is reasonable), though the constraints on the leaseholder are greater. He must observe rules defined in his lease, and some formal obligations to the freeholder. This nuanced lack of absoluteness—in the country whose historic development Pipes defines as the most opposing case to Russia's, the case that best exemplifies a long tradition of secure and transparent property rights—certainly makes the variability and complexity of Soviet ownership seem to be legitimate versions of property rights.

A variety of tenurial arrangements was therefore a common feature of European systems—even within their state sectors. The post-1945 (capitalist) welfare states transformed the balance of housing ownership. In Britain local councils became major owners within the national fund. Between 1919 and 1939, municipal government was the owner of 28.4 percent of new housing construction, and between 1945 and 1965, of 57.8 percent.[43] Yet for all the nuance of English property law, the nature of council ownership involved a particularly crude tenurial division between state and private; people were council tenants, private tenants, or home-owners.

In Sweden, West Germany, and France, state involvement was more pervasive yet more diffuse than in Britain, creating something more akin to a basic tripartite tenure. In Sweden state housing was constructed by "nonprofit housing corporations" rather than directly by local government; cooperatives and a private sector also existed. Genuine communes were created from time to time, but were on the whole still less popular than they had been in the Soviet Union in the 1920s.[44] The private sector was divided into owner-occupiership, construction for rental, and construction by employers for rental to employees. Even the private sector made use of cheap state loans. State involvement was thus not a heavy-handed matter of local authorities' undertaking construction and then distributing housing according to rigid norms; it depended on responsive relationships between state bodies, public corporations, employers, and individuals, moderated by accessible state finance.[45] In France, the Habitations à Loyer Modéré (Housing at Moderate Rents) were reestablished in 1947. These were independent specialist housing agencies that supervised construction, effectively on behalf of the arguably less effective local authorities. France also had an "intermediate or semipublic sector of housing construction," by which owner occupiers could obtain extra and cheap finance from the state via the Crédit Foncier.[46] In West Germany after the war, the private sector enjoyed generous state subsidies, and public housing was constructed by "social housing companies," which responded to the investment, demands, and strategies of central government, *Länder* government, and local authorities.[47]

The governments of the Eastern European satellites manipulated tenurial arrangements, whose categories partly though not entirely derived from Soviet example, in order to maximize construction output. In East Germany, state tenures were responsible for 79 percent of construction in 1957, fifteen percentage points higher than in the USSR.[48] The Bulgarian housing stock had an opposite profile: over 80 percent of construction fell within "private" and cooperative tenures between 1957 and 1963.[49] Even in East Germany, however, where requisition of housing space had proceeded ruthlessly according to the terms of the Reconstruction Law of 1950, novel methods were used to release citizens' savings, such as distributing some apartments on the basis of a lottery, to which one could buy in with voluntary working hours, sometimes on construction sites.[50] In 1960–1961, as a major housing program got under way in Hungary, the national Writers' Association organized the so-called Family House Debate, assessing the virtues of individual house construction against the new mass approaches to apartment block design.[51] The individual approach remained popular; as the 1960s progressed, the variety of credit arrangements diversified, tenurial forms became more flexible, and "private" construction expanded, still accounting for 60 percent of output in the late 1970s.[52] Similar trends emerged in Yugoslavia.[53]

Such variable penetrations by the state in Western and Eastern Europe alike paralleled some of the formal structures of ownership in the Soviet Union. But there was a major point of difference. Although important similarities existed in the Eastern European satellites, the Soviet Union was distinctive in allocating a high level of individual ownership to residents who, by law, were tenants. In (Western) welfare states, state and private tenants held much more limited rights of possession, and no real rights of ownership at all.[54] The particularity of the Soviet case partly lies in the way that law and state agencies collaborated with citizens in the process of enlarging the scope and volume of individual ownership. In the Soviet Union, individual ownership was a crucial practical mechanism for delivering a major share of urban housing construction, for guaranteeing a certain level of ongoing maintenance, and could be justified in principle in terms of socialist morality.

Individual ownership is a multifarious notion. These comparisons and contexts help to show that the Soviet Union was part of the European tradition of property, and that the highly distinctive and diffuse ways in which individuals occupied urban housing in the Soviet Union were, indeed, modes of ownership. Such modes show that Soviet citizens, Russians and non-Russians alike, were not debarred from understanding what individual ownership meant. Yet they also illuminate what was particular about the Soviet case and provide the basis of the chronologically focused discussion that follows. These forms of individual ownership had a major historical effect. More than any other factor, they explain the urban housing program.

Individual Ownership, Welfare, and the Soviet Order

As a citizen of the Soviet Union, I have the right to live and
work . . . I have the right to housing space.

—**Resident of Minsk, April 1954**

We would have made more progress if our citizens had been
more demanding in asserting their rights.

—**Khrushchev, discussing the housing program in his memoirs**

One day in December 1952, a group of workmen from the housing administration of Moscow's Kirov district entered the communal apartment room of a sixty-two-year-old cleaner. They erected a partition, which deprived her and her husband of much of their housing space. She had already lost her son in the war; her husband died a fortnight after the reduction of their room. The action was invasive and intolerable, subjectively and objectively assessed. As she conducted a careful war with the bureaucracy, the cleaner's arguments rested on emotion and law. While she emphasized her tragic circumstances, she also insisted that her "rights" had been contravened, citing directives that forbade such a deprivation of space without warning, agreement, and the permission of the central Moscow Soviet. Although she was not the formal owner of her dwelling, she showed that she had been, at least formally, the victim of a kind of expropriation. The outcome of her case is difficult to trace, but it is her sense of property rights that is of lasting historical interest.[1]

A constitutional right to housing existed only from 1977, and the panoply of rights that were presented in the constitution of 1936 only had traction on paper.[2] Yet the change brought in by the 1977 constitution was merely recognition of a reality that came about during the years of Khrushchev's leadership. Three genres of rights had been built into Soviet law from the 1930s.[3] They became newly prominent as a result of the Great Fatherland War but only gained force and meaning after Stalin's death. Socioeconomic rights were supposed to define a predictable standard of living and the right to a job; individual rights proclaimed freedom of conscience; and political rights made possible formally equal participation in elections. Courts or officials did not protect any of these rights consistently or apply any of them universally, and some were rhetorical absurdities until the late 1980s; overall, these rights scarcely formed a secure and logical system as they did, for example, in some other parts of Europe and the United States. But the shift from sacrifice to beneficence and then to paradise in the sphere of Soviet housing was based absolutely on giving real meaning to the various rights to housing: the right to "have" shelter, to obtain the norm through fair and nonarbitrary distribution mechanisms, to enjoy security of occupancy in line with rules of tenancy or personal property, to pay only minimum housing charges, to keep one's housing space during work secondments in other parts of the country (*komandirovki*), and the right to conduct an exchange.[4] Rational systems, such as those informing the methods of distribution, were the basis of the functioning of rights; the consolidation of a beneficent housing economy after Stalin's death made this possible. But it was in the context of Khrushchev's would-be paradise—in which new economic and political conditions combined with the creation of "moral-community" (*moral'no-obshchestvennye*) relations—that primitive legal rights and social guarantees cohered.[5] True, some people continued to enjoy institutionalized housing privileges, such as the workers who moved to inhospitable regions.[6] Corruption and the benefits of being well-connected remained endemic, and higher elites were always privileged. However, wide social "estates" with legally defined status and particular privileges did not exist, and the legal system was not, as such, biased against the individual citizen. In this system of housing rights, the right to ownership and the right to welfare trumped other rights and formed a tough nexus, which by the era of impending paradise was the core characteristic of the urban housing program.

Back in 1952, the cleaner in her reduced communal apartment room did not yet have access to this system of rights. But even then, rights of ownership gave her some power in her dealings with the local housing administration. The elements of ownership on which her housing space rested were divided between the resident and various state agencies; rights of occupancy, use, management, and formal title were split in complex ways. Meanwhile, the appeal of emotion, of wartime loss and recent bereavement, added a dimension of deserving to this resident's legal status. This kind of subjective appeal was especially crucial during the arbitrariness of Stalinism, when the scope of rights was confined to rhetoric. But even during the late Stalinist era, the components of individual ownership that were embedded in all housing tenures were intensified. The Great Fatherland War expanded, relegitimated, and strengthened the existing scope of individual ownership. It did so by raising the permitted level of autonomy that citizens could exercise within the urban housing economy, and by creating a more systematic relationship between these autonomous activities and the functions of state bodies. This made it easier, for example, for citizens to build their own house and own it as their personal property, or to make justifiable claims for the return of state housing space claimed by another citizen during wartime evacuation. Yet agencies of the state also used various mechanisms to strengthen their grip over the housing fund. The sanitary norm, which was the formal ration or limit of housing space allocated to a citizen, and the propiska, or internal passport residence registration, were two of the most important mechanisms. Autonomous citizens manipulated even these limiting mechanisms to increase their share of individual ownership.

Yet by the peak of Khrushchev's dominance, when communism was beckoning, personal property was increasingly sidelined and housing cooperatives were reintroduced. This marked an ideological shift, but in practice the possibilities of individual ownership simply migrated from one tenure to the other. Although residents invested their own savings and made use of state credits in order to obtain cooperative housing, cooperatives formed a part of the "socialist" state tenures. Thanks to expanded rights of occupancy, the possibility of individual ownership of a standard state apartment, formally owned by a soviet or department, also became more deeply entrenched during the Khrushchev era, and it was in some ways more stable than an individual's direct ownership of a house as personal property. As the residency of soviet and especially departmental apartments was now replicated on a considerably growing scale, mass security of occupancy was the result.

Citizens had real property rights during the late Stalinist and Khrushchev eras, which were in part the consequence of a high level of permitted autonomy. These property rights were matched and reinforced by welfare rights, of which the centerpiece was the right to expect the state to provide one's family with a separate apartment in the foreseeable future (within ten or twelve years of the 1957 decree). The growing strength of welfare rights in the sphere of housing depended on an expanded conspectus of state provision, whose shape, in the high Khrushchev era, derived from the demands of the transition to paradise. Such paradoxes—property and welfare, citizen autonomy and the encroaching state—created a favorable setting in which individual ownership and proto-communism could not only coexist but depend on each other. This essential connection between property and welfare was the defining feature of the Soviet urban housing economy during the two postwar decades. The nexus of property and welfare goes back to the war, before which the ruthless suppression of workers' living standards made such a nexus meaningless, but during which the housing program began to take shape.

War, Reconstruction, and the Expansion of Individual Ownership

Patterns of property ownership changed as a consequence of the war, and while they evolved further during the Khrushchev era, it was the war that signaled the major shift. The crisis of mass destruction occasioned by the conflict was so intense and widespread and even had such sharp ramifications in the housing profiles of cities thousands of kilometers from the fighting that central government was obliged, for the first time in Soviet history, to develop housing construction policies that had discernible mass effects. Yet this was a time of national emergency, when the domestic construction industry was enfeebled and the resources that might be committed to rebuilding were tightly circumscribed. The solution was to engage the initiative of citizens in the amelioration of their own personal housing crises: to use state credits and other forms of assistance to mobilize the potential of the existing tenure of personal property. Results were variable, but they made an essential contribution to postwar reconstruction. What was new was the political commitment, not the existence of the tenure.

Not only did personal property (effectively encoded into the foundations of the Soviet urban housing economy) date back to original revolutionary settlements, but the 1944 scheme itself had a prewar analogue. Decrees of October 1937 and April 1939 made it possible for individual citizens to claim credits for housing construction.[7] This was part of prewar Stalinism's apparent consolidation of personal property. Yet in the absence of plausible levels of investment or the political seriousness that could tighten the chain of policy implementation between center and locality, such decrees only had a marginal effect on the urban housing shortage. They did, however, show that officials were aware of how personal property could be manipulated, and that new policies were effectively consolidating the tenure's status.

Thus in Soviet cities the possibility of individual ownership survived not just the revolution but the urban upheavals of the 1930s. Personal property continued to account for one-third of the urban housing stock, and newly constructed separate houses, owned as personal property, were objects of aspiration. In the 1930s the stereotypical purchaser or individual builder of such a house was someone who had the income of a Stakhanovite or a factory director.[8] Yet citizens who were able to call in favors, make use of stolen materials, and undertake physical construction themselves with the assistance of their neighbors might reduce the costs of a ten-thousand-ruble house by a factor of ten, according to a postwar refugee recalling her experience of 1938.[9] Individual housing construction and personal property were important aspects of the urban economy of prewar Stalinism, though in chaotic form. In the changed political and transformed physical circumstances wrought by the war, the 1944 decree, expanding and regulating the personal sector, was one of several possible housing policies that could have been drafted, but in the context of official and popular attitudes to property during prewar Stalinism, it was certainly a likely one.

For all the variable success of the 1944 scheme, it was directly or indirectly responsible for a major share of postwar reconstruction.[10] While the system's basic legal attitude to individual forms of property was not dissimilar before and after 1944, the war caused a major expansion in the construction of individually owned urban houses. The proportion of new urban construction held as personal property was 16.0 percent in the last complete prewar five-year plan (1933–1937); during the 1946–1950 plan, it was 38.2 percent.[11] This caused the ownership of individual houses to spread across more categories of the population than before; a Soviet legal scholar noted that it had been confined to the "prosperous" in the 1920s and 1930s.[12] The penetration of personal property into the urban housing funds of five Soviet republics in 1950 is illustrated in table 5.1.[13] These data show the high proportion, and in some places the dominance, of personal property in cities across the Soviet Union. Variability reflected cultural conditions and contingent circumstances. In Latvia personal property was proportionately the least significant, despite the long tradition of building separate urban houses. This paradox flowed from the new local soviets' mass appropriation of dwellings, many of whose owners had fled during the war (though expropriation was the fate of many who stayed as well). Soviet responses to Uzbek culture, meanwhile, were consistent with almost two-thirds of urban housing being held as personal property.

Not only did the stock of personal property physically grow as a result of the war, but so did the emotional force with which citizens related to it.[14] People referred to their experience of war as a legitimating basis for their ownership. Throughout the postwar world, people's specific aspirations to own their home, as well as their more general yearning for an enclosed domestic space and a family hearth, grew markedly.[15] In the Soviet Union, individual construction expanded as a response to two separate but mutually reinforcing imperatives: the urgent need for shelter and the emotional desire to keep secure hold of that shelter once it had been obtained. During the chaos of the postwar emergency, many people came back from years away to find someone living in their house. They had recourse to the courts, but these were overburdened and worked ineffectively.[16] Z. M. Zil'berman, a factory worker from Zaporozh'e, was evacuated during the war with her father and sister. The women's husbands had gone to the front. Their father died in Omsk while the war was still on, and the sisters inherited the family home, a house that the father

TABLE 5.1. URBAN HOUSING HELD AS PERSONAL PROPERTY
IN THE SOVIET UNION, 1950

	Percentage of total urban housing stock held as personal property
USSR	39.6
RSFSR	34.4
Belorussia	54.7
Latvia	19.6
Georgia	53.9
Uzbekistan	61.2

Source: RGAE f. 1562, op. 14, d. 2031, l. 1; d. 2027, ll. 74, 79, 88, 94.

had built himself. On their return from evacuation, however, their attempts to claim their inheritance failed; the sisters were excluded from their home by those who had lived in it during the war. Zil'berman went to court nineteen times during two years to try to recover it. Unable to obtain a satisfactory outcome, she petitioned Malenkov. In her letter she emphasized her father's work record and her family's wartime sacrifice as further reasons to view her case favorably. As well as these justifications of law, labor, and service, she also defined her property rights with reference to acute need. "We just can't live here any longer," she wrote of the thirty-six-square-meter room in which twelve people, her family and strangers, were now settled. And she reinforced this with a powerful and repeated expression of unjustly thwarted ownership, writing of "our house."[17] These imperatives were entwined in a combination that is commonly expressed in archival documents.

The increase in the numbers of individual house owners occurred in the context of a dynamic relationship between individuals and agencies of the state, particularly at a local city level. Officials frequently legitimized individuals' informal strategies for solving, or ameliorating, their own housing crises. For historians, analysis of this practice might knock down the artificial conceptual barrier that renders "state" and "society" antagonistic partners, tied in a relationship where the latter was forced to break the rules imposed by the former in order to obtain its desired commodities. In the circumstances of the postwar urban housing emergency, what might have been considered resistance was sometimes more akin to mutual collaboration, though the process was complex and evolved over time.

Perhaps unauthorized (*samovol'noe*) construction illustrates this best. Very often the only shelter people could find after the war was what they built for themselves, outside the law, without waiting for credit, on whatever plot of land might be available, and sometimes using stolen materials. Such survival strategies are universal and do not reflect a particularly Russian anarchic spirit. Between 1945 and 1950, officials estimated that one in six individual houses in Stalingrad was built without authorization.[18] In Vladimir, at least eighteen individual houses were approved in 1950 by the local soviet as the personal property of their occupiers, even though they had originally been built without authorization.[19] Unauthorized dwellings, lacking formal title, might paradoxically become bargaining chips in dealings between citizen and local housing administration. In a workers' settlement near Astrakhan' toward the end of the late Stalinist period, several workers went ahead and built houses, without having obtained legally allotted plots of land, propiski, construction plans, or credit. They built the houses in an unsuitable area prone to flooding, which lacked basic infrastructure. But in the absence of sufficient funds to rehouse all of them immediately, the executive of the provincial soviet (*oblispolkom*) was obliged to argue vigorously that their employer, the Ministry of Communications, should pay for the infrastructure that would make the area properly inhabitable, and that the houses should then be retrospectively formalized as their occupiers' property.[20] Similarly, one Sh. E. Iakhtel, who was serving in the army, had built not so much a house as a temporary shelter (*vremianka*) in Groznyi. Oil pipes passed through the plot of land. In 1956 the executive of the city soviet (*gorispolkom*) would not change its mind about pulling down the house, as safety here was a much more acute and chronic problem than in Astrakhan', but promised to allot another plot of land and give assistance to the family in setting up home there.[21]

State tenants related equally strongly to their dwellings and also defined the relationship in the terms of individual ownership. After coming back from the war, veterans or civilians commonly argued that they owned the housing space they had occupied before, even though this was formally the property of a state body. In many cases, however, a stranger now lived in the space, and the original resident had to go to court to get it back. The would-be owners pursued legal process for two reasons. Their former home might be the only housing they had any chance of obtaining, and securing its return would be their only means of escaping from the misery of wherever they had found shelter in the meantime. But they often wanted the return of their former home to the exclusion of reasonable alternatives because, simply, they believed it was theirs. In such instances, citizens and officials alike broadly used terms of citizen-ownership.

A woman called P. A. Latyeva came back to Moscow in 1945, following her evacuation to Ufa in 1941. Another citizen, L. A. Agranovskaia, was living in her former housing space. Latyeva went to law. Eventually, a court in the city's Leningradskii raion ordered Agranovskaia's eviction. But Agranovskaia appealed. She made use of several legal channels and took advantage of technicalities. A year after the Leningradskii court had ordered the eviction, Agranovskaia remained ensconced and Latyeva's life was still in abeyance. She was seventy-three. Two of her sons had been killed in the war, one was a disabled veteran, and the last was still in the army. In despair she wrote to Malenkov: "I can't get any help from anyone in my old age, wandering from corner to corner and leaving no stone unturned in the courts." She wanted her home back: "I ask you, comrade Malenkov, as my deputy, to help me get back my housing space, where I lived with my son who was killed in the defense of the motherland." Malenkov pursued the case, asking the Leningradskii raion soviet to arrange the return of "her" housing space; the officials wrote back that she was now living in the housing space that "previously belonged to her."[22]

At the same time, the acuteness of the postwar shortage meant that many people had renewed possibilities for renting out "corners" of their housing space. Citizens who should have expected housing from a department were very often obliged to seek it out in the "private sector." More than half the students attending Voronezh's Agriculture Institute in 1953 lived in privately rented "corners"; student numbers, moreover, were growing, while construction continued to be neglected.[23] Indeed, in 1952 in Kasimovo, Riazan' oblast', a number of citizens were found to have charge of both a state apartment and a personally owned house and were renting out the latter. One of them paid 10 rubles a month for the rent of her "state" apartment and obtained 250 rubles from the tenant in her "private" house. Surprisingly, it was difficult for jurists to make a coherent civil case, based on property law, against what was nevertheless criminal speculation. It seemed that the civil law did not foresee such a situation.[24] Private landlords had property rights, too, at least by default; though it is no accident that the woman who rents out a room in *Spring on Zarechnaia Street* (1956) is one of the most negative characters in the film, a relic in an otherwise modernizing town.[25]

It was very difficult to obtain reasonable housing during the dreadful postwar shortage, but it was equally difficult to be thrown out. People were aware, of course, that a soviet- or department-owned dwelling did not formally belong to them, but they consistently invoked different strategies to assume extended rights of possession over it. They occupied state housing space, whether soviet or departmental tenure, on exceptionally advantageous terms, of which difficulty of eviction was the most important.[26] Formally, a tenant could be evicted for such infractions as not paying apartment charges, damaging the space, or using it for nonhousing purposes. This amounted to security of occupancy, because apartment charges were little more than 5 percent of income.[27] Such lack of reversionary rights severely undermined the practical claim of a soviet or department to a dwelling that was formally their property. These institutions often struggled to pursue legal proceedings to a satisfactory conclusion, even though a substantial—if disparate—body of law gave them the right to take back space still occupied by former employees.[28] Unlike the private tenants who dominated the housing funds of Western Europe, state tenants in the USSR, who were the majority of the population, enjoyed some of the characteristics of de facto owners during late Stalinism and the first few post-Stalin years.

Negotiating the Limits of Tenure

Agencies of the state, nevertheless, retained considerable formal rights. Citizens were protected, by law and accepted practice, against eviction from socialist property or the alienation of personal property; as anywhere, however, they could not do just what they wanted in or with their dwelling. In usual circumstances, perhaps the most common reason for losing one's home was the failure to maintain it in a proper state of repair. This was a serious issue in an economy where urban housing was precious because it was so scarce. Newspaper campaigns about looking after one's housing space, whatever its tenure, were frequent.[29] Officials in Moscow's Kalininskii raion soviet repeatedly warned one F. A. Panteleeva that her continuing refusal to maintain her house, which had led to its irretrievable dilapidation, would result in her losing it. And she did lose it in 1954.[30] En route to this outcome, she received multiple warnings, and soviet officials never doubted that the alienation of her property could only take place in a court.

Yet Soviet citizens were also vulnerable to the vicious caprice that underwrote so many late Stalinist transactions. A. P. Gura had been a highly decorated railroad worker in Krasnodar in the 1930s, and a client of Kaganovich. In 1936, as part of the public celebration of his work, the Krasnodar city soviet received instructions to award Gura a house. He was, at least temporarily, a local celebrity. The soviet bought a large house and transferred it to Gura, which he then owned as personal property.

However, in 1948, his house reentered the housing fund of the city soviet, apparently because he had failed to maintain it to the required standard of repair. It is also possible that the extreme local housing shortage made the comfortably accommodated Gura, once the beneficiary of the local politics of clientelism and vulnerable to the politics of envy, an obvious target for bringing into line with the housing ration, or sanitary norm. The order was revoked the following year by the oblast' soviet, but it was only in 1956 that the situation was apparently finally confirmed in Gura's favor.[31] Gura's case is particularly colorful and illustrates both the vulnerabilities and the residual strength of personal property, as well as the differences between arbitrariness during the years of late Stalinism and greater administrative regularity in the Khrushchev era.

While citizens vigorously and inventively expanded or protected their possibilities of individual ownership, soviets and state departments sought to produce the opposite outcome through their regulation of housing space. Here citizens and state agencies could stand in opposition to each other, and citizens' autonomous responses were not of the explicitly permitted type.[32] The "sanitary norm" and the propiska or residency registration were the two most powerful routine administrative tools at the citizen's disposal. They could, perversely, exploit these mechanisms to strengthen their share of individual ownership, by exploiting informal practices and determinedly acting on their customary understandings of Soviet rights.

Soviet law stated that every citizen should occupy a maximum ration of square meters. This ration was known as the sanitary norm. It was variable, in limited ways. Some categories of the population, including those who were obliged partly to work at home, such as artists, enjoyed a higher norm. Republics and cities could have different norms, though city soviets that wanted to reduce theirs below the republican level had to make a persuasive case. In August 1947, the norm was set at nine square meters for the towns and cities of the RSFSR.[33] But such a level was an aspiration. Many cities had averages below four square meters.[34] The norm was thus not really an entitlement. It was a mechanism that helped planners to calculate construction and renovation targets. And it was a limit: if a citizen happened to be living beyond the norm, the law obliged him to give up the excess. Regulations stated that the "alienation" of housing space had to be accompanied by the construction of partitions to safeguard a minimum of family life and could not cause a woman to share a room with an unknown man. Such niceties aside, citizens had to give up the excess.[35]

State tenants fought back, using a variety of strategies to soften the effects of the sanitary norm, or even to turn it to their advantage and thus regain elements of individual ownership from the formal state owner. One way to defend the integrity of one's home was by deploying professional prestige. Following the death of the well-known architect D. S. Markov in 1943, his widow and son remained in the family apartment on Marx Street, together with a maid. The apartment was relatively luxurious; each resident's space was now even further beyond the norm. By 1947 the local housing administration was insisting that the family give up some of their home. The widow Markova made use of her husband's name and called in his connections and was eventually allowed to keep the apartment in its present form. She did not lose rooms to other tenants, and it did not become a communal apartment. In effect she and her son retained their "ownership" of the dwelling.[36] Using another characteristic tactic, one Aleksei Mandryka tried to invoke the prestige of academic and scientific work to keep his three-room apartment as a discrete family home. The logic of the sanitary norm threatened to turn it into a communal apartment following his mother-in-law's impending death. Writing to Voroshilov in 1953, Mandryka argued that these conditions would deny him the chance to complete his higher doctoral dissertation. He also claimed that the family would anyway live in line with the norm by 1957, by which time his daughter would have attained majority and he would be enjoying the greater entitlement associated with academic elevation.[37]

The other routine way of regulating tenancy rights and reducing the resident's share of individual ownership was the propiska. This was the stamp in the internal passport with which local housing administrations registered Soviet citizens at their home address. It was an absolute legal requirement, which was incidentally checked during unrelated bureaucratic processes, from starting a job to getting married.[38] Propiska rules could infringe the individual's sense of ownership, sometimes violently. The regulations' blindness to the intentions of citizen-"owners" magnified the effect. In 1947 the local soviet denied a demobilized senior lieutenant, I. A. Karachevtseva, a propiska in her mother's Moscow room. As another adult and child were now living with her mother in this space of twenty square meters, the simple mathematics of the norm made it impossible to grant the propiska. The mother could not allow the daughter to live in her home. In her letter of petition to Malenkov, the daughter wrote: "Don't I deserve, after serving for three years in the army, to live quietly and with my family? Respected Comrade Malenkov, I very much request that you allow me to be granted a propiska at my mother's home."[39] Long absences from home, even in wartime, caused propiski to lapse. The Supreme Court (USSR) emphasized in November 1946 that a citizen could not reclaim housing space simply by virtue of having a propiska at that address.[40] Yet many citizens did recover their former homes because officials acknowledged—and ordinary people insisted on—elements of citizen-"ownership," notwithstanding formal rules and exemplary court judgments.

Citizens exploited even the propiska regulations to secure or defend ownership and exclude the unwanted. Individual family members could have dreadful power. In 1929 one E. A. Radygina got married and had a child. A dozen years later, with the war underway, her husband was evacuated with his factory, first to Siberia, and then in 1943 to Serpukhov in Moscow Region, where he had to stay until 1952. After his return to Moscow, his daughter successfully obstructed his attempts to regain his propiska at the family housing space on Manège Street. E. A. Radygina was distraught, condemning the objection as "not right," "mercenary, not principled." She worried he would go off with another woman. The authorities eventually took her side, finding that the daughter's objection to the granting of propiska was inadequate grounds for the father's exclusion.[41]

This case contains a paradox that illuminates the problem of ownership. Citizens and authorities alike could assume that one resident of a dwelling had the power to exclude another person, even a parent, from that individual's housing space. This was a mistaken assumption, but where it existed it lent real power to an individual's "direction" of his room or apartment. The case also shows that a careful application of the law actually made it difficult to evict one resident if another resident objected on the grounds of a lapsed propiska. This formally correct position, where it was applied, injected other elements of ownership into a person's rights over his or her housing. Both halves of the paradox—the mistaken but influential assumption and the proper use of law alike—nourished the vitality of individual ownership, the first in favor of one type of resident, the second in favor of another.

A gentler propiska regime emerged during the Khrushchev era, in the context of the further formal rights that state tenants started to enjoy. Yet paradox and ambiguity persisted as the benign environment in which elements of individual ownership flourished. In this environment, personal property would be reduced in scope while the individual "ownership" of state apartments expanded. The most direct means of achieving this outcome was by shifting the balance between personal and cooperative tenures sharply in favor of the latter.

The Personal—Cooperative Balance

During the first year that followed the introduction of the keynote 1957 decree, personal property was at its most robust. It was probably never stronger during the entire history of the Soviet Union. According to published statistics, the total volume of urban housing held as personal property reached its postwar peak in 1958 at 39.9 percent.[42] Moreover, at what in retrospect was a climactic moment for the tenure, officials were looking to enhance its security further. In 1957 Gosstroi discussed measures for "providing help for individual house-builders in the rapid construction of their houses" and for constructing individual houses for sale to citizens in cities, workers' settlements, and rural localities. The officials also proposed that construction plans and appropriate building materials should be more easily available.[43] Increasing the number of sales would further regularize personal property transactions and would firm up personal property rights. Officials were only interested in making the construction of separate houses more efficient, and in streamlining the single transaction of the purchase of a new dwelling by a citizen from a state institution. They were consolidating something opposite to a housing market, while developing a flexible system that depended on autonomous actions by citizens.[44] In 1958 Gosstroi officials were discussing the establishment of a network of three hundred new warehouses to be administered by the Ministry of Trade, where citizens would be able to buy construction kits and parts. Officials were also considering how best to set up proper public information (*reklama*) to ensure that people knew what opportunities were available to them. The Gosstroi officials wanted the Ministry of Finance to increase the size of the maximum loan to fifteen thousand rubles.[45] Kucherenko, the head of Gosstroi, favored the perpetuation of a substantial role for individual housing construction in the mass housing program. The policy allowed mass economies of scale, intensive applications of professional expertise, and effective regulation of urban growth to combine with the further efficiencies associated with permitting a substantial level of citizen autonomy. But things changed after 1958; it did not happen as Kucherenko saw it.

The limited scale of postwar reconstruction depended heavily on individual building and personal property, but the mass construction that began in the second half of the 1950s could not proceed without the very focused activity of agencies of the state and the dramatic expansion of soviet and especially departmental tenures. Most characteristic of the program were five-story apartment blocks owned by departments such as industrial enterprises. Although personal property remained important throughout the Khrushchev era, its proportional contribution declined from 25.9 percent of new urban construction in 1959 to 16 percent in 1964.[46] This striking fall, the result of urban modernization and neo-Leninism, foreshadowed the tenure's marginalization in the cities of the 1970s and 1980s.

New modern microdistricts were often built on the rubble of old neighborhoods of individual houses, which might have looked like shanty towns or might have possessed a more established, but partly rural, feel. Personal property was shattered as a workable large-scale concept. Yet this was not mass requisition; the principle of ownership was respected. While citizens were required to give up their homes, they were immediately compensated by the provision of state housing, in accordance with the norm and usually superior in quality. People swapped tumbledown shacks for indoor plumbing. In Moscow, at least, the executive committees of district soviets preceded each individual demolition with the legal transfer of the owner's housing space from personal to soviet tenure.[47] The Kalininskii raion soviet (raisovet) promulgated a typical resolution on 15 June 1960: "On accepting into the housing fund of the raisovet the privately-owned [*chastnovladel'cheskii*] house no. 147, Shosse Entuziastov."[48] This named the particular house owner, gave the date of the final handover, and confirmed the provision of soviet housing in compensation. Another resolution, of 28 December 1961, stated that since 1946 one L. Z. Severinova had owned "a 7/100 share of house 37/17 Perovskii Passage [*proezd*], namely, one room of size 10.9 square meters." Severinova shared the room with a family member, and both were guaranteed appropriate, and probably significantly more modern, housing from the raion soviet.[49] By 1961 the wholesale demolition of houses owned as personal property was in full swing in Moscow.[50]

Such demolitions prepared urban land for the quick construction of new housing. The practical effects were partly comparable to the slum clearance taking place elsewhere in Europe.[51] But this was not just another example of modernization. It was also an ideological attack on personal property as a legal category and the individual urban house as the symbol of a backward-looking way of life. Legislative measures between 1958 and 1963 removed individual housing construction as a significant instrument of policy. The switch was directly associated with Khrushchev, who spoke enthusiastically in favor of it.[52] Kucherenko, at Gosstroi, was uneasy, thinking that the marginalization could threaten total construction output, whereas Khrushchev seemed to celebrate it on the basis of ideological advance. Nevertheless, the vision of Khrushchev and the technocratic concerns of Kucherenko contained common aspects. Both men wanted the highest possible and most efficient level of construction, and both understood that agencies of the state could not achieve it by themselves. Yet for Khrushchev, personal property could no longer fulfill this function because it would not bring the communist future closer. It constrained his priority. In the late 1950s, with the capacity of state construction newly enormous, overall output still depended, through individual construction and personal property, on citizens' physical resources and especially their savings. The loss of this input could not be recovered by the so-called Gor'kii method, by which a collective of workers built an apartment block in return for housing space.[53] This procedure had some ideological appeal, but spare-time construction work could not provide what was really needed, which was a modern financial mechanism for releasing and channeling people's savings.

Housing construction cooperatives, reintroduced in decrees of March 1958 and June 1962, answered the technical demand but within new collective structures.[54] Citizens (often employees of the same institution) would come together to invest their savings—reinforced by cheap state loans—in a cooperative charged with the construction and management of an apartment block. These blocks were modern, often completed to a particularly high standard, and like conventional state housing, they were embedded in local infrastructure and planned neighborhoods. The 1958 decree envisaged that cooperatives would be a complement to individual housing, and that both forms would increase overall construction.[55] By 1962 the ideological drive of the communist future had placed further burdens on cooperatives; they should start to do the job of individual housing. The first aim of the decree was "To realize in the near future the steady transition from building individual separate houses in cities and workers' settlements to the building of well-appointed cooperative apartment blocks, using the population's resources."[56] Individual construction must still make a contribution, but it was visibly declining. Its status during late Stalinist reconstruction had been transformed. The point is underlined with the statistical evidence presented in table 5.2.

By 1964 it seems that there were 224,355 shareholders in 3,009 housing cooperatives throughout the USSR, which suggests that fewer than a million people lived in cooperative apartments at the end of the Khrushchev era.[57] The numbers of cooperatives increased dramatically through to the end of the 1960s, and they became increasingly important in the 1970s and 1980s. This suggests that the permitted autonomy that citizens exercised in the housing economy further transmuted and remained essential during the Brezhnev era.

Cooperatives were based on a different principle of property relations than personally owned individual houses. An apartment block built by a housing-construction cooperative was socialist property.[58] The occupants of each apartment

TABLE 5.2. PROJECTIONS FOR INDIVIDUAL AND COOPERATIVE
CONSTRUCTION, RSFSR, 1963–1965

	Cooperative housing (millions m²)	Individual housing (millions m²)
1963	1.5	12.0
1964	2.4	10.0
1965	3.1	5.4

Source: GARF f. A-259, op. 42, d. 9593, l. 3 (Gosplan data).

were members of the cooperative, which as a whole retained the rights of direction over each apartment.[59] It was the cooperative, not the resident, that was the property owner (*sobstvennik*), though the resident was a member and had a vote in the cooperative's general meeting.[60] Neither higher agencies of the state nor the individual members of the cooperative had greater control than the cooperative itself. Not only could a cooperative shareholder not sell his apartment or use it to raise collateral, but he could not formally exchange it either. If he wanted to live somewhere else, the first stage was to leave the cooperative, forfeiting his membership, at which stage his investment would be returned to him.[61]

Members of cooperatives, like the owners of individual houses, had invested their own money. But their "ownership" of their apartments was much more akin to the "ownership" enjoyed by state tenants than that of the holders of personal property. Housing-construction cooperatives were not part of soviet or departmental tenures, but like them, they fell into the category of "socialist property," which stood in contradistinction to personal property. Like state tenants, cooperative members could not transfer their dwelling or part of their dwelling by sale or gift directly to another citizen. Cooperative members could bequeath their dwelling (and its financial investment) in line with the laws banning the accumulation of dwellings, but this was effectively paralleled by the substantial rights of occupancy enjoyed by the family of a deceased state tenant, which amounted to de facto inheritance rights (elaborated below). Trade unions (*profsoiuzy*) often instigated the formation of cooperatives and retained influence over their operation. This reduced the individual exercise of property rights and increased the scope within which systemic patronage networks could flex their power. Voinovich's comic novella *The Ivankiad* (*Ivankiada*, 1975) recounts the epic quest of a resident to assert a measure of individual property rights in a cooperative block of the Academy of Writers.[62]

For all these paradoxes, people were keen to invest their savings in cooperatives. In 1961 the Moscow Soviet approved a cooperative for "circus artists."[63] The following year employees of the Ministry of Foreign Trade set up a cooperative in Moscow, as did employees of the Academy of Medical Sciences.[64] Around the same time the Moscow Soviet also discussed cooperatives for employees of the Ministry of Foreign Affairs and the KGB.[65] Workers who had spent many years in climatically unfavorable regions were sometimes given priority in applications for cooperative shareholding in a more comfortable part of the country; when this was mooted in 1963 in Sakhalin oblast', 2,500 long-term workers applied.[66] In general, privileged citizens invested their savings in order to obtain an apartment more quickly than they could by waiting for soviet or departmental housing.[67] They paid with cash to jump from a long queue to a shorter one. What they were precisely not doing was literally purchasing an apartment or acquiring private property, which would have made no legal, ideological, or practical sense. Ultimately, the cooperative shareholder's principal claim to an individual form of ownership derived from occupancy. This was the same for residents in other types of "socialist property" housing.

Cooperatives were the most recognizable consequences of the diffusion into the "socialist" fund of the individual ownership that had been associated with the rapidly diminishing tenure of personal property. But they were not the only consequences. More broadly, the already existing possibilities of individual "ownership" of soviet and departmental housing were deepening.

Individual Ownership on a Mass Scale

By the last years of the Khrushchev era, the right to "own" a state apartment became more vigorous and sustainable than rights associated with personal property had ever been. In Khrushchev's USSR, therefore, de facto forms of ownership outperformed de jure forms, and their substance and force persisted for the rest of the Soviet period. Personal property became controversial during communist transition and, for some contemporary scholars, theoretically unstable.[68] It had always been a temporary form, resting on a city soviet's limited-term approval of the plot of land on which the house was to be built. In the era of impending communism (and indeed its chronological successor, the endless stasis of developed socialism), a citizen would "own" his state apartment within the eternal time frame of communist promise. One citizen wrote in a letter of 1960 that new apartment houses must be sufficiently comfortable so that a person "doesn't feel like a temporary resident but a resident who loves his housing so much that he would refuse to move from it. That will be doing things the right way, as if we are the owners [*Tak to budet po-khoziaiski*]."[69] Ideological imperatives and practical needs converged on the objective of complete security of occupancy. More people were "owning" what they occupied because society was rhetorically moving toward communism.

The third party program made clear that an essential sign of the transition to communism was every citizen's occupancy of a separate family apartment in little more than a decade.[70] While the promise was unrealistic, citizens did now have a newly reasonable expectation of obtaining a separate family home within a foreseeable time frame. When they obtained the dwelling, moreover, it would be secured by explicit rights of occupancy and use. Both these changes were post-Stalin phenomena and ultimately depended on the shift from beneficence to paradise. The legal specialist A. G. Potiukov commented in 1962, "The basic tendency of housing legislation is the strengthening of the guarantee of rights of all users of housing space." He argued that legislation passed by the Supreme Soviet in December 1961 was emblematic. State tenants could now only be evicted if they had been offered alternative housing space, or if they had committed an "acute violation" of tenancy agreements. The tenant should "as a rule" be able to appeal in a court.[71] By the high Khrushchev era, the elements of ownership of state apartments were split in such a way as to favor the tenant, decisively. Occupancy of a state apartment was certainly not the same as the right to private property, but it was the most convincing case of individual ownership hitherto in the urban housing economy.[72]

It was a de facto form of ownership, but not less powerful for that. Agencies of the state still held the title to state apartments. Tenants could not sell, gift, or pass on the housing space that was theirs by close to secure right. But tenants did have some limited rights of transfer. Two were notable: the formal right of exchange and the effective right of a kind of inheritance. The occupants of one apartment could exchange their dwelling with the occupants of another. This seemed a purer socialist transaction than the purchase or sale of personal property (though legal scholars had shown that even this was entirely justifiable in terms of socialist morality), and it boosted the efficiency of the regular system of distribution. Exchange bureaus were a part of the late Stalinist housing economy.[73] Until the late 1950s, however, those who sought exchanges were faced with a seemingly impenetrable system. In October 1955 G. A. Gurok was looking to exchange the room in a communal apartment that he shared with his wife. Gurok had joined the party in 1917. His career had ranged from service in the brigade of the legendary Chapaev during the Civil War to employment in Magnitogorsk during the industrial revolution of the 1930s. Now he held a senior position in the Moscow Region Pedagogical Institute, where he was working on a textbook. His wife was writing a candidate's dissertation. It was difficult for them to complete their "academic and teaching" work while living in a communal apartment. The conditions there exacerbated Gurok's "various" age-related illnesses (he would soon be sixty). For all these reasons, he wanted to exchange his twenty-four-square-meter room for a thirty-square-meter apartment. He sought the patronage of Maksim Saburov, first deputy chairman of the Council of Ministers, because "to do this without the help of a high-ranking organization is almost impossible." Gurok wrote, "My work during all my time in the party gives me the basic hope that you will want to help me." Saburov did.[74]

In the late 1950s and the early 1960s, however, the exchange system was enlarged and its processes were regularized. The bulletin that listed the details of those who wished to exchange dwellings in Moscow was physically expanded.[75] A representative decree of the Moscow Soviet in September 1961 called on exchange bureaus to work more effectively.[76] In Moscow, 27,000 exchanges took place in 1961.[77] The system was still inadequate, overcomplicated, sometimes very difficult to get going, and intensely stressful, and while it was possible to exchange between cities, this would usually involve an extremely vulnerable chain.

Iurii Trifonov's 1969 novella *The Exchange* (*Obmen*) reflects the system that was set up under Khrushchev, though it bears an unmistakable imprint of the Brezhnev era. Dmitriev's mother, Ksenia Fedorovna, is badly ill. His wife, Lena, suggests that they exchange both Ksenia's spacious separate apartment and their own communal-apartment room for a single, larger dwelling, so that they can all live together. Lena's real aim, however, is to factor into the transaction her mother-in-law's housing space while this can still happen, in explicit anticipation of her death. After a terrible moral, emotional, and practical struggle, Dmitriev and Lena carry out the scheme. For Trifonov, personal morality dissolved in the bureaucratic solvent, leaving Dmitriev not just conscience-stricken but physically ill. Trifonov wanted to indict a system that was not working well enough: that did not match the promise of 1917.[78]

Yet for all the system's considerable inadequacies, the possibility of conducting an exchange, and the existence of a rudimentary infrastructure within which it could be organized, were real. These rudiments of organization, combined with the use of an agent (*makler*), that ambiguously permitted entity, as well as the information and contacts provided by the networks spanning out of one's workplace collective and one's other acquaintances, made for an example of how individual ownership worked during the Khrushchev era. The "state" was now a more powerful and effective player in the urban housing economy than it had been during the late Stalinist period and before. Citizens, however, still cooperated with its agencies in ways that were unofficial yet permitted, and ways that were straightforwardly legal, in order to attain their objects.

The other type of property transfer was inheritance. Where personal property remained, so did formal inheritance.[79] A cooperative apartment was also an inheritable item.[80] In 1963 a legal commentator could still maintain, "The right of inheritance has enormous significance for the workers of the USSR, because it is connected with the preservation of their existing property [*imushchestvennykh*] interests." Its role in preserving these interests "increases their material and cultural well-being and constructs communism" and "has major significance in strengthening the Soviet family."[81] Citizens could not use inheritance laws to amass property; these laws had to maintain the consumption character of the tenure. Yet for the growing majority who lived in state apartments, inheritance was a partly redundant problem, solved by circumstances. When a resident died, the other family members who were registered by propiska at the same address continued to live there by right.[82] Fewer people would now occupy the same number of square meters. Sometimes each person's share would move ahead of the sanitary norm, though the new separate apartments were usually sufficiently small to avoid the invasive implications that could otherwise arise. But even when the norm was overtaken, the rights of occupancy were assured. By the early 1960s, in such situations of "inheritance," or when a family member left home, the soviet or department could not allocate housing space to a stranger in the apartment. If each remaining family member's space was now much higher than the norm, then the institutional owner could resettle the family elsewhere, but only in another separate apartment.[83] Often this was not worth the trouble. In reasonable cases, elaborate petitioning like that in 1947 of the widow Markova of Marx Street was no longer necessary. This was because citizens' rights to "own" the state apartment that they occupied were effectively becoming formalized. But these rights were divided further among those who were registered to live in the dwelling; they were not invested in a single "owner" or pair of "owners." Property law as well as architecture made this truly the separate family apartment.[84]

Security of occupancy, the relative inviolability of private space, and the practice of inheritance are elements of ownership; by the early 1960s the elements were accumulating and consolidating, and extra millions of people were enjoying them in new separate apartments every year. This strengthening of individual ownership coincided with its growing invisibility in public culture. The rhetoric of "ownership" was marginalized during the high Khrushchev era. It seemed harmful in a society that was looking toward communism. This reflected the ideological recalibrations associated with the high point of the Khrushchev years and chimed with the idealism and optimism symbolized by Iurii Gagarin's conquest of space. Yet it was also part of the ambiguous but workable compromises on which the whole Soviet edifice was sustainably constructed.

The exclusion of "ownership" as a positive category in Khrushchev-era rhetoric is illustrated by a case stretching from 1952 to 1957, in which one Comrade Khavkina and her husband acted as viciously aggressive proprietors of "their" state apartment. According to the norm, the apartment was too big for them, and a woman called Lebedeva was allocated space there. One day in 1952 she knocked at the door, ready to move in. The Khavkins would not open up. After a two-hour stand-off, representatives of the housing administration succeeded in allowing Lebedeva to gain access. The three of them now shared what had become a communal apartment. Lebedeva commented that she and Khavkina were both the "ladies of the house" (*khoziaiki*), which suggested common rights of proprietorship. But Khavkina did not see it that way and prevented Lebedeva from properly preparing food, washing clothes, or using the bathroom and even called her a "Soviet prostitute." In November 1956, one Comrade Kurnosova came to live in the apartment. Khavkina treated her in a similarly abusive way, accusing her of being a hooligan, a drunk, a member of the Black Hundreds, and a fascist (suggesting anti-Semitism). Khavkina expressed her sense of ownership in unstable and aggressive ways but still acted like a property owner whose rights had been infringed. That was how the commission (*Obshchestvennaia komissiia*) charged with investigating the case saw it, concluding in April 1957 that Khavkina had behaved "like an old house-owner." Such behavior was thus anachronistic; it was deemed prerevolutionary. The report defined the opposing qualities, suitable for a Soviet citizen, as the ability to "respect human characteristics and observe normal mutual relations."[85]

Such a criticism of "private" property and proprietorial attitudes was more frequently expressed in official and popular discourse by the end of the 1950s and the start of the 1960s. D. Ia. Buriak, the chief economist of the Leningrad Housing Planning (Lenzhilproekt) Institute argued in 1960 that, still, "the obstacles of private property constrain the possibilities of ordered town planning."[86] Mislabeling personal property as "private" gave a brief rhetorical intensity to his professional quest to craft proto-communism. A member of the public, L. G. Pokrovskaia, wrote in a letter to architects the same year that private gardens, which might have been attached to individual houses or indeed to dachas, were "terribly evil [. . .] kulak-like."[87] The same point underwrote the comment of a legal scholar in 1962: "private-property [*chastnosobstvennicheskie*] tendencies are especially intolerable in modern conditions, when the basic direction of ideological work is . . . building communism."[88]

No real breach divided a public culture that condemned mentalities of ownership from an urban housing economy that encouraged them. The rhetorical conventions of Stalinism had always propagated the notion that a citizen should look after his housing space, as well as the areas of common use that surrounded it. This approach persisted during the Khrushchev era, but for those city dwellers who lived in the new housing, it now took on a particular focus. The microdistrict was the communally inspired setting in which the possibility of individual ownership had reached its highest level. Similarly, the public culture of the collective became more vivid just as private life was expanding. The power of the collective was present in the communal and state management structures of the urban microdistrict, which had some invasive potential over the home. Personal life and collective life were thus not considered separate during these years but, as Susan Reid has shown, "part of a continuum: the boundaries were supposed to be transparent and permeable."[89] Features of an enclosed domestic life existed somewhere on this continuum, but they were subject to particular intrusions and pressures. Likewise, the elements of ownership of state housing were divided. Some elements were held by the occupiers of the apartment, others were controlled by the agencies of the state. Yet even at the peak of Khrushchevian proto-communism, the trend was unmistakable. On the continuum of property relations, the place of the individual was becoming more favorable.

The Link to Welfare—Rights and Surveillance

Between 1944 and 1964, therefore, the sum of individual ownership increased. As a general trend more citizens possessed more elements of ownership, creating a range of distinctively Soviet forms of individual property. Citizens' property rights grew, while the standard of living of the Soviet population as a whole improved. As the societal sum of individual ownership increased, so did the volume of welfare provision. Since the revolution of 1917, property had been transformed from a profit-generating commodity into a welfare good. While housing space was held by citizens on increasingly secure terms, their access to it derived from mechanisms of state welfare (with its deliberate incorporation of types of citizen autonomy). The nexus between property and welfare grew tighter during the Khrushchev era. Rights lay at the center of this nexus. Not only were property rights absolutely linked to welfare rights, they were almost the same thing.

The origins of the welfare-property nexus went back to the revolution, and more recently to late Stalinism, when beneficence unevenly and uncertainly overtook sacrifice as the motor of housing policy. But the nexus only tightened when it was characterized by rights that citizens could actually exercise rather than merely express. Rights were embedded into law and rhetoric under Stalin, especially in the 1936 constitution and with greater discursive frequency as a result of the experience of the war, but they did not exist as practically useful tools. Quite the contrary. If they were to act in such a way—as real things—rather than as just the symbols of empty rhetoric, rights required the end of arbitrary rule, or at least its minimization. This crucial step could only accompany the end of Stalinism as a full system, which broadly coincided with the four years following the death of Stalin. While aspects of the housing program date from the 1940s, when beneficence had started to replace sacrifice as the basis of policy, the rights on which the program ultimately depended could only emerge from the mid-1950s. In other words, rights began to take hold when the polity as a whole was moving away from arbitrariness, radical unpredictability, and acute personal insecurity, and when the housing economy was starting to experience greatly increased volumes of construction and the entrenchment of rational mechanisms of policy and technique.

But these rights gained greater substance during the height of the Khrushchev era, when the aspiration of paradise became the leading impetus behind the program. Some scholars have seen a renewed and even expanded totalitarianism in Khrushchev's visions of paradise. The new microdistricts, for example, contained novel structures of mutual surveillance. Their invasive implications are easy to exaggerate and were of secondary importance, however. The shift to paradise had a more significant result than this. It was the desire to create paradise—defined by plenty, equality, and proto-communist consciousness—that assured the great extent of Khrushchevian construction, demanded the relative rationality that underpinned its distribution, and increased the security with which it was "owned" by its occupiers, though it also exacerbated the failures of central planning on which the whole project was based. The nexus of property and welfare rights locked together in the shadow of Khrushchev's would-be paradise.

In general terms, property rights and property relations have a direct impact on the welfare of a population. All postwar welfare states—that is, the capitalist democracies of the West—manipulated property in the formulation of their housing programs. Trade-offs took place, most simply, between private owners and state tenants, in which taxation and urban planning encroached on the rights of owners in order to secure the rights of tenants. While property owners derived other social advantages from living in a welfare state, their crude material interests were hardly coincidental with those of welfare claimants—indeed, they were often antithetical. In the postwar Soviet Union, with its socialist political economy, property rights and welfare rights generally increased within an intertwined trajectory, in contrast to the West where the two sets of rights could not by definition increase in the same direction or at the same pace. By the high Khrushchev era, this trajectory was explicitly directed at paradise. During this last attempt to remake the Soviet person in the early 1960s, principles of individual ownership were entirely consistent with communist morality, because individual property rights and social welfare were so tightly wound together.

The Soviet urban housing economy offered universal rights and was constructed in such a way as to distribute housing space in a generally equal way. In the welfare states of the West, only a very limited number of benefits were universal; typically they were associated with children and health.[90] To make the point reductively but basically accurately, welfare states provided housing only for those citizens who were unable to obtain comparable housing conditions with private resources; the means tests varied in severity but often maintained high thresholds. For most people, housing distribution was regulated by a market that was entirely insensitive to equal outcomes. But constant redistributions still took place, according to which the tax system effectively made minor reductions in the property rights of private owners in order to increase the welfare rights of state tenants.[91] This minority lived in housing estates that, by the early 1960s, had become dominated by problems associated with poverty. The tenants had rights of possession of variable force, but none of ownership. Rights were simply not distributed in this way, and those citizens who lived in state housing lacked the political strength to push for such a switch. The relationship between property and welfare rights was not quite a zero-sum game, but the two sets of rights certainly traveled in different directions.

In the USSR the principle was completely different, for welfare and property rights were intertwined and effectively worked in the same way for everybody. Welfare rights extended to all, even in terms of housing. As the Khrushchev era progressed, it became increasingly possible to talk meaningfully of a general system of rights, or at least of aspects of such a system. In terms of housing, people formally had the right to a separate family apartment (or to a place on an equitably regulated queue for such an apartment), and construction was so extensive that the practical results yielded by this right were not fictional. This was in direct contradistinction to late Stalinism. The war changed people's conceptions of their rights and the perceptions of some officials about how society should be governed; it thus generated a discourse of rights and entitlement. But those "rights" existed only as words. It is impossible to prove their empirical reality.[92] Late Stalinist rule never lost its repressive instincts and remained in essence arbitrary.[93] The mildly beneficent late Stalinist urban housing economy had most meaningfully been structured by a discourse of gratitude and gift. People were forced to fall back on patronage and, at least until the mid-1950s, continued to argue that misfortune was a result of lack of justice rather than of rights abused.

On the night of 12 March 1954, for example, M. V. Mal'tinskii, a citizen of Minsk, turned up at the doors of the Belorussian State Theatre of Opera and Ballet. Inside, Maksim Saburov, the chairman of Gosplan and the city's representative in the Supreme Soviet, was due to give a speech. Mal'tinskii was grasping a letter that outlined the housing situation that was afflicting his life, and which he hoped to press in person on his deputy. Instead, he had to hand his letter to a duty cleaner; nobody else would take it. Mal'tinksii saw her give it to a militia officer, who was standing on the threshold of the room where Saburov was speaking. This was the pointless fate of yet another of his letters to yet another substantial organization or senior official. Mal'tinskii had suffered serious injuries during the war, which made it desperately difficult for him to walk up to his fifth-floor apartment. He was a well-informed citizen, aware of the law and writing to all the right places, but more than a year after Stalin's death, he still wrote, "Giving me a room on the fifth floor is unfair. With will, it could be possible to give me a room in this house on a low floor. . . . I pressingly ask . . . I ask you, help me." In a subsequent letter to Saburov he stated, "only your strict instruction will stop my torture."[94] Mal'tinksii's frame of reference, when he had reached bottom, was bound by an arbitrary conception of justice, not of rights.[95]

Stopping "torture" in the urban housing economy by creating rights was an explicit policy during the Khrushchev era. The combination of the July 1957 decree and the third party program enshrined the principle that every family had the right to a separate apartment, and the reality of mass construction gave some meaning to families' expectations. This was not just a matter of mass construction but of its equal distribution. Organs of government self-consciously modified their relationship to those who were queuing for new housing and those who had recently received it. Crucially, a new system of appeal was instituted, making the distribution and construction authorities more accountable to new residents, and making more than a token shift toward the obtaining of housing on the basis of rights (in theory, practice and discourse) rather than on gratitude.[96]

"Property rights" did not create an autonomous class of property owners; these rights depended on the system's constant willingness, which it could withdraw or modify, to tolerate autonomous actions by individual citizens. Much of the state operated from within society; the second economy and the official economy depended completely on each other; the top 1 percent and the rest were bound not in a contract as such but, in the housing economy, by a shared experience of property rights (though the very apex, fannng off from the central committee, had a different set of privileges). Welfare rights, within the realm of urban housing, were not something that flowed from an explicit or implicit social contract between "classes" or between rulers and ruled but were entirely connected to the indispensable exercise of ownership. A state tenant's "ownership" was governed by his tenancy agreement. The same document activated his welfare entitlement from the housing administration of the soviet or department that held the formal title. A public information source explained in 1963, "rights and duties are defined in the tenancy contract. . . . Having signed the contract, the tenant knows that he can demand from the house management [the exercise] of whatever duties are invested in it for the use of the housing space."[97]

The universality of welfare and property rights had totalizing aspects. Inside housing districts, the interests and competences of the housing administrations increased beyond what was practically necessary. In July 1963 the Moscow Soviet Executive Committee and the Moscow City Soviet of Trade Unions passed a resolution about "Health Day," in which ZhEKi were to play an important role, alongside other organizations, in "propagandizing medical and hygiene knowledge among the population."[98] The way in which the mass construction program operated, with its intense systemic obsession with economy, was a force for surveillance in itself. At its most banal, the state peered into citizens' underwear drawers, investigating in 1959 the most efficient way for citizens to store different types of clothing and kitchen items.[99] Regardless of its benign or malign effects, this was a particular trend and can be associated with a broadened conspectus of surveillance.

Surveillance seems to fit urban housing and the organizations that administered it more tightly inside a matrix of welfare provision. It sounds like the consolidation of a welfare-state bureaucracy that became more effective, and thus more intrusive, under Khrushchev than it had been under Stalin. All post-1945 urban housing programs required this type of bureaucratic surveillance, but in the Soviet Union, unlike the welfare states, surveillance was an aim of housing policy as well as a necessary mechanism for its fulfillment. Oleg Kharkhordin also emphasizes the power of surveillance outside its usual penal context, but in a different way, and with sometimes brilliant conceptual originality, in analyzing the status and interplay of individual and collective during the length of Soviet history. Yet by the time his survey reaches the Khrushchev era, his reliance on published sources and analysis of discourse generate conclusions that are inconsistent with a broader evidential and methodological approach. From his reading of Khrushchev-era official documents, Kharkhordin argues that "the reforms associated with Khrushchev's name aimed at heightening the collectivization of life to the utmost," that they aimed to establish newly extensive and intensive "mutual surveillance," in which (workplace) collectives of citizens were utterly pervasive, and membership of them effectively compulsory. This is how he describes the effect of the people's patrols (druzhiny): "they were the people policing itself, and thus escape was hardly possible from their omniscient gaze and omnipresent power."[100]

This contention, together with Kharkhordin's general argument that the Khrushchev era was the Soviet Union's peak of "totalitarian" surveillance, are scarcely possible to sustain. No historian has uncovered the evidence to make credible claims about the significance of druzhiny to the era's "totalitarian" design. Conceptually, moreover, the claim does not accurately represent the incentives that drove people during the contrasting eras of Stalinism and post-Stalinism.[101] While it is possible to exaggerate the extent of mutual surveillance in the 1930s, life and death incentives existed, at certain times and in certain places, for people to spy on and betray their neighbors and colleagues. Aggressive participation in Khrushchev-era druzhiny, though entirely explicable in terms of universal desires to accumulate moments of power, to put down others, to pry and gossip, was driven by much weaker forces than the first-rank incentives of protecting self and family, defending career, and acquiring important items of consumption that prompted popular acts of surveillance and denunciation in the morally disrupted crucible of Stalinism. It was therefore likely to be much less widespread and effective.

True, other legislation intruded on people's everyday lives, such as the dronery law that defined appropriate Soviet behavior and condemned apparent parasites. The revamped comrades' courts were another such example. Little historical research, however, has been completed on the overall extent of patrol druzhiny, the actual work they did and the motives of their members. Generalizing about their real power is a hazardous enterprise. Indeed, such patrols were only one form of popular mobilization. Local housing administrations encouraged voluntary, socially minded activity in more practical types of druzhiny, whose functions were exclusively connected with repair and maintenance, and which might well have been more widespread during the peak of Khrushchevian voluntary activity than the subpolice groups on which Kharkhordin's analysis focuses. They certainly better exemplify the connections between state power and citizen autonomy, and between property and welfare, that have been documented in the present study. Many more people's lives were affected by another surveillance mechanism—the propiska, which connected property, surveillance, and welfare. A propiska expressed a person's right to inhabit a dwelling, magnified the capacity of housing administrations and police actively to keep track of residents, and assured residents access to a range of welfare services.

The propiska regime was an instrument of official surveillance, but it was also a crude mechanism for regulating housing conditions, for checks and controls acted not just on the citizen but also on housing space.[102] Possessing propiska, moreover, a citizen had the right to demand something from his local housing administration. The administration, backed up by militia and courts, was legally obliged to protect the citizen's access to that particular space. If the space disappeared (if the building within which it was located became uninhabitable, say), then the citizen had the right for that space to be replaced with something comparable. The propiska regime brought together property rights, welfare rights, and the intrusive bureaucratic gaze; it also exemplified the web of bureaucratic ties between state agencies, such as raion housing administrations and local police stations, which citizens had to penetrate in order to get what they wanted.

In September 1952 Liudmila Levina was in trouble, looking at this web and unable to negotiate it. She was a young student at the First Moscow Pedagogical College. Until 1950, when they moved to Sakhalin for a fixed three-year term, she had lived with her mother at Meshchanskaia Street in Moscow. In January 1952, however, Levina's mother died, and she came back to live with her only surviving—but not close—relative, a Muscovite aunt. The household she joined consisted of the aunt, her three children, and their grandfather. Levina obtained the consent of aunt and grandfather and applied for her propiska there, but the housing administration refused it on the grounds that as the building was undergoing capital repair, sooner or later the family would have to move out temporarily, and the housing administration would then become responsible for finding comparable space for her during that interim. She insisted that she could stay with friends from her college during the interval, but the officials at the administration were adamant.[103] Welfare rights were a tenuous concept during late Stalinism, and the actual operations of housing administrations were often arbitrary, repressive, and poverty-inducing, but Levina's propiska would give her a formal relationship with the raion soviet based on a rights-based "welfare" entitlement to housing. Her protestations of future self-help were irrelevant because she would have inalienable legal rights. Given the extent of the housing shortage, the raion soviet wanted to ration the numbers of citizens with whom it had such a relationship.

This created a paradox, because the possession of welfare rights as they applied to housing, and as they were expressed within the rubric of propiska, seemed to be a privilege that a local soviet could dispense. Yet the governing motif of beneficence makes sense of the paradox during late Stalinism; limited rights were things for which citizens were effectively obliged to express gratitude and humbleness if party-government awarded them. Late Stalinist rights were thus figments of legal formality and political discourse rather than valid practical categories, but they were a crucial jurisprudential basis for much more substantial post-Stalin developments. The bureaucracy was, moreover, capable of interpreting the rules in particularly cruel ways, not least because of the pressure the housing shortage placed upon its officials. The inflexible application of propiska regulations, formally on the grounds of welfare considerations, could lead to brutal outcomes.

In September 1951 V. M. Dubrovskaia was an engineer-economist in one of the main administrations of the Ministry of Light Industry (USSR) in Moscow, where she had been working for two years. She lived with a female relative on the Kropotkinskaia embankment, where she had with "great difficulty" obtained a temporary propiska. The militia refused to renew it on the grounds that her workplace would not be able to offer her any spare housing space in the foreseeable future. High-level endorsement from the deputy minister of light industry apparently did Dubrovskaia little good. The militia now prevented her from staying with her relative, and she was forced to appeal to colleagues on a night-by-night basis to give her a place under their roofs. She continued working at the main administration, but its housing office could not promise her a room soon, and her only chance of renewing the propiska was through petition to high authority (she wrote to Kosygin).[104] Such a rigid interpretation of the rules aggressively swept away any vestige of personally autonomous status for Dubrovskaia within the city's housing economy; it was the consequence of a welfare authoritarianism in which the system seemed blind to the subjective outcome. The morally neutral enforcement of rules is a principle of all bureaucracies, but an additional explanatory factor for Dubrovskaia's plight is the specific context of urban late Stalinism: the extreme housing shortage, the residual regulatory chaos, and the purposeful or incidental cruelties of local bureaucracy.[105]

By the late 1950s, when the housing shortage, though serious, was receding, and the postwar emergency had demonstrably passed, space existed in which the bureaucracy that governed the urban housing economy could better breathe. This was the time in which housing policy joined the new route to communism, with the party-government's promise to end the housing shortage by 1969. Ending the shortage was effectively defined as fulfilling the right of every family to have its own separate apartment. The language of rights and their testable practice now explicitly governed the relationship between the citizen and the local housing administration. Yet propiska rules still produced consequences that were inconsistent with a coherent system of rights. While the rights that Levina had been denied in 1952 were now more widely shared (and existed inside a complex of other, newer citizen rights within the urban housing economy), propiska regulations persisted in delivering their problematic outcomes. As Dubrovskaia had experienced, the flip side of the propiska regime's desire to control was its mission to check, and by the end of the 1950s, the results of this were less arbitrary, but still ambiguous.

When propiska rules were tightened at the peak of the Khrushchev era, focus was lent to property rights, and to welfare rights, too. Stricter policing of citizens' propiska documents (the relevant stamp in the internal passport) reduced the number of criminal infractions, and expulsions caused the population of Moscow to fall by ten thousand in the first half of 1958. This might seem to support Kharkhordin's reading of the Khrushchev era. Yet the expellees were often the victims not just of the apparently totalizing ambitions of the officials who ran the housing economy but also of the more prosaically economic interests of the industrial managers for whom they might be working in Moscow. The discovery of infringements of propiska regulations at industrial enterprises was in some cases an exposure of worker exploitation. At the end of summer 1958, it was reported that a leading manager in Moscow's Gidromontazh trust was employing thirteen workers who did not have a propiska, accommodating them in barely habitable conditions.[106] Police investigations found that at the well-known Moscow Electrode Plant, twenty-seven workers, in-migrants from various regions of the country, were living in the enterprise's housing without a propiska.[107] In 1963 further drives to investigate passport abuses revealed similar cases within ZhEKi themselves. Comrade Simoian, the head of ZhEK number 1 in Kirovskii raion in Moscow took on workers illegally and unofficially allocated them housing in basements, which were by then considered uninhabitable: "Despite repeated warnings, comrade Simoian not only did not take measures to dismiss and evict those citizens illegally employed but did not stop similar practices involving a range of workers." Meanwhile, in October 1961, the head of ZhEK number 22 in Moscow's Frunzenskii raion employed as stokers three people who had abandoned their collective farm in Smolensk oblast' and allowed them to live in the boiler room.[108]

People's access to housing depended on their propiska, from which they derived some of their property and welfare rights. Lacking a propiska, these illegal in-migrants to Moscow did not enjoy the associated rights to which it gave rise. When the police or housing administration authorities uncovered the absence of a propiska and eliminated a particular set of unspeakable working and housing conditions, they did not have an obligation of welfare toward the "victim," precisely because he had no propiska (though this obligation existed elsewhere in jurisprudence and in the bureaucracy). Those boiler workers from Smolensk thus experienced a triple misfortune, losing job, housing space, and city of residence. The propiska regime showed how property and welfare rights were connected but also revealed some of the inconsistencies that undermined the system of rights. The propiska's exclusionary and exclusive characteristics reduced the universality of housing rights that were the apparent mark of the Soviet system. Meanwhile, the duo of workplace management and trade union determined many people's access to the triad of employment, housing, and thus, propiska, which expanded the potential for patronage ties. When these ties were not systemically regularized, as the party-government could hardly achieve even in the less arbitrary years of Khrushchev, rights were further diluted with privileges.

These qualifications are added in an effort to lend realism to the picture, rather than to disorder its composition. The argument remains—to a unique degree, welfare rights clarified and consolidated property rights in the Soviet Union. This was the nexus of property and welfare that did not exist in (capitalist) welfare states. It was the defining conceptual feature of the Soviet urban housing experiment between 1944 and 1964.

Excavating the urban property relations of the period from 1944 to 1964, which have lain hidden under other historiographical priorities and the reflex interpretation that the Bolsheviks abolished all forms of individual ownership of housing, helps to explain both the extent of housing construction and the particular experience of Soviet citizens. Study of the nature of individual ownership provides additional evidence for the existence of a positive citizen autonomy, according to which Soviet citizens acting in the urban housing economy did not always resist the state—although they sometimes did—but more frequently cooperated in a mutually advantageous project. By the Khrushchev era, the acquisition of a decisive number of the elements of ownership had made Soviet citizens not an autonomous class of property owners, masters of their own fate and major players in a civil society that did not exist in the Western sense, but substantial figures in a thoroughgoing welfare system. And property rights were closely tied to welfare rights. Even the surveillance functions of welfare, particularly pervasive as they were, were bound up with rights. Comparative history and longer-term perspectives sharpen the distinctiveness of this nexus of property and welfare. They bring into precise relief a particularly unexpected explanation of the Soviet urban housing program: that, in Soviet cities, private property had been abolished but the imperative of individual ownership was utterly integral to policy, and life.

Paradise in Grey

> Citizens of the USSR have the right to housing.
>
> —Constitution (Fundamental Law) of the USSR, 1977, article 44

On 14 October 1964, the day Khrushchev fell from power, several thousand Soviet citizens obtained new apartments.[1] Thousands more moved in the following day, the day after that, and every future day of Soviet rule. This was the result of a substantial reorientation in housing policy, which derived not just from the post-Stalin settlement but also from the Great Fatherland War. On 14 October 1964, those thousands of citizens were taking part in the most large-scale and intensive state housing program of the period. Yet the particularity of their experience was crucially conditioned by the possibility of exercising an individual form of ownership over their housing space. Their very particular property rights were powerfully reinforced by a related set of welfare rights. This nexus of property and welfare was one of the causes of the Soviet Union's largely unthreatened endurance in the twenty-seven years that followed Khrushchev's fall.

In considering the origins of the housing program, historians have tended to focus on raw construction figures and their immediate social impact. They have therefore explained the onset of the program as a product of the shift in policy priorities that followed Stalin's death. Such an approach reinforces the paradigmatic separation between the late Stalinist and post-Stalin eras. By studying the mass construction that began in the mid-1950s in light of the reconstruction that dates from the mid-1940s, however, a more complex explanation can be set out. This explanation also better fits the general tendency of recent scholarship to draw out the continuities in Soviet life across 1953.

The argument of this book is that the mass destruction wrought by the war forced citizens and officials to interact in the implementation of a more substantial housing policy than the Soviet Union had hitherto seen. During late Stalinist reconstruction, output was high in comparison with the 1930s, though still much lower than it would be a decade later; it was simultaneously unprecedented and dreadfully inadequate. Tens of millions of people continued to languish in terrible conditions. The immediate postwar era was important, therefore, not so much for increased construction of housing (though this was also a fact) but for the assembly of many of the aspects of a latent proto-program. This was a time of crucial developments in policy, administration, and technology that were very unevenly implemented, and of groundbreaking professional and political discussions that foreshadowed and enabled later action. In the early 1950s, after officials recognized anew the scale of the postwar housing emergency, these developments accelerated, forming the essential foundation of the Khrushchev-era program. In addition, Stalinism bequeathed a complex Soviet attitude to concepts of separateness and communality. It encouraged the aspiration to have a separate home and at critical moments demanded that local populations participate in the maintenance of the districts where they lived. The semi-enclosed nature of family life, wrought by the proliferation of separate apartments in a context of simultaneous local mobilization, was not, therefore, exactly a Khrushchevian innovation. Yet Stalinism had another, objectively malign influence. The economic levers that controlled the housing program were never really de-Stalinized; instead, they continued to be driven by highly overcentralized planning and giantist targets.

As stated most concisely in the keynote housing decree of July 1957, the aim of Khrushchev's housing policy focused purely on output, in the first instance, radically expanding construction in order to eliminate the housing shortage within a dozen years. Despite many imperfections, the result was a considerable overall rise in standards of living and a bolstering of equality. But the apparently rational aim of the 1957 decree, measured with material precision, was hindered by the Stalinist dynamics of its delivery. These dynamics overemphasized housing space itself at the expense of all other construction categories, including essential local infrastructure. The target-induced requirement to build so quickly also reduced the quality of the completed dwellings. During the build-up to the twenty-second congress in 1961, moreover, the aim of housing policy broadened. It should now have the potential to transform people's consciousness. Policy demanded the introduction of elaborate structures of communality into the new urban arena of the mikroraion. Although additional research is required into the everyday operation of these systems, they were for a time an essential counterpoint to the apparently enclosed nature of family life in the new separate apartments.

The enormous volume of construction, and the particularities of its ideological foundations, make much more sense from inside a lengthened chronology. Yet for all its origins in wartime and late Stalinism, the mass housing program was decisively a Khrushchev-era phenomenon. Stalin would never have committed the extensive resources that the program required because his rule was based on fundamentally different principles. While a change took place during and after the war in the way that a growing number of enlightened officials treated the basic aspirations of the population, there is no evidence that their concerns were shared by Stalin, who continued to direct policy. More generally, the meaningful exercise of rights was absent during late Stalinism; the actions of party-government were admittedly more beneficent than before, but they were still capricious and required the population's ritualistic gratitude. Under Khrushchev, by contrast, the occupancy of a separate family apartment, accessible via an orderly and accountable queuing system, became a right.

These rights to improved housing were entirely wrapped up in property relations. Private property was abolished in 1917, but forms of individual ownership survived, thanks to multiple tenures and the favorable terms on which state tenants occupied their housing space. These forms of ownership were strengthened as a consequence of the Great Fatherland War: reconstruction was partly driven forward by the expansion in the stock of personal property, while people related to the possession of their housing with more determination, or defensiveness, a sentiment that some officials were prepared to protect and nurture. Under Khrushchev, people's occupancy of state apartments on the basis of rights become so secure as to amount to a substantive form of ownership, while the phasing out of personal property in favor of cooperatives actually added to the total of individual ownership in the urban housing economy. Yet the mechanisms that governed the operation of the urban housing fund were by the peak of the Khrushchev era those of a universalizing and embracing system of welfare. Welfare rights and property rights made for an internally consistent form of social organization, each strengthening the other, in a nexus that was unique to the USSR. For instance, the registration system of propiska gave citizens the right to have residency at an address and to receive welfare goods from the local housing administration; it also manifested the surveillance function of a maximalist welfare system.

People's capacity to exercise forms of individual ownership of their own housing space had crucial implications. The resulting property relations help to explain the extent of construction. They conditioned people's relationship with their housing. But they were also emblematic of one of the main driving forces of the urban housing economy: citizen autonomy and initiative. To a major extent, the Soviet people made their own housing program. The system always depended on the energies of those who built their own houses, or paid off state credits, or used their savings in cooperatives, or took risks to exchange their apartments, or moved to inhospitable regions in return for a better salary and a shorter housing queue. Most often, the otherwise centrally rigid program was specifically designed to incorporate these energies. This was the essential workable paradox at the heart of the centrally planned economy as it related to urban housing.

So what were the longer-term consequences of the program? How did life evolve for those who obtained new apartments on Khrushchev's last day in power? What did it look like ten or twenty years after? The archival research for this book ends in 1964. But some preliminary comments on later developments help to clarify what had gone before. According to published figures, urban construction output continued to grow until the early 1970s, though without repeating its earlier giant strides, and annual output stabilized thereafter at about 75 million square meters through to the mid-1980s.[2]

By 1964 the direction of the urban housing economy had been set and would not change. This was true not only of the volume of construction but also of patterns of ownership and general social impact. Even apparent changes such as the considerable expansion in cooperative housing during the 1970s and 1980s reflected the operation of the system that had been set up under Khrushchev. A 1979 public information booklet for foreign readership described the mechanics of Soviet housing in ways that would have been entirely recognizable fifteen years earlier.[3] Those famous districts of five-story apartment houses were an instantly familiar trace of the Khrushchev era, but each successive model of apartment block, growing taller and sometimes wider, was also a direct consequence of the system that developed between 1944 and 1964.[4]

Something was lost from the urban housing program after its idealistic peak in the early 1960s. Elements of a futuristic urbanism persisted in public culture—but only for a time—and were no longer expressed in communist terms. Georgii Natanson, in his 1968 film *Once More in Love*, depicts a dynamic Moscow, with its pulsing highways, space-age nightclubs, and international modernist interiors. More widely, goals of material advance remained, and a renewed beneficence guided policy makers and planners. Housing construction was considerable, yet it no longer induced a heady feel or seemed inspired by a utopian vision. Partly thanks to continued improvements in standardization, capital investment in housing dropped in proportionate terms.[5] Life in mikroraiony changed, and future historians will measure the extent of social provision within them in the 1970s and 1980s. An impressionistic view suggests, however, that locally integrated networks of kindergartens, schools, and polyclinics formed one of the Soviet system's advanced achievements in comparison with many parts of the West. The eclipse of paradise by the eternal beneficence of developed socialism meant that urban housing and the social infrastructure that surrounded it were measured only in terms of material improvement, without reference to their capacity to alter human behavior and craft communism. In Daneliia's 1979 film *Autumn Marathon* (*Osennii marafon*), the new housing districts of Leningrad are echoing, deserted spaces, a contrasting vision to his film of sixteen years earlier, *I Walk around Moscow* (*Ia shagaiu po Moskve*, 1963), where the city is vigorously modern, not tired. It is likely that neighborliness and spontaneous mutual dependence between urban dwellers remained considerable, especially in comparative international terms. Yet the whole infrastructure of urban life, with housing at its center, seems to have lacked the energy and possibility that existed in the early 1960s.

Foreign visitors to post-Khrushchev Soviet cities and to similar cities in other socialist countries employed recurring tropes of unsightliness, greyness, and monotony in their descriptions. For the American journalist Hedrick Smith, resident in the Soviet Union between 1971 and 1974, Moscow had "a drab, grey visage." John Simpson, a BBC journalist, first came to Moscow in 1978 and later recalled, "Even in the summer sunshine it looked crude and forbidding. . . . The apartment blocks of brown brick were huge and undifferentiated, the shops carried no name other than their function. . . . All the fine detail, all the decoration, all the attraction of existence seemed to have been stripped away here . . . this first sight of it was gloomy and depressing." Colin Thubron, who traveled across European Russia in the early 1980s, described Moscow's apartment blocks as having "desolate similitude." In Malcolm Bradbury's novel *Rates of Exchange* (1983), a closely observed satire of an archetypal Eastern European socialist city, a visiting academic "looks out at the apartments, which look duller from the ground than from the air. Dust blows between the blocks; there is the Eastern European spectacle of much vacant open space." Everything is desolate and on a scale little fit for human living: "Few cars are parked here, few people walk, no children play; no shops are visible, and on the ends of the apartments are great maps of the complex for the guidance of the residents." Margaret Thatcher noted that her famous walkabout in Moscow in March 1987 was around "a bleak suburb"; John Simpson watched her and mentioned "a dreary block of flats."[6]

Novelists who wrote about espionage found the contrast with Western urban life an obvious background for their intriguers and fellow travelers. In the 1970s Graham Greene described an English defector in Moscow: "From the window on the twelfth floor of the great grey building, Castle could see the red star over the university. There was a certain beauty in the view as there is in all cities at night. Only the daylight was drab." During perestroika, John le Carré wrote of an English Russophile's glimpse of "the sad flatland of Moscow's outskirts."[7]

Analogous observations can be found for the earlier period. But their extent and repetitiousness—and their counterparts, to some extent, in Soviet cultural production—suggest that by the 1970s something had changed. In turn, they clarify the real-time consequences of the urban housing program of the period 1944–1964. They reinforce the argument made in this book that the housing program was driven by the powerful energies of its time: first, the emergency imperatives associated with reconstruction, then the determination to improve popular conditions on a systematic and mass scale, and finally the idealized visions of Khrushchev's short-lived and luckless march to communism. In the years of late socialism that followed, it seems likely that what was left was an undramatic beneficence, modulated by "cultured" qualities and a rhetoric of fair equality, expressed in socialist terms. In Riazanov's film *Garazh* (1979), at a meeting of a garage cooperative at which members must be ejected, one of the shareholders ambiguously describes the process as "worse than the market," but it is the chairwoman who loses her position, and the decision is approved by lot. Yet for all its comic qualities, the film is deliberately claustrophobic. Paradise had gone for good.

This book began with the paradox that the party-government in the USSR combined violence and welfare inside a coherent but also evolving system. Mass terror in its multiple guises was the bottom line of Soviet history. For Solzhenitsyn the Great Terror was the Soviet Union under maximum magnification, at sharpest clarity. He was surely right for the period before 1941. But there were several Soviet Unions, and it plays hooliganism with metaphors to argue that the USSR and Nazi

Germany were two sides of the same coin. At the simplest level of chronology, the Great Fatherland War created the basis of a highly modified Soviet system, and in 1953 the shift to a substantially new kind of polity really began. The post-Stalin system was infused with some, but only some, of Stalinism's characteristics. It was also partly defined by the common European historical inheritance. What emerged was a vastly less desirable variant than capitalist democracy, though one that was indefinitely viable. The history of the urban housing program from the 1940s to the 1960s illustrates how this viability took hold: how the Soviet Union survived the catastrophic destruction of the war, and then the death of Stalin.

An extraordinary achievement by determined people, the program was the red star in the elaborate social system of the post-Stalin age. It was one of the great social reforms of modern European history. Yet it was built amid the rust and ashes that were the Soviet Union's other signal products.

Introduction—Limits of Sacrifice

1. For the story of the activist and the geography of Moscow's killing grounds, see Timothy J. Colton, *Moscow: Governing the Socialist Metropolis*, 286, 588, and David Remnick, *Lenin's Tomb: The Last Days of the Soviet Empire*, 136–40. The epigraphs are from Aleksandr Solzhenitsyn, *Sobranie sochinenii*, vol. 5, *Arkhipelag Gulag, 1918–1956: opyt khudozhestvennogo issledovaniia I-II*, 98; N. S. Khrushchev, *Vospominaniia: Vremia, liudi, vlast'*, 1:101. Unless otherwise noted, all translations from the original are my own.

2. Steven A. Barnes, "Soviet Society Confined: The Gulag in the Karaganda Region of Kazakhstan," 31.

3. The two recent studies are Steven E. Harris, "Moving to the Separate Apartment: Building, Distributing, Furnishing, and Living in Urban Housing in Soviet Russia, 1950s–1960s," and Christina Varga-Harris, "Constructing the Soviet Hearth: Home, Citizenship, and Socialism in Russia, 1956–1964." The other full-length treatments of the program were conducted by social scientists. While they were based on very different types of evidence and governed by different scholarly agendas, they are still essential introductions: Timothy Sosnovy, *The Housing Problem in the Soviet Union*; Gregory D. Andrusz, *Housing and Urban Development in the USSR*; Alfred DiMaio, *Soviet Urban Housing: Problems and Policies*. See also the series of articles written by Timothy Sosnovy, Alexander Block, and Henry Morton that are cited in the bibliography. The most distinguished historical study of a cognate phenomenon is Stephen Lovell, *Summerfolk: A History of the Dacha, 1710–2000*. Scholarly articles that address aspects of the program, full-length studies that are primarily concerned with housing in other periods of Soviet history, scholarship that partly intersects with the program, and investigations of property relations are discussed elsewhere in the book and can be found in the bibliography.

4. The Khrushchev era certainly ended with Khrushchev's ousting in 1964, but historians can date it variously from 1953 when Stalin died, from 1955 when Khrushchev became dominant in a collective leadership, from 1956 when he imprinted the epoch with the Secret Speech, or from 1957 when he removed his opponents. Note that the singular of *khrushchevki* is *khrushchevka*.

5. *Dolgie provody*, dir. Kira Muratova.

6. Vladimir Paperny, *Architecture in the Age of Stalin: Culture Two* (written in 1970s).

7. See, for example, *The German Ideology* (1846) and *The Critique of the Gotha Program* (1875).

8. Karl Marx and Friedrich Engels, *The Communist Manifesto*, 235; Friedrich Engels, *The Housing Question*, esp. 36. For the Bolsheviks, see for example, *KPSS v rezoliutsiiakh i resheniiakh s''ezdov, konferentsii i plenumov tsentral'nogo komiteta* (1970), 1:61.

9. V. I. Lenin, *The State and Revolution*, in *Collected Works*, 47 vols, 25:381–492 (434). This is expressed more gently in Lenin, *Will the Bolsheviks Maintain Power?* 63–66. For the early revolution in housing, see, for example, Hubertus F. Jahn, "The Housing Revolution in Petrograd, 1917–1920," 212–27.

10. "Packing in" is a literal rendition of the term of the time, *uplotnenie*.

11. Andrei Ikonnikov, *Russian Architecture of the Soviet Period*, 117–36. For the Narkomfin building, see Victor Buchli, *An Archaeology of Socialism*.

12. *KPSS v rezoliutsiiakh* (1983), 2:90. Similarly, the popularization of the program by Bukharin and Preobrazhenskii in their *ABC of Communism* looked to straightforward material advances: "huge [apartment] houses with all the comforts" or "well-appointed small houses for workers." N. Bukharin and E. Preobrazhenskii, *Azbuka kommunizma: populiarnoe ob''iasnenie programmy rossiiskoi kommunisticheskoi partii bol'shevikov*, 296.

13. The term "personal property" (*lichnaia sobstvennost'*) had an analogue in the Stolypin-era land reforms. This new tenure extended certain rights of land sale and mortgage to peasants but imposed other limits on ownership. More extensive than Soviet personal property, and of course not informed by socialist morality, it was "still far from private right." See George Yaney, *The Urge to Mobilize: Agrarian Reform in Russia, 1861–1930*, 263.

14. Mark Meerovich, by contrast, insists that the housing shortage and thus the communal apartment and the apartment block itself (rather than individual houses) were deliberately used as repressive tools by the regime, rather than being simply the manifestations of the imperative of urgent economy. His wide-ranging analysis is hindered, however, by his narrow empirical base and focus on published decrees, which he frequently interprets as if their implementation precisely reflected their prescripts. See Mark Grigor'evich Meerovich, *Kvadratnye metry, opredeliaiushchie soznanie: Gosudarstvennaia zhilishchnaia politika v SSSR, 1921–1941gg*, 10–11, 115.

15. For economic examples of the failure of housing construction in the 1930s, see R. W. Davies, *Crisis and Progress in the Soviet Economy, 1931–1933*, 470.

16. Sosnovy, *Housing Problem in the Soviet Union*, 276.

17. John Scott, *Behind the Urals: An American Worker in Russia's City of Steel*, 90, 92. His memoirs were first published in 1942.

18. *KPSS v rezoliutsiiakh* (1970) 4:546.

19. Ibid. (1983) 7:75, 77.

20. Calculated from Colton, *Moscow*, 796.

21. *Dom, v kotorom ia zhivu*, dir. Lev Kulidzhanov and Iakov Segel'.

22. Timothy Dunmore pioneered this branch of argumentation when the available documentary base was considerably narrower. See his *Soviet Politics, 1945–1953*.

23. A. A. Danilov and A.V. Pyzhikov, *Rozhdenie sverkhderzhavy: SSSR v pervye poslevoennye gody*.

24. Aleksandr Pyzhikov, *Khrushchevskaia "ottepel'."*

25. Rudol'f Pikhoia, *Moskva, Kreml', Vlast': Sorok let posle voiny, 1945–1985*.

26. Yoram Gorlizki and Oleg Khlevniuk, *Cold Peace: Stalin and the Soviet Ruling Circle, 1945–1953*.

27. Julie Hessler, *A Social History of Soviet Trade: Policy, Retail Practices, and Consumption, 1917–1953*, 297.

28. Ethan Pollock, *Stalin and the Soviet Science Wars*.

29. Alexander Titov, "The 1961 Party Program and the Fate of Khrushchev's Reforms."

30. Andrew Elam Day, "Building Socialism: The Politics of the Soviet Cityscape in the Stalin Era."

31. Elena Zubkova, *Russia after the War: Hopes, Illusions, and Disappointments, 1945–1957*; Mark Edele, "Strange Young Men in Stalin's Moscow: The Birth and Life of the *Stiliagi*, 1945–1953," 37–61; Juliane Fürst, "Prisoners of the Soviet Self? Political Youth Opposition in Late Stalinism," 353–76.

32. All statistics are debated, but this is the lowest probable figure for military and civilian deaths and excludes knock-on demographic effects. See Michael Ellman and S. Maksudov, "Soviet Deaths in the Great Patriotic War: A Note," 671–80. Seventeen hundred towns and seventy thousand villages are the most commonly cited figures for destroyed settlements.

33. Mark Edele and Michael Geyer, "States of Exception: The Nazi–Soviet War as a System of Violence," 345–95 (380).

34. Amir Weiner, *Making Sense of War: The Second World War and the Fate of the Bolshevik Revolution*; Robert Service, *Stalin: A Biography*, 491. Service argues that late Stalinism, if it really existed, should be traced to the greater rationalization that followed the Terror, from 1938. *Stalin*, 372, 375.

35. Gorlizki and Khlevniuk, *Cold Peace*, 105.

36. Many ordinary people reciprocated and rethought their relationship with power. Some historians have argued that they did so within the language of "entitlement" and even of rights (though rights especially had no real, practical existence during late Stalinism). See, for example, Mark Edele, "Soviet Veterans as an Entitlement Group, 1945–1955," 111–37; Shaun Morcom, "Social Workings of Soviet Power: State-Society Relations in Postwar Russia, 1945–1953."

37. Nancy Condee, "Cultural Codes of the Thaw," 160–76.

38. Stephen V. Bittner, *The Many Lives of Khrushchev's Thaw: Experience and Memory in Moscow's Arbat*; Iurii Aksiutin, *Khrushchevskaia "ottepel'" i obshchestvennye nastroeniia v SSSR 1953–1964gg*.

39. Miriam Dobson also raises a "challenge" to the metaphor, in *Khrushchev's Cold Summer: Gulag Returnees, Crime, and the Fate of Reform after Stalin*, 15.

40. For a discussion of this term, see Polly Jones, "Introduction," in Polly Jones, ed., *The Dilemmas of De-Stalinization: Negotiating Cultural and Social Change in the Khrushchev Era*.

41. Stephen Kotkin, *Magnetic Mountain: Stalinism as a Civilization*, ch. 5.

42. Weiner, *Making Sense of War*, 368.

43. See, for example, Igal Halfin and Jochen Hellbeck, "Rethinking the Stalinist Subject: Stephen Kotkin's *Magnetic Mountain* and the State of Soviet Historical Studies," 456–63.

44. For Fitzpatrick's description of her position vis-à-vis Kotkin and related scholars, see *Tear Off the Masks! Identity and Imposture in Twentieth-Century Russia*, 6–9. She discusses her status as a revisionist and social historian, and her engagement with the totalitarian school in the long run, in "Revisionism in Retrospect: A Personal View," 682–704. Note that several of Fitzpatrick's students have produced dissertations and monographs to which, by topic, this work is particularly closely related: Steven E. Harris, P. Charles Hachten, Stephen V. Bittner, and by period, many others including Julie Hessler and Mark Edele.

45. Sheila Fitzpatrick, *Everyday Stalinism: Ordinary Life in Extraordinary Times, Soviet Russia in the 1930s.*

46. Mark Edele, "Soviet Society, Social Structure and Everyday Life: Major Frameworks Reconsidered," 349–73.

47. Hessler, *Social History of Soviet Trade.*

48. Sarah Davies, *Popular Opinion in Stalin's Russia: Terror, Propaganda, and Dissent, 1934–1941.*

49. Donald Filtzer, *Soviet Workers and Stalinist Industrialization: The Formation of Modern Soviet Production Relations.* See the bibliography for his other works, which elaborate this theme. These have been a very rich secondary source for the present book.

50. Moshe Lewin, *The Making of the Soviet System: Essays in the Social History of Interwar Russia.*

51. Jeffrey Rossman, *Worker Resistance under Stalin: Class and Revolution on the Shop Floor.*

52. For examples of how NEP-era and Stalinist structures of housing management through to 1937 made use of citizen involvement in the running of housing stock, see Yasuhiro Matsui, "Housing Partnerships, ZhAKTy, or Housing Trusts? A Study of Moscow's Housing Management System, 1917–1937," 109–39. For the existence of a "public" of autonomous local residents, see the same author's analysis of local involvement in the running of canteens in a district of Moscow during the 1930s: "Stalinist Public or Communitarian Project? Housing Organizations and Self-Managed Canteens in Moscow's Frunze Raion," 1223–46. These examples are not as deep, as "organic," or as widespread as the trends isolated here from 1944.

53. Cf. Deborah A. Field's argument about the closeness between "state" and "society" during the Khrushchev era, in *Private Life and Communist Morality in Khrushchev's Russia,* 7. See also Mary Fulbrook on the 'honeycomb state' in East Germany, esp. from the 1970s, in *The People's State: East German Society from Hitler to Honecker.*

54. John Barber and Mark Harrison, *The Soviet Home Front: A Social and Economic History of the USSR in World War II.*

55. For a more detailed discussion of patronage ties in Russian and Soviet history, see Geoffrey Hosking, "Patronage and the Russian State," 301–30; Fitzpatrick, *Everyday Stalinism,* 109–14. On *kollektivy* (the collective units, usually formed of workplace colleagues, to which people belonged), see Aleksandr Zinov'ev, *Kommunizm kak real'nost'*; on favors and *blat* (the informal exchange of favors or exercise of "pull"), see Alena Ledeneva, *Russia's Economy of Favours: Blat, Networking, and Informal Exchange.*

56. Jeffrey Brooks, *Thank You, Comrade Stalin! Soviet Public Culture from Revolution to Cold War.*

57. Stephen Kotkin, "Modern Times: The Soviet Union and the Interwar Conjuncture," 111–64. Other dimensions of the modernity paradigm are explored by associated scholars: see Weiner's contributions in Amir Weiner, ed., *Landscaping the Human Garden: Twentieth-Century Population Management in a Comparative Framework*; Peter Holquist, "'Information Is the Alpha and Omega of Our Work': Bolshevik Surveillance in Its Pan-European Context," 415–50.

58. Kotkin, *Magnetic Mountain,* 20. Historians as various as Robert Service, Martin Malia, and Moshe Lewin use "welfare state" to describe the USSR. Fitzpatrick writes uncritically that the "Soviet welfare state" is a "given" in post–1991 historiography. "The Soviet Union in the Twenty-First Century," 63.

59. Asa Briggs, "The Welfare State in Historical Perspective," 18–31 (18).

60. See, for example, Pyzhikov, *Khrushchevskaia "ottepel'," * ch. 4.

61. Götz Aly makes the maximalist case for Third Reich welfare (with welfare in vari-

ous guises partly funded by wartime plunder) in *Hitler's Beneficiaries: Plunder, Racial War, and the Nazi Welfare State.* His case is convincingly dismantled by Adam Tooze, who argues that welfare was far from all-embracing, that the economy was tilted in favor of rearmament throughout much of the 1930s, and that the state's attention to the well-being of its citizens was much lower than Aly suggests. See Tooze, *The Wages of Destruction: The Making and Breaking of the Nazi Economy.* Maria Sophia Quine, meanwhile, characterizes the "welfare state" of Fascist Italy as "overly ambitious and deeply unfocused," distorted by the attempt radically to reduce working-class autonomy. *Italy's Social Revolution: Charity and Welfare from Liberalism to Fascism,* 298 and passim.

62. This view applies to Rodney Lowe, *The Welfare State in Britain since 1945,* 16, and Paul Spicker, *The Welfare State: A General Theory,* 178ff.

63. Claus Offe, *Contradictions of the Welfare State,* 147.

64. In later historiography, the most effective proponent of this view was Martin Malia, *The Soviet Tragedy: A History of Socialism in Russia, 1917–1991.*

65. For example, see the *Problems of Communism* symposium on "Toward a 'Communist Welfare State,'" *Problems of Communism* (1960): 1, with subsequent discussion by correspondence (1960): 3. Note contributions by Nove, Wolfe, de Jouvenal, and Schapiro.

66. Some institutions were in formal terms semi-detached from the "state," like trade unions or professional organizations, but they also owned housing space.

67. On the Khrushchev era, Susan E. Reid has made perhaps the most significant contribution to the study of the domestic interior. Her work in this area includes but is not limited to Susan E. Reid, ed., "Design, Stalin, and the Thaw"; Susan E. Reid, "The Khrushchev Kitchen: Domesticating the Scientific-Technological Revolution," and "Women in the Home."

68. For the problem of "distortion" in an analysis of the limits of archival industrial data in Estonia, see Olaf Mertelsmann, "Was There a Stalinist Industrialization in the Baltic Republics? Estonia—an Example," 151–70 (152–53). For more detail about the problem of statistics, and summaries of ongoing debates for the period before late Stalinism, see S. G. Wheatcroft and R. W. Davies, "The Crooked Mirror of Soviet Economic Statistics," in R. W. Davies, Mark Harrison, and S. G. Wheatcroft, eds., *The Economic Transformation of the Soviet Union, 1913–1945,* 24–37.

1—Reconstruction and Its Legacies, 1944–1950

1. The epigraph is from a letter to Maksim Saburov, in GARF f. 5446, op. 68, d. 5, l. 38.

2. GARF f. A-259, op. 6, d. 55, l. 56. These data, like most in this book, refer to *zhilaia ploshchad'*, the housing space in a dwelling excluding bathroom, kitchen, hallway, and walk-in cupboards. The overall total space is described as *obshchaia ploshchad'.*

3. RGAE f. 1562, op. 14, d. 2767, l. 2.

4. Ibid., d. 2695, l. 2.

5. Ibid., d. 2726, l. 2.

6. GARF f. A-259, op. 6, d. 37, l. 81.

7. Ibid., d. 84, ll. 4, 6, 18, 20.

8. RGAE f. 9432, op. 1, d. 13, l. 73.

9. See, for example, RGAE f. 8627, op. 13, d. 1467, ll. 2–3.

10. Paul W. Ward, *Life in the Soviet Union: Reprinted Articles from the Sun,* 51.

11. Zdeněk Mlynár, *Night Frost in Prague: The End of Humane Socialism,* 10.

12. Report by Australian chargé d'affaires, 6 July 1953, in TNA: PRO: FO 371/106588: 1–2.

13. GARF f. R-5446, op. 85, d. 9, ll. 34, 35.

14. Ibid., d. 15, ll. 10–12. Malenkov was also a deputy chairman of the Council of Ministers (USSR).

15. Ibid., d. 1, l. 132.

16. Gorlizki and Khlevniuk, *Cold Peace*; J. Eric Duskin, *Stalinist Reconstruction and the Confirmation of a New Elite, 1945–1953*, 129–38.

17. TsAGM f. 490, op. 1, d. 49, l. 141.

18. Compare with this the existence of an enlightened officialdom during authoritarian rule at the time of Nicholas I, as described in Richard Wortman, *The Development of Russian Legal Consciousness*; W. Bruce Lincoln, *In the Vanguard of Reform: Russia's Enlightened Bureaucrats, 1825–1861*.

19. The impact on housing was mixed, and the impact in other areas of socioeconomic life sometimes harmful; "suppressing consumption" in response to the 1947 famine was hardly beneficent or enlightened. See Donald Filtzer, "The 1947 Food Crisis and Its Aftermath: Worker and Peasant Consumption in Non-famine Regions of the RSFSR," 343–85 (346).

20. *Vecherniaia Moskva*, 18 May 1945, 3.

21. RGASPI f. 397, op. 2, d. 21, l. 13.

22. The delivery of promises to veterans was sporadic and disappointing, however. See Mark Edele, *Soviet Veterans of the Second World War: A Popular Movement in an Authoritarian Society, 1941–1991*, esp. part 1.

23. GARF f. R-5451, op. 30, d. 462, l. 31.

24. GARF f. A- 259, op. 6, d. 2752, ll. 95–96.

25. E. S. Seniavskaia, *Frontovoe pokolenie: istoriko-psikhologicheskoe issledovanie*; Morcom, "Social Workings"; Mark Edele, "More than just Stalinists: The Political Sentiments of Victors, 1945–1953"; Elena Zubkova, *Obshchestvo i reformy, 1945–1964*.

26. GARF f. R-5446, op. 85, d. 6, l. 46.

27. E. Iu. Zubkova et al., eds., *Sovetskaia zhizn', 1945–1953*, 292 (doc. 92).

28. GARF f. 7860, op. 5, d. 401, ll. 21–24.

29. Zubkova, *Obshchestvo i reformy*.

30. Paul Kesaris, ed., *CIA Research Reports: The Soviet Union, 1946–1976*, reel 1, report 3, 6 January 1947, "Revised Soviet Tactics in International Affairs," 3.

31. Iurii Trifonov, *Studenty*, in *Sobranie sochinenii*, vol. 1.

32. A. S. Kiselev, ed., *Moskva poslevoennaia, 1945–1947: Arkhivnye dokumenty i materialy*, 434 (doc. 113).

33. N. F. Khomutetskii, *Leningrad: ocherk arkhitektury*, 156–58.

34. Richard Davenport-Hines, ed., *Letters from Oxford: Hugh Trevor-Roper to Bernard Berenson*, 236.

35. V. Dudintsev, *Ne khlebom edinym*, *Novyi mir*, 8:31–118, 9:37–118, 10:21–98. Vera Dunham, *In Stalin's Time: Middle-Class Values in Soviet Fiction*.

36. Cynthia V. Hooper, "A Darker 'Big Deal': Concealing Party Crimes in the Post-Second World War Era." Local officials could seek personal profit at the expense of a local population that was lacking in almost everything. Jones, for example, reveals the printing and sale of hundreds of thousands of additional ration cards in Rostov around 1946. Jeffrey W. Jones, "'People without a Definite Occupation': The Illegal Economy and 'Speculators' in Rostov-on-the-Don, 1943–1948," 236–54 (244).

37. For the early planning on prestige cities, see Andrew Day on Stalingrad, in "Building Socialism," and Karl D. Qualls on Sevastopol, in "Raised from Ruins: Restoring

Popular Allegiance through City Planning in Sevastopol, 1943–1954."

38. For the fruits of this, see *Stalingrad: Al'bom dokumental'nykh fotoilliustratsii o gorode-geroe.*

39. GARF f. A-259, op. 6, d. 2751, l. 21.

40. I. V. Stalin, *Sochineniia* 16:18.

41. GARF f. A-259, op. 6, d. 2743, l. 6.

42. A Council of Ministers (RSFSR) decree of November 1948, "On Measures of Help for the Housing-Municipal Economy of the Towns of Kalinin oblast," in ibid., d. 5340, l. 88.

43. Ibid., d. 5341, l. 1.

44. Ibid., d. 5339, l. 54.

45. For Tomsk, ibid., d. 6954, ll. 27–32 (for 1948); for Penza, ibid., d. 5330, ll. 44–45 (1948); for Krasnodar, ibid., d. 6949, ll. 32–34 (1950).

46. Ibid., d. 3136, l. 76.

47. This is one of the core arguments of Gorlizki and Khlevniuk, *Cold Peace.*

48. TsAGM f. 490, op. 1, d. 50, l. 150.

49. As noted by the architect N. Ternovskaia to *Vecherniaia Moskva*, 12 May 1950, 2.

50. GARF f. R-5446, op. 85, d. 27, l. 16.

51. The decree is published in *Sobranie postanovlenii i rasporiazhenii pravitel'stva SSSR*, 1 July 1944, 149.

52. For detail on the operations of the Municipal (Communal) Bank (Tsekombank), and on banking in general, see O. Kuschpèta, *The Banking and Credit System of the USSR*, esp. 35–86.

53. GARF f. R-7676, op. 6a, d. 197, ll. 2, 7, 8. This provides an example of how transport workers received various kinds of help from trade union (and, by extension, enterprise) in exploiting the scheme.

54. GARF f. R-5451, op. 30, d. 23, ll. 6–7.

55. Individual housing construction also took place during the 1930s (see chapter 5). When it did, the effects on urban space were particularly chaotic, as Heather DeHaan shows for the city of Nizhnii Novgorod/Gor'kii. Heather Diane DeHaan, "From Nizhnyi to Gor'kii: The Reconstruction of a Russian Provincial City in the Stalinist 1930s," 309–10.

56. *Vecherniaia Moskva*, 3 January 1945, 4.

57. Donald Filtzer, *Soviet Workers and Late Stalinism: Labour and the Restoration of the Stalinist System after World War II*, 96.

58. GARF f. R-5451, op. 30, d. 10, l. 57.

59. GARF f. A-259, op. 6, d. 5320, l. 35. For problems in Rostov, see RGAE f. 9028, op. 1, d. 589, l. 22.

60. RGAE f. 9028, op. 1, d. 589, l. 45.

61. For Rostov, GARF f. A-259, op. 6. d. 55, l. 129; for Leningrad, ibid., l. 135; for Magnitogorsk, ibid., d. 80, ll. 17, 36.

62. Ibid., d. 4501, ll. 1–2: at least 410,000,000 rubles, compared to 27,000,000 devoted to "measures for widening the capacity of municipal enterprises."

63. RGAE f. 1562, op. 14 d. 1169, l. 1; d. 1175, l. 4 (1944); d. 2030, l. 2 (1950). Note that these figures are national totals for existing housing space, not for construction, and that increases were the consequence not just of new construction but also of repair, new settlement of derelict property, and other factors. It is not entirely clear how accurate wartime housing figures could possibly be. Data for 1944, meanwhile, exclude housing in the Baltic States, Moldavia, and Kareliia that is included in 1950. The figures for personal property are

74,446,072 and 125,916,608; for soviets, they are 69,080,800 and 85,246,137 square meters.

64. GARF f. A-259, op. 6, d. 4501, l. 13.

65. Sosnovy, *Housing Problem in the Soviet Union*, 117.

66. RGAE f. 1562, op. 14, d. 1212, l. 1; d. 2030, l. 2.

67. GARF f. A-259, op. 6, d. 5718, l. 46 (15,063,000 of 44,595,000 square meters).

68. Ibid., d. 4501. ll. 3–4.

69. Kees Boterbloem, *Life and Death under Stalin: Kalinin Province, 1945–1953.*

70. GARF f. A-259, op. 6, d. 5340, l. 103.

71. Ibid., d. 5718, l. 46.

72. RGAE f. 9432, op. 1, d. 13, l. 15.

73. Iu. L. Kosenkova, *Sovetskii gorod 1940-kh—pervoi poloviny 1950-kh godov: Ot tvorcheskykh poiskov k praktike stroitel'stva*, 217.

74. *Vecherniaia Moskva*, 12 January 1946, 2.

75. TsAGM f. 534, op. 1, d. 40, l. 70.

76. His obituary in *Pravda*, 31 October 1981, contains biographical information.

77. RGAE f. 9432, op. 1, d. 12.

78. But note Harris, "Moving to the Separate Apartment," 51, which follows Day, "Building Socialism," in drawing attention to important architectural precursors even in the 1930s.

79. Some technologies were developed earlier, producing some medium-rise apartment blocks in the early 1930s. See, for example, G. Konstantinopol'skii, "Doma, dostoinye stolitsy," in L. Kovaleva, ed., *Moskva*, 442–45. But the war forced a much more substantial and coordinated change.

80. See, for example, *Stroitel'naia gazeta*, 26 July 1964, 4.

81. For a biographical sketch, see www.sovarch.ru/arch/m/195/ (accessed 16 August 2009).

82. For Mordvynov at the 1937 congress, see Hugh D. Hudson, *Blueprints and Blood: The Stalinization of Soviet Architecture, 1917–1937*, 194.

83. RGAE f. 9432, op. 1, d. 12, ll. 21–22.

84. TsAGM f. 534, op. 1, d. 62, ll. 33, 35. GlavAPU was the Main Architectural-Planning Administration of the Moscow Soviet.

85. See *Sovetskaia arkhitektura, ezhegodnik* for numerous examples of neoclassical designs. For example, see an award-winning grandiose design of 1950 by G. A. Petrov on Rostov-on-Don's Engels Street in ibid. (1953): 81.

86. *Vecherniaia Moskva*, 25 January 1945, 2.

87. Ibid., 30 May 1945, 1.

88. GARF f. A-259, op. 6, d. 2809/a.

89. Ibid., d. 5099, ll. 38–40.

90. For example, photographs showing Khrushchev-era-style blocks that had been completed earlier, under Stalin, in *Zhilishchno-kommunal'noe khoziaistvo* (1953): 6.

91. For a characteristic example of shifts in architectural priorities in the Belorussian republic, see Kosenkova, *Sovetskii gorod*, 268.

92. RGAE f. 1562, op. 14, d. 1122, l. 15 (1943); ibid., d. 1527, l. 9 (1947).

93. This point is difficult to make statistically, though it was frequently raised in published or semipublic sources. It is discussed in the Ginzburg speech of 1943, and it continued to be a matter of concern in the Khrushchev era. See, for example, *Zhilishchno-kommunal'noe khoziaistvo* 5 (1956): 5–8.

94. Here I take issue with Meerovich, in *Kvadratnye metry*, who does not provide convincing evidence for the contrary position. Kotkin argues the same point as Meerovich

without particular evidence, seeming to attribute the distribution of square meters of "living space" rather than discrete dwellings as a deliberate and manipulative policy of repression rather than the by-product of a shortage of funds. Kotkin, *Magnetic Mountain*, 158, 161.

95. Catriona Kelly, *Refining Russia: Advice Literature, Polite Culture, and Gender from Catherine to Yeltsin*; Vadim Volkov, "The Concept of *kul'turnost'*: Notes on the Stalinist Civilizing Process," 182–209.

96. *Vecherniaia Moskva*, 21 January 1945, 2.

97. Ibid., 21 May 1945, 2.

98. Ibid., 11 January 1949, 2.

99. Kenneth M. Straus, *Factory and Community in Stalin's Russia: The Making of an Industrial Working Class*, 243.

100. Katerina Gerasimova, "Public Privacy in the Soviet Communal Apartment," 207–30. For other aspects of this historiographical debate, see the somewhat contrary position of Svetlana Boym, *Common Places: Mythologies of Everyday Life in Russia*, introduction.

101. Kotkin, *Magnetic Mountain*, ch. 4; Lynne Attwood, *Creating the New Soviet Woman: Women's Magazines as Engineers of Female Identity, 1922–1953*.

102. Susan E. Reid argues in a similar way and at much greater length for the Khrushchev era: see various works cited in the bibliography.

103. For a discussion of the traditional peasant experience, see David Moon, *The Russian Peasantry, 1600–1930: The World the Peasants Made*, ch. 5.

104. GARF f. R-5446, op. 85, d. 1, l. 251.

105. *Vecherniaia Moskva* 20 June 1949, 2.

106. Ibid., 8 April 1950, 2.

107. See Brooks, *Thank You Comrade Stalin!*

108. One of the first published references to "mikroraion" is in an article by A. Kasianov, in *Arkhitektura SSSR* (January 1957): 22–25.

109. RGAE f. 9432, op. 1, d. 192, l. 1.

110. Ibid., l. 25.

111. Ibid., l. 26.

112. Ibid., d. 194, l. 93.

113. Ibid., d. 193, l. 5.

114. *Vecherniaia Moskva*, 9 December 1947, 2.

115. Ibid., 8 October 1947, 1.

116. David L. Hoffmann, *Peasant Metropolis: Social Identities in Moscow, 1929–1941*; Geoffrey Hosking, *Rulers and Victims: The Russians in the Soviet Union*, 115.

117. *Vecherniaia Moskva*, 27 January 1945, 3.

118. Ibid., 2 February 1945, 2.

119. Ibid., 11 April 1945, 2.

120. Ibid., 9 March 1945, 2.

121. Ibid.

122. Ibid., 5 February 1945, 2.

123. TsAGM f. 490, op. 1, d. 23, ll. 65–66, 101.

124. GARF f. A-259, op. 6, d. 3136, ll. 2–3.

125. Ibid., ll. 4–5.

126. TsAGM f. 490, op. 1, d. 25, l. 5.

127. Ibid., d. 27, l. 44.

128. Ibid., d. 61, l. 159.

129. The failures of such community-mindedness are discussed by M. N. Potemkina, *Evakonaselenie v Ural'skom tylu (1941–1948gg)*, ch. 3. I would like to thank the author for the gift of her book.

130. TsAGM f. 490, op. 1, d. 23, l. 36.

131. Cf. Geoffrey Hosking, *Russia: People and Empire, 1552–1917*.

132. Zubkova, *Obshchestvo i reformy*.

133. GARF f. R-5446, op. 85, d. 5, l. 130.

134. Kiselev, *Moskva poslevoennaia*, 431 (doc. 109). From information presented to G. M. Popov, head of Moscow Soviet.

135. For the transformation of urban space in Tashkent between the Terror and the earthquake, see Paul Stronski, "Forging a Soviet City: Tashkent, 1937–1966." For life in Tashkent during the evacuation, see Rebecca Manley, "The Evacuation and Survival of Soviet Civilians, 1941–1946."

136. GARF f. R-5446, op. 59, d. 92, ll. 30–31.

137. See, for example, Eugène Zaleski, *Stalinist Planning for Economic Growth, 1933–1952*, 483–86.

138. R. W. Davies, "Industry," in Davies, Harrison, and Wheatcroft, *Economic Transformation of the Soviet Union*, 131–57 (152).

139. Alec Nove, *Was Stalin Really Necessary? Some Problems of Soviet Political Economy*, 120 (though Nove makes the argument for the post-Stalin period).

140. Aleksei Tikhonov and Paul R. Gregory, "Stalin's Last Plan," 159–92 (175).

141. GARF f. A-259, op. 6, d. 4543, l. 16. For a detailed analysis of failures of sanitation and water supply across a wider geographical sample, see Donald Filtzer, "Poisoning the Proletariat."

142. GARF f. A-259, op. 6, d. 5718, l. 46.

143. GARF f. A-259, op. 6, d. 37, l. 49.

144. Ibid., l. 50.

145. For example, see GARF f. A-259, op. 6, d. 5718, l. 17, for Kaliningrad oblast' in 1949; and ibid., ll. 55–58, for Stalingrad in 1949, where other factors are also blamed.

146. Ibid., d. 37, l. 131.

147. Ibid., d. 2751, l. 21; d. 5078, l. 3.

148. Ibid., d. 7749, l. 41.

149. Ibid., d. 2789, l. 3.

150. Ibid., d. 2747, l. 1.

151. Ibid., l. 3.

152. Ibid., d. 37, ll. 65–66.

153. Ibid., d. 5091, l. 41; d. 6910, ll. 20–21.

154. Ibid., d. 2745, l. 3.

155. TsAGM f. 490, op. 1, d. 24, ll. 1–3.

156. Ibid., d. 34, l. 10. The Moscow Soviet's housing administration also controlled those housing construction cooperatives and dacha construction cooperatives that still existed following the 1937 shift away from the cooperative principle.

157. For Moscow in November 1944, see, for example, TsAGM f. 490, op. 1, d. 22, l. 53.

158. GARF f. A259, op. 6, d. 793, l. 27.

159. Ibid., d. 793, l. 52.

160. "On measures for the reconstruction of cities in the RSFSR which were destroyed by the German invaders": see GARF f. A-259, op. 6, d. 55, l. 18.

161. Ibid., d. 3184, ll. 95–96.

162. Ibid., d. 5340, l. 87.

163. As claimed in a *profsoiuz* report. See GARF f. R-5475, op. 25, d. 378, l. 6.

164. On the repression and exploitation of the workforce, see the essential work of Donald Filtzer, *Soviet Workers and Late Stalinism.*

165. TsAGM f. 490, op. 1, d. 23, l. 113.

166. For example, TsAGM f. 490, op. 1, d. 47, l. 3.

167. Donald Filtzer, "From Mobilized to Free Labour: De-Stalinization and the Changing Legal Status of Workers": 154–70 (157ff.). Filtzer draws a distinction between the FZOs and the trade colleges (*remeslennye uchilishcha*, or RUs) whose programs were more thorough and prestigious, though he still considers their graduates, at least in the earlier period, to be part of the indentured workforce.

168. TsAGM f. 490, op. 1, d. 47, l. 129.

169. GARF f. A-259, op. 6, d. 2751, l. 12.

170. Ibid., d. 5341, ll. 13, 19, 22.

171. Ibid., d. 3184, l. 112. Other failing cities discussed in this source include Smolensk, Viaz'ma, Rostov-on-Don, Novorossiisk, Sevastopol, Voronezh, Novgorod, Velikie Luki, Kalinin, Briansk, Vezhits, Orel, Kursk, and Murmansk.

172. Ibid., d. 5711, l. 10. For example, the trust Stalingrazhdanstroi fulfilled its spending plan by just 50 percent while increasing its costs by 26 percent.

173. For a comparable situation with materials during wartime, see Potemkina, *Evakonaselenie v Ural'skom tylu*, 93.

174. For an example in the Ruhr Valley, see Mark Roseman, "The Uncontrolled Economy: Ruhr Coal Production, 1945–1948," 93–123 (108). For Japanese shantytowns, see John Dower, *Embracing Defeat: Japan in the Aftermath of World War II*, 50.

175. GARF f. A-259, op. 6, d. 5711, l. 16.

176. Ibid., d. 3155, l. 39.

177. Ibid., d. 4119, l. 1.

178. GARF f. R-5446, op. 59, d. 88, l. 44. Kosygin helped her.

179. Roseman, "Uncontrolled Economy"; Ian Connor, "The Refugees and the Currency Reform," 301–24 (310).

180. Roger H. Duclaud-Williams, *The Politics of Housing in Britain and France.*

181. Ann Waswo, *Housing in Postwar Japan: A Social History*, 59.

182. See, for example, Patrick Dunleavy, *The Politics of Mass Housing in Britain, 1945–1975: A Study of Corporate Power and Professional Influence in the Welfare State*, 34–41.

183. See a typical newspaper reference of 1952, which quotes the head of Moszhilstroi. *Vecherniaia Moskva*, 12 January 1952, 2.

2—The Launch of the Mass Housing Program, 1951–1957

1. *Arkhitektura SSSR* (October 1957): 29–34 (29). The epigraphs are from a confidential report by the Australian chargé d'affaires, 6 July 1953, in TNA: PRO: FO 371/106588; and *KPSS v rezoliutsiiakh* (1970) 7:283.

2. For the text of this set-piece decree of the Central Committee and the Council of Ministers, "On the development of housing construction in the USSR," see *KPSS v rezoliutsiiakh* (1970) 7:278–94 (293, 283).

3. See conclusion of chapter 1 for her story.

4. The Politburo of the Central Committee was renamed the Presidium in 1952 and remained as such until 1966.

5. GARF f. R-5446, op. 59, d. 93, ll. 128–30.

6. GARF f. R-7523, op. 37, d. 12, ll. 161–68.

7. The statistics quoted in this paragraph are taken from such reports; similar data presented in chapter 1, although consistent with these, were gathered from the files of the Central Statistical Administration (TsSU).

8. RGAE f. 9510, op. 3, d. 18, l. 155.

9. RGAE f. 9510, op. 3, d. 131, l. 178. For the contrast with the apparently complete or near-complete reconstruction of another prestige city, Minsk, see chapter 1.

10. RGAE f. 9510, op. 3, d. 140, l. 1.

11. Ibid., l. 3.

12. For example, GARF f. A-259, op. 6, d. 8400, l. 10.

13. For center-periphery relations during the prewar period especially, see James Harris, *The Great Urals: Regionalism and the Evolution of the Soviet System*.

14. GARF f. R-5446, op. 59, d. 97, l. 30.

15. In Tallinn, for example, see RGAE f. 9510, op. 3, d. 140, l. 9.

16. Ibid., l. 7.

17. GARF f. A-259, op. 7, d. 159, l. 26.

18. For Iakutskii ASSR and the city of Murmansk, see ibid., d. 1926, ll. 2ff, 32ff; for Gor'kii, ibid., op. 6, d. 8333 passim; for Chkalov, ibid., op. 7, d. 1906, ll. 22, 24.

19. "On the work of construction organizations of the Ministry of Housing-Civil Construction RSFSR in 1953," ibid., op. 7, d. 1911, ll. 1–4.

20. Ibid., d. 5227, ll. 7–8.

21. Ibid., d. 4025, ll. 9, 25. Khrushchev, though, was enthusiastically investigating the provision of sinks even in the 1930s. See Hudson, *Blueprints and Blood*, 190.

22. GARF f. A-259, op. 7, d. 5227, ll. 7–8.

23. Ibid., d. 865, l. 6.

24. RGAE f. 4372, op. 53, d. 783, l. 23. Assuming an average family size of 3.5, this would be an average of four square meters per person.

25. GARF f. A-259, op. 7, d. 4019, l. 1.

26. TsAGM f. 2852, op. 1, d. 13, l. 51; GARF f. A-259, op. 6, d. 7750, ll. 1, 8.

27. RGAE f. 9510, op. 3, d. 140, l. 7.

28. RGAE f. 339, op. 1, d. 638, l. 34.

29. RGAE f. 293, op. 1, d. 483, l. 1.

30. *Zhilishchno-kommunal'noe khoziaistvo* (June 1953).

31. GARF f. A-259, op. 7, d. 5252, ll. 12–13.

32. See, for example, RGAE f. 8216, op. 3, d. 2, ll. 16–17, 20–25, 32–33.

33. *Arkhitektura SSSR* (December 1953).

34. TsAGM f. 716, op. 1, d. 27, l. 20.

35. RGAE f. 339, op. 1, d. 638, ll. 38–42, 64–66.

36. Ibid., ll. 14, 33.

37. Ibid., d. 1256, l. 6; d. 1257, ll. 24, 26. A professional consensus would by the end of the decade condemn such use of ground floors as excessively expensive and hence irrational; but correspondence of 1956 shows that even then this conclusion was still some way off. See ibid., op. 3, d. 81, ll. 15–17.

38. As illustrated in *Sovetskaia arkhitektura, ezhegodnik* (1953): 67–71.

39. TsAGM f. 534, op. 1, dd. 230, 301.

40. *Stroitel'naia gazeta,* Moscow, 1 December 1954 (and subsequent issues). In full, the event was entitled the "All-Union Conference of Builders, Architects, and Workers of the Industries of Construction Materials, Construction, Road and Car Manufacture, and Science-Research Organizations."

41. For example, 400 construction workers to Kuibyshevstroi and 500 to Sevosetinstroi in 1951. GARF f. A-259, op. 6, d. 7754, ll. 3, 12.

42. Ibid., op. 7, d. 183, l. 3.

43. Donald Filtzer, *Soviet Workers and De-Stalinization: The Consolidation of the Modern System of Soviet Production Relations,* ch. 2.

44. TsAGM f. 716, op. 1, d. 1, l. 17.

45. GARF f. A-259, op. 7, d. 161, l. 17.

46. Ibid., l. 12.

47. Ibid., d. 7773, ll. 1, 4.

48. Ibid., d. 156, l. 13.

49. TsAGM f. 716, op. 1, d. 1, l. 109.

50. Numerous similar cases include one in Moszhilstroi, March 1954. TsAGM f. 589, op. 1, d. 171, l. 134.

51. GARF f. A-259, op. 7, d. 5231, l. 84.

52. "On measures of struggle with unauthorized construction in cities and workers' settlements of the RSFSR," ibid., op. 6, d. 7785, ll. 83–84. Residence documents included *domovye knigi* and propiski.

53. GARF f. 7523 op. 58, d. 114, l. 160.

54. TsAGM f. 2852, op. 1, d. 25, l. 6.

55. GARF f. A-259, op. 7, d. 811, ll. 16, 56, 91.

56. Calculated from ibid., d. 6154, l. 103.

57. TsAGM f. 2852, op. 5, d. 46, l. 16.

58. GARF f. A-259, op. 6, d. 7760, l. 5.

59. *Vecherniaia Moskva,* 7 October 1949, 2. "Gigantic" (*gigantskoe zhilishchnoe stroitel'stvo*) is from a meeting of the *aktiv* of the Moscow city organization of the Communist Party, held at the Columned Hall of the House of Unions, 30 August 1951. Ibid., 31 August 1951.

60. RGAE f. 293, op. 1, d. 481, l. 1.

61. *KPSS v rezoliutsiiakh* (1970) 6:357–58, 366 (360 for housing).

62. See, for example, Gorlizki and Khlevniuk, *Cold Peace.* Reconstruction (narrowly conceived) and rationing ended in 1948.

63. Transcript of meeting between Wilson and Khrushchev, 12 January 1956, in TNA: PRO: PREM 11/1604/6.

64. N. S. Khrushchev, *The Last Testament,* 122.

65. Khrushchev, *Vospominaniia,* 4:7–21.

66. For discussion of Khrushchev's work in construction further back, in the mid-1930s, see R. W. Davies and Melanie Ilic, "From Khrushchev (1935) to Khrushchev (1956–1964): Construction Policy Compared." Thanks go to Melanie Ilic for sending a copy of the chapter in advance of publication.

67. Khrushchev wanted to import urban standards of living—and some urban forms— into rural areas. His position on the *agro gorod,* which he broached in 1949 to near disastrous effect, was implemented in heavily revised form during his leadership. It chimed with a long

tradition of Soviet discussion of mixed urban-rural forms, which dated to the "disurbanist" debate of the late 1920s. For this, see, for example, S. Frederick Starr, "Visionary Town Planning during the Cultural Revolution," 207–40.

68. RGASPI f. 397, op. 2, d. 21, l. 4.

69. Ibid., ll. 10–11.

70. Khrushchev, *Vospominaniia*, 4:17.

71. RGASPI f. 397, op. 2, d. 22, l. 15.

72. Ibid., l. 18.

73. Khrushchev, *Vospominaniia*, 4:24.

74. Ibid., 34.

75. My source is *Vecherniaia Moskva*, 5–12 January 1951. Khrushchev was also ultimately responsible for a smaller and shorter conference of architects, engineers, and builders, held by the Moscow Soviet on 24–25 August 1950.

76. Khrushchev, *Vospominaniia*, 4:26.

77. Not only was Khrushchev put in his place in *Pravda* the day after he made his speech on the *agro-gorod* in 1949 (a humiliation from which he was lucky to recover), but three years later, the notion was condemned by Stalin in his *Economic Problems of Socialism* (1952).

78. See William Taubman, *Khrushchev: The Man and His Era*, 230.

79. Stephen V. Bittner, "Exploring Reform: De-Stalinization in Moscow's Arbat District, 1953–1968," 165.

80. Speech of Khrushchev, *Stroitel'naia gazeta*, 29 December 1954, 2–4 (3).

81. Sir William Hytner to Sir Anthony Eden, 31 December 1954, in TNA: PRO: FO 418/95.

82. For example, *Zhilishchno-kommunal'noe khoziaistvo* editorial (January 1955); *Arkhitektura SSSR* (June 1955), editorial.

83. RGAE f. 4372, op. 53, d. 332, l. 8.

84. TsAGM f. 534, op. 1, d. 351.

85. GARF f. A-259, op. 7, d. 6150, ll. 1–2.

86. TsAGM f. 490, op. 1, d. 185, l. 34; GARF f. A-259, op. 7, d. 7029, l. 58; d. 8345, ll. 20, 26; RGAE f. 339, op. 3, d. 80, l. 158; d. 352, ll. 66, 95–98, 153.

87. TsAGM f. 490, op. 1, d. 199, l. 5; d. 185, l. 46; d. 200, l. 36.

88. RGAE f. 339, op. 3, d. 359, ll. 59–65.

89. *KPSS v rezoliutsiiakh* (1970) 7:278–94.

90. There are also points that deal only with housing in rural areas; those are excluded from this analysis.

91. *KPSS v rezoliutsiiakh* (1970) 7:282.

92. Ibid., 292.

93. TNA: PRO: FO 371/116805.

94. Ibid., 116804. See also TNA: PRO: PREM 11/1021.

95. Khrushchev did so even when discussing Kucherenko's equally "talented" brother, one of the designers of the T-34 tank. Khrushchev, *Vospominaniia*, 1:282.

96. *Vecherniaia Moskva*, 29 November 1963, 1; *Stroitel'naia gazeta*, 29 November 1963, 3.

97. *Pravda*, 30 November 1963, 3.

98. To some extent, this draws on the acutely formulated analytical categories delineated in David Priestland, *Stalinism and the Politics of Mobilization: Ideas, Power, and Terror in Inter-war Russia*.

99. David L. Hoffmann discusses Soviet modernity and its particular location in a

common Enlightenment project in his "European Modernity and Soviet Socialism," in David L. Hoffmann and Yanni Kotsonis, eds., *Russian Modernity: Politics, Knowledge, Practices*, 245–60.

100. Priestland, *Stalinism and the Politics of Mobilization*.

101. David L. Hoffman, *Stalinist Values: The Cultural Norms of Soviet Modernity 1917–1941*.

102. Philip Hanson, *The Rise and Fall of the Soviet Economy*, 58–60, 70.

103. RGASPI f. 397, op. 2, d. 22, l. 21.

104. For example, Khrushchev, *Vospominaniia*, 4:17.

105. RGASPI f. 651, op. 1, ll. 1–54 (for 1958–1959).

106. See also Catherine Cooke with Susan E. Reid, "Modernity and Realism: Architectural Relations in the Cold War," 172–94.

107. See also Davies, *Crisis and Progress*, 490–99. For an overview from the 1920s to the 1980s, see Sari Autio-Sarasmo, "Soviet Economic Modernisation and Transferring Technologies from the West," 104–23. The single most prominent example of this process followed the end of the Khrushchev era. This was the Fiat-inspired Togliatti car plant, which effectively created a new Soviet city. See Lewis H. Siegelbaum, *Cars for Comrades: The Life of the Soviet Automobile*, ch. 3.

108. RGAE f. 339, op. 3, d. 827, ll. 39–40.

109. Ibid., ll. 41, 43.

110. Ibid., d. 80, ll. 38–43.

111. For an example of the complex relationship between East–West exchange and the Cold War, see Susan E. Reid, "Who Will Beat Whom? Soviet Popular Reception of the American National Exhibition in Moscow, 1959," 855–904.

112. RGAE f. 339, op. 3, d. 369, ll. 23–24 (Scandinavia); d. 368 (Germany).

113. Ibid., d. 369, ll. 23–24.

114. Ibid., d. 365, ll. 242–57.

115. For a detailed discussion of such conferences and their significance for postwar renewal, domestic hope, and the Cold War, see Greg Castillo, "Domesticating the Cold War: Household Consumption and Propaganda in Marshall Plan Germany," 261–88.

116. RGAE f. 339, op. 3, d. 827, ll. 1–7.

117. Gorlind Staemmler, "East Germany (The German Democratic Republic)," 220–46 (224).

118. See, for example, Lennart J. Lundqvist, *Housing Policy and Tenures in Sweden: The Quest for Neutrality*.

119. GARF f. A-259, op. 6, d. 7785, l. 9.

120. Ibid., op. 7, d. 6150, ll. 17, 20, 30.

121. RGAE f. 339, op. 3, d. 359, l. 65.

122. GARF f. A-259, op. 7, d. 6150, ll. 17, 20, 30.

123. RGAE f. 4372, op. 53, d. 333, ll. 56–57.

124. GARF f. A-259, op. 7, d. 6151, l. 1.

125. Ibid., d. 8775, l. 4.

126. RGAE f. 339, op. 3, d. 351, l. 5.

127. Ibid., d. 365, ll. 2–15.

128. Ibid., d. 366, l. 118.

129. Ibid., d. 367, l. 126.

130. The value of socialist competition for various categories of output, including

housing construction, was demonstrated in a report of 1951 (RGAE f. 9166, op. 2, d. 518). For a further, famous example of Stalin-era socialist competition, see Lewis H. Siegelbaum, *Stakhanovism and the Politics of Productivity in the USSR, 1935–1941.*

131. For example, RGAE f. 339, op. 3, d. 250; d. 252, ll. 1, 5; d. 253; d. 277, l. 19; d. 467; TsAGM f. 490, op. 1, d. 185, l. 9; TsAGM f. 605, op. 1, d. 228, l. 229.

132. TsAGM f. 2852, op. 1, d. 23, l. 18.

133. RGAE f. 339, op. 3, d. 245, ll. 41–73.

134. Ibid., d. 251, ll. 131, 149.

135. Ibid., d. 465, ll. 3, 28.

136. Ibid., d. 240, l. 55.

137. Ibid., ll. 41–44 (Kareliia); ll. 140–51 (Voroshilovgrad); d. 242, ll. 111–16 (Magnitogorsk).

138. Fitzpatrick, "Patrons and Clients," in *Tear Off the Masks!* 182–202 (188). Historians such as Geoffrey Hosking and sociologists such as Alena Ledeneva rightly stress its importance throughout the Soviet period.

139. Writers and creative artists were another category. See Vera Tolz, "Cultural Bosses as Patrons and Clients: The Functioning of the Soviet Creative Unions in the Postwar Period," 87–105; Kirill Tomoff, *Creative Union: The Professional Organization of Soviet Composers, 1939–1953.*

140. The property dimensions are explored in detail in chapter 5. GARF f. R-7523, op. 58, d. 127, ll. 77–78.

141. GARF f. R-7523, op. 58, d. 126, ll. 130–34. Voroshilov was chairman of the Presidium of the Supreme Soviet between 1953 and 1960, a position that gave him some ceremonial but not first-rank political authority, and in which capacity he often received such letters.

142. RGAE f. 339, op. 1, d. 902, l. 2.

143. Ibid., d. 1257, l. 61.

144. Ibid., op. 3, d. 79, l. 196.

145. RGANI f. 5, op. 30, d. 134, l. 63.

146. GARF f. R-5446, op. 59, d. 98, l. 58.

147. RGANI f. 5, op. 30, d. 267, ll. 65–70.

148. Miriam Dobson argues that many ex-prisoners tried to show they were "endlessly devoted to the cause" in such letters and constructed their life narratives accordingly. Dobson, *Khrushchev's Cold Summer*, 77.

149. GARF f. R-7523, op. 58, d. 142, l. 36.

150. Ibid., l. 9.

151. Fitzpatrick, "Supplicants and Citizens," in *Tear Off the Masks!* 155–81 (173).

152. His story is told in Ilya Zbarsky and Samuel Hutchinson, *Lenin's Embalmers.*

153. GARF f. 7523, op. 58, d. 142, ll. 28–29.

154. "On the priority supply of housing space to those who have been rehabilitated," see GARF f. 5451, op. 30, d. 462, l. 33. See also Christine Varga-Harris, "Forging Citizenship on the Home Front: Reviving the Socialist Contract and Constructing Soviet Identity during the Thaw," in Jones, *Dilemmas of De-Stalinization*, 101–116 (107).

155. Nanci Adler, *The Gulag Survivor: Beyond the Soviet System*, 153–54.

156. Solzhenitsyn, *Sobranie sochinenii*, 7:445.

157. Evan Mawdsley and Stephen White, *The Soviet Elite from Lenin to Gorbachev: The Central Committee and Its Members, 1917–1991*; Polly Jones, "From Stalinism to Post-Stalinism: De-mythologizing Stalin, 1953–1956"; Dobson, *Khrushchev's Cold Summer.*

3—To the Communist Future, 1958–1964

1. Aleksandr Iakovlev, *Omut pamiati: ot Stolypina do Putina*, 1:175. The epigraph from Vasilii Promyslov is from *Stroitel'naia gazeta*, 17 April 1964, 3.

2. For example, Blair Ruble's criticism of the program, "From *khrushchoby* to *korobki*," is somewhat impressionistic, unlike his major social science work, *Leningrad: Shaping a Soviet City*. Harris, "Moving to the Separate Apartment," though much more empirically secure and overall an essential study, effectively derives some principal conclusions from evidence found in letters of complaint, a directly loaded source. Kulavig's chapter on housing in the Khrushchev era is based on letters of complaint, making his case for popular discontent with, especially, the distribution system somewhat circular. Erik Kulavig, *Dissent in the Years of Khrushchev: Nine Stories about Disobedient Russians*.

3. *Arkhitektura SSSR* (April 1959): 2–4.

4. *Zhilishchno-kommunal'noe khoziaistvo* (December 1962): 1.

5. *Pravda*, 10 December 1963. Khrushchev's claim is rhetorical and explicitly does not refer to people who obtained new apartments. In line with similar statements, it is probably about 20 percent over the mark, and some of the people in question might not actually have improved their conditions by much.

6. Harrison E. Salisbury, *A New Russia?*, 7.

7. There are no yearly published data for before 1951 (see the introduction).

8. Israel and Hong Kong both experienced major housing crises, which verged on catastrophe, after the Second World War. In the case of Israel, this prompted a rapid construction drive. Government data suggest that the corresponding statistics to those featured in chart 3.3 are, on average, 12.45 during 1955–1959, 10.69 during 1960–1964, and 10.38 during 1965–1969. Calculated on basis of Naomi Carman and Daniel Czamanski, "Israel," 517–36 (532). About 80 percent of "housing starts" in 1950s Israel were "public," which included inputs by state construction, state assistance, and "quasi-public" bodies. See Rachelle Alterman, *Planning in the Face of Crisis: Land Use, Housing, and Mass Immigration in Israel*, 53–54. In Hong Kong, where housing was required for the many Chinese refugees who had fled Communist rule, the colonial government became involved in public housing projects in the mid-1950s—and with increasing vigor in the 1960s and 1970s. By 1990, approximately 2 million people (41% of the population) consequently lived in housing owned or subsidized by the government. See Michael Scott Houf, "The Re-invention of Hong Kong during the Post-War Period," 205, 243–53.

9. The data published by the Central Statistical Administration (TsSU) in its annual yearbooks from 1956 (which show yearly figures from 1951, but no further back) do not precisely accord with those that can be found in the TsSU's archival records. When extracting all-union data for state tenures, the 1952 archive figure can be seen as 83.1 percent of the published figure, and that of 1960 is 81.7 percent.

10. Note that it is republic and city (as opposed to all-union) figures that are more consistently recorded in the somewhat uneven archival fund of the Central Statistical Administration (RGAE f. 1562).

11. I could not locate figures for the RSFSR for 1961–1964.

12. Calculated from RGAE f. 1562, op. 14, d. 1424, l. 9; d. 1934, l. 50. Between the end of the war and July 1947 alone, the state urban housing fund increased by 47.9 percent (calculated from ibid., d. 1424, l. 9; d. 1527, l. 12).

13. Ibid., d. 2767. For more detail on the impact of the war on Minsk, and developments in the city's history since 1945, see Thomas Bohn, *Minsk—Musterstadt des Sozialismus*.

Stadtplanung und Urbanisierung in der Sowjetunion nach 1945. Thanks go to the author for introducing me to his work and for sending me chapters from the forthcoming Russian translation.

14. RGAE f. 1562, op. 14, d. 1212, l. 2; d. 1682, l. 109; d. 2397, l. 1; d. 2799, l. 205; d. 3004, l. 5.

15. As individual and cooperative housing depended on state credits and a whole range of financial, construction, and communications infrastructures that were directed by the state, the existence of tenurial variety and the possibilities of individual ownership (discussed in part 2) do not reduce the status of the mass urban housing program as a major *state* initiative.

16. Kesaris, *CIA Research Reports*, reel 3, report dated 20 March 1963, "Soviet Economic Problems," 1–2.

17. *Narodnoe khoziaistvo, statisticheskii ezhegodnik* (1958), 902; (1959), 802; (1962), 636; (1964), 771. Cf. Hanson, *Rise and Fall*, 101.

18. RGAE f. 7733, op. 47, d. 891, l. 45.

19. GARF f. A-259, op. 42, d. 971, ll. 36, 109–112. Note that enterprise directors were subject to a malformed structure of incentives that could discourage them from spending all of their budgets.

20. For research institutes, see RGAE f. 339, op. 3, d. 537, l. 28 (March 1958); for journals, see ibid., ll. 80–81, 125; for the all-union construction conferences of 1958 and 1960, for example, see numerous references, including ibid., l. 115 and dd. 1046–51.

21. For example, in Leningrad in 1959, see ibid., d. 780, l. 150.

22. For example, see ibid., d. 922, l. 2; d. 1188, l. 29. Successful outcomes were reported in Moscow; see TsAGM f. 490, op. 1, d. 213, l. 23; d. 228, l. 103. The Frunzenskii raion housing administration considered socialist competition the reason for the overfulfillment of their capital repair target in August 1960. TsAGM f. 490, op. 1, d. 244, l. 22.

23. Typically, an order (*prikaz*) of Moscow's Sverdlovskii raion soviet of October 1961 discussed the "confirmed [training] plan for the preparation and improvement of cadres" of the housing economy. TsAGM f. 2852, op. 5, d. 87, l. 53. In September 1961, a senior engineer at Glavmosstroi, A. P. Goldyrev, was honored and rewarded for "long and conscientious service [*rabota*]" on the occasion of his sixtieth birthday. TsAGM f. 605, op. 1, d. 650, l. 75. For the prompt investigation of workplace accidents, see the characteristic example, TsAGM f. 589, op. 1, d. 224, l. 14.

24. GARF f. A-259, op. 7, d. 8777, l. 7. Output by soviets was particularly impressive at 46 percent. Cf. RGAE f. 339, op. 3, d. 829, l. 34.

25. GARF f. A-259, op. 7, d. 8777, l. 13.

26. Ibid., op. 42, d. 9468, l. 36.

27. Ibid., ll. 10–11.

28. RGAE f. 339, op. 3, d. 925, l. 182.

29. V. R. Skripko et al., eds., *Zhilishchnoe zakonodatel'stvo v SSSR i RSFSR*, 25.

30. GARF f. A-259, op. 42, d. 9593, l. 74.

31. "On housing construction and dacha construction cooperatives," *Sobranie postanovlenii i rasporiazhenii pravitel'stva SSSR* (May 1958): 115; "On individual and cooperative housing construction" (December 1962): 283–86 (283).

32. GARF f. A-259, op. 45, d. 1086, l. 92.

33. RGAE f. 233, op. 1, d. 215, ll. 1–3.

34. GARF f. A-259, op. 45, d. 1086, ll. 41–49.

35. RGAE f. 339, op. 3, d. 561, ll. 161–66.

36. As seen, for example, in the way that local administrations modified and improved policy during implementation; see TsAGM f. 2852, op. 1, d. 166, l. 8.

37. Cooperatives had been built between 1924 and 1937, but on an entirely different scale.

38. RGAE f. 339, op. 3, d. 554, ll. 231–35.

39. Ibid., d. 1046, l. 10.

40. *Zhilishchno-kommunal'noe khoziaistvo* (January 1962): 7.

41. RGAE f. 339, op. 3, d. 829, l. 40.

42. Ibid., d. 1046, l. 24. Note the inconsistency with Gosstroi estimates.

43. GARF f. A-259, op. 45, d. 2512, ll. 1–4.

44. RGAE f. 339, op. 3, d. 829, l. 42.

45. For example, see discussions of 1958 in the Council of Ministers (RSFSR), in GARF f. A-259, op. 42, d. 960, ll. 2–4.

46. TsAGM f. 2852, op. 1, d. 164, l. 25.

47. See, for example, RGAE f. 9492, op. 1, d. 3207, l. 47.

48. Vladimir Voinovich, *Khochu byt' chestnym.*

49. GARF f. R-5462, op. 32, d. 412, ll. 41–51.

50. It was also a new socialist-imperial city, with similar housing districts constructed in cities across the Soviet sphere of influence, most notably in Eastern Europe.

51. Laurens van der Post, *Journey into Russia*, 73.

52. Interesting discussions include V. E. Khazanova, "Massovoe i unikal'noe v arkhitekture sovetskikh obshchestvennykh sooruzhenii poslevoennogo perioda"; Stephen V. Bittner, "Remembering the Avant-Garde: Moscow Architects and the 'Rehabilitation' of Constructivism, 1961–1964," 553–76; Bittner, *Khrushchev's Thaw*, ch. 4.

53. M. V. Posokhin, *Dorogi zhizni: iz zapisok arkhitektora*, 75.

54. *Ia shagaiu po Moskve*, dir. Georgii Daneliia.

55. *Katok i skripka*, dir. Andrei Tarkovskii.

56. Stephen Spender, *Journals, 1939–1983*, 213.

57. Van der Post, *Journey into Russia*, 73.

58. RGAE f. 339, op. 3, d. 1053, l. 56.

59. The best-known joke about the uniformity of the Soviet city is the theme of a famous late socialist film, *Ironiia sud'by, ili s legkym parom!* (*The Irony of Fate, or How was the Sauna?*), dir. E. Riazanov, where the drunken main character finds himself one new year's night in a district of Leningrad precisely resembling his own part of Moscow—the key fits the lock of the identical apartment he thinks is his home—with comic and heartwarming consequences.

60. *Arkhitektura SSSR* (January 1958): 38–40. 61. Ibid. (April 1959): 5–13.

62. *Zastava Il'icha* (also known as *Mne dvadtsat' let*), dir. Marlen Khutsiev.

63. *Nash dom*, dir. Vasilii Pronin.

64. The question of rights will be addressed in more detail in part 2.

65. Some architects were certainly aggrieved. See, for example, the documentary film *Khrushchevki.*

66. TsAGM f. 534, op. 1, d. 480.

67. RGASPI f. 397, op. 2, d. 49, l. 4.

68. RGAE f. 339, op. 3, d. 366, ll. 114–17.

69. Such pictures regularly appeared in journals such as *Zhilishchno-kommunal'noe khoziaistvo* and newspapers such as *Vecherniaia Moskva.*

70. "On the development of large panel housing construction, 1959–1964," RGAE f. 339, op. 3, d. 925, ll. 65–69.

71. Ibid., d. 1200, l. 3.
72. Ibid., d. 1267, ll. 37–38.
73. GARF f. A-259, op. 42, d. 4021, ll. 65–66.
74. Ibid., d. 5989, ll. 18–19.
75. Ibid., op. 45, d. 2490; op. 42, d. 971, ll. 9–11; op. 42, d. 4021, ll. 65–66; RGAE f. 339, op. 3, d. 1187, ll. 68–69.
76. The theme of the domestic interior has been studied by various historians, notably Susan Reid, and I will not venture further indoors here. See the introduction for a brief historiographical discussion.
77. RGAE f. 339, op. 3, d. 820, l. 57.
78. For example, ibid., d. 827, l. 112.
79. *Arkhitektura SSSR* (February 1960): 36–38.
80. RGANI f. 5, op. 30, d. 393, l. 70.
81. RGAE f. 339, op. 3, d. 803, l. 41.
82. GARF f. A-259, op. 42, d. 5979, l. 32.
83. See, for example, ibid., d. 5989, ll. 18–19.
84. See Colton, *Moscow*, 374–76. Also *Arkhitektura SSSR* (February 1958): 20ff.
85. Colton foregrounds the ninth experimental district, and it features in the architectural press of the time. See, for example, *Arkhitektura SSSR* (June 1958): 37; (January 1959): 36–43. Other pioneering projects were also undertaken in Novye Cheremushki, however, including the experimental kvartal 10-S, which brought together various design bureaus and institutes. RGAE f. 339, op. 3, d. 1267, ll. 3–9.
86. *Cheremushki*, dir. Herbert Rappaport.
87. *Zhilishchno-kommunal'noe khoziaistvo* (January 1962): 7–9 (7).
88. *The Programme of the Communist Party of the Soviet Union Adopted by the Twenty-second Congress of the CPSU, October 31, 1961*, 46.
89. Ibid., 63–64 (amended translation).
90. Ibid., 68.
91. *Arkhitektura SSSR* (September 1955): 46–47 (46).
92. Ibid., (August 1958): 6.
93. Katherine Anne Lebow, "Nowa Huta, 1949–1957: Stalinism and the Transformation of Everyday Life in Poland's 'First Socialist City,'" 235–71. See also, for example, David Turnock, "Housing Policy in Romania," in J. A. A. Sillince, *Housing Policies in Eastern Europe and the Soviet Union*, 135–69 (esp. 151–57).
94. *Arkhitektura SSSR* (January 1957) is one of the first examples of this kind of public discussion of mikroraion.
95. S. Khan-Magomedov, "O roli arkhitektury v perestroike byta," *Arkhitektura SSSR* (February 1958): 45–46.
96. *Zhilishchno-kommunal'noe khoziaistvo* (February 1962): 9.
97. One example is RGAE f. 339, op. 3, d. 360, ll. 34, 37.
98. GARF f. R-5451, op. 30, d. 439, ll. 93–97.
99. RGAE f. 339, op. 3, d. 1051, l. 53.
100. Ibid., d. 1053, l. 8.
101. Ibid., d. 1046, l. 202.
102. TsAGM f. 2852, op. 1, d. 65, l. 4.
103. Relevant evidence is cited in the discussion of obshchestvennost', below.
104. *Zhilishchno-kommunal'noe khoziaistvo* (April 1958): 4–5. In Moscow's Kalininskii

raion in June 1959, nine ZhEKi were formed from fifty-nine *domoupravleniia*. TsAGM f. 2852, op. 1, d. 78, l. 73.

105. *Zhilishchno-kommunal'noe khoziaistvo* (December 1959): 13–14. For the advantages to ZhEKi in using efficiency savings to improve the skills of personnel, see TsAGM f. 2852, op. 1, d. 78, l. 73; d. 76, l. 17. For the emphasis on financial discipline, see TsAGM f. 2852, op. 5, d. 82, l. 32.

106. For example, TsAGM f. 2852, op. 1, d. 129, l. 34.

107. *Zhilishchno-kommunal'noe khoziaistvo* (April 1958): 4–5.

108. From a Mosgorispolkom resolution of July 1958. TsAGM f. 490, op. 1, d. 212, ll. 13–14.

109. *Zhilishchno-kommunal'noe khoziaistvo* (September 1960): 5.

110. For discussion of some parallel Khrushchev-era reforms, and an engagement with scholarly discussion thereof (such as the work of Oleg Kharkhordin), see chapter 4.

111. TsAGM f. 490, op. 1, d. 214, l. 28.

112. TsAGM f. 2852, op. 5, d. 109, l. 8.

113. See Mary Buckley, "The Untold Story of Obshchestvennitsa in the 1930s," 569–86; *Zhilishchno-kommunal'noe khoziaistvo* (November 1963): 7, 10.

114. TsAGM f. 2852, op. 1, d. 143, ll. 115–16.

115. *Zhilishchno-kommunal'noe khoziaistvo* (February 1960): 6.

116. An idealized account of obshchestvennost' in Kishinev, including mass attendance at a *voskresnik*, is in *Zhilishchno-kommunal'noe khoziaistvo* (January 1962): 7–9.

117. TsAGM f. 2852, op. 5, d. 75, l. 32.

118. For example, *Zhilishchno-kommunal'noe khoziaistvo* (April 1963): 4–5. There is a discussion of the *druzhiny* (citizen patrols) in chapter 5.

119. *Zhilishchno-kommunal'noe khoziaistvo* (April 1961): 5–6.

120. Andrei Bitov, "Bezdel'nik" (1961–1962), in *Sobranie sochinenii*, 1:86.

121. For a vivid description of the American case, which can be used as comparison for the Soviet Union, see Michael Harrington, *The Other America: Poverty in the United States*, 141–47.

122. *A esli eto liubov'?* dir. Iulii Raizman.

123. Donald Filtzer, *Soviet Workers and Late Stalinism*. On the demographic context of poverty, see Andrei Markevich, "Urban Households in the USSR, 1941–1964: The Legacy of War," 35–51.

124. Varga-Harris, "Constructing the Soviet Hearth," ch. 4; Steven E. Harris, ""I Know All the Secrets of My Neighbors': The Quest for Privacy in the Era of the Separate Apartment."

125. To some extent at least, the sympathetic analysis of Medvedev and Medvedev in the 1970s is borne out by the archival record. See Roi Medvedev and Zhores Medvedev, *Khrushchev: The Years in Power*.

126. For the implications of this, and the famous exhibition at which it took place, see Cristina Maria Carbone, "Building Propaganda: Architecture and the American National Exhibition in Moscow of 1959."

127. Cf. Avner Offer, *The Challenge of Affluence: Self-Control and Well-Being in the United States and Britain since 1950*.

128. Lev Lur'e and Irina Maliarova, *1956 god. Seredina veka*, 360.

129. Overcrowded conditions took a toll on family life, and when divorcees were forced to continue cohabiting because of the shortage of space, the toll persisted on post-family life. See Deborah A. Field, "Divorce and Conceptions of Private Life in the Khrushchev

Era," 599–613. Yet the separate apartment offered some scope for a "legal" strengthening of the family. See chapter 5 for the argument that the rights of different family members over the dwelling could even be characterized as a form of family ownership.

130. Victoria De Grazia, *Irresistible Empire: America's Advance through Twentieth-Century Europe*, 361; Robert Gildea, *France since 1945*, 95.

131. TsAGM f. 2433, op. 8, d. 43, l. 17.

132. GARF f. A-259, op. 42, d. 5983, ll. 34–35.

133. Ibid., d. 6920, l. 3. For dreadful conditions in Rostov (including in Novocherkassk), see ibid., d. 7687, ll. 28–30. Construction workers remained particularly unfortunate: see ibid., op. 45, d. 2530, ll. 7–8.

134. Nursultan Nazarbayev, *My Life, My Times, and the Future*, 25–26.

135. See Vladimir Kozlov, *Neizvestnyi SSSR: Protivostoianie naroda i vlasti, 1953–1985gg*, parts 1, 2.

136. RGAE f. 339, op. 3, d. 1046, l. 196.

137. Another correspondent discusses the implications of apartment design for health and hygiene, in ibid., l. 217.

138. Ibid., l. 204.

139. For example, ibid., l. 104. Although the inaccessibility of coffins was a cliché, this can hardly have lessened its impact on people's lives.

140. Ibid., l. 254.

141. Ibid., d. 1047, l. 183.

142. Ibid., d. 1053, l. 3.

143. This was another common subject of complaint. See ibid., d. 1046, l. 61; d. 1051, ll. 75–76.

144. RGAE f. 339, op. 3, d. 1046, l. 209.

145. Ibid., l. 230.

146. Ibid., d. 1051, l. 71.

147. Ibid., d. 1046, l. 87.

148. See, for example, RGANI f. 30, op. 5, d.192, ll. 38–39 for this rhetoric of "*pochelovecheski*."

149. RGAE f. 339, op. 3, d. 1046, l. 54.

150. Ibid., d. 1018, l. 13.

151. TsAGM g. 605, op. 1, d. 650, l. 96.

152. RGAE f. 339, op. 3, d. 1367, ll. 18–19.

153. Harris, "Moving to the Separate Apartment," ch. 8.

154. Exceptions include Geoffrey Hosking, *A History of the Soviet Union*, 353.

155. Filtzer, *Soviet Workers and De-Stalinization*.

156. Malia, *Soviet Tragedy*.

157. Mikhail S. Lipetsker, *Property Rights of Soviet Citizens*, 10.

158. Samuel H. Baron, *Bloody Saturday in the Soviet Union: Novocherkassk, 1962*. Vladimir Kozlov shows that this type of reaction, and its manifestation as disturbance, was not isolated. See Kozlov, *Neizvestnyi SSSR*.

159. See, for example, Steven Solnick, *Stealing the State*.

160. For the consequences of relative equality in the housing fund of Togliatti after the end of the Khrushchev era, see Siegelbaum, *Cars for Comrades*, 122.

161. RGANI f. 5, op. 30, d. 222, ll. 167ff. The sample was made up of 14,869 families of workers; 2,678 families headed by engineering-technical staff; and 1,249 families of white-

collar industrial employees (380 of teachers, 99 of doctors, and 278 of "mid-level medical personnel"). Family members make up the grand total.

162. GARF f. A-259, op. 42, d. 5983, ll. 12–13. See also Lovell, *Summerfolk*.

163. RGANI f. 5, op. 30, d. 267, ll. 3–5.

164. For example, Jeremy Smith, "Khrushchev and the Path to Modernization through Education," 221–336.

165. This is expressed in a citizen's letter emphasizing that fair and ordered distribution is a communist principle. RGAE f. 339, op. 3, d. 1051, ll. 149–50.

166. Cf. a resolution and an order of the Moscow Soviet about reform to the city's Housing Queue and Distribution Administration in spring 1958, in TsAGM f. 2433, op. 8, d. 20, l. 48; d. 31, ll. 15–16.

167. GARF f. 5451, op. 30, d. 462, ll. 29–40. All the evidence in this paragraph and the next is taken from this report.

168. See chapter 2 for more discussion of the 1955 decree that should have guaranteed their housing conditions.

169. TsAGM f. 2433, op. 8, d. 35, ll. 18–19.

170. GARF f. A-259, op. 45, d. 2531, ll. 7–10. Further research might clarify how effectively the legal system worked in punishing such individuals.

171. GARF f. R-5451, op. 30, d. 462, l. 37.

172. Ibid., d. 449, ll. 85–88. Unless specifically cited, subsequent evidence in this paragraph comes from this source.

173. TsAGM f. 2433, op. 8, d. 48, l. 62; d. 54, l. 33.

174. RGAE f. 51, op. 3, d. 1108, ll. 7ff.

175. Bittner, "Exploring Reform," 44. See also Stephen V. Bittner, "Local Soviets, Public Order, and Welfare after Stalin: Appeals from Moscow's Kiev Raion," 281–93.

176. GARF f. R-5451, op. 30, d. 462, l. 39.

177. Ibid., d. 449, l. 87.

178. A. A. Tomsen, "Zhilishchnyi vopros pri kapitalizme i v SSSR," 10.

179. *Zhilishchno-kommunal'noe khoziaistvo* (January 1962): 5–7.

180. M. A. Shipilov, *Zhilishchnyi vopros pri kapitlizme i sotsializme*, 4.

181. Vasilii Aksenov, *Kollegi*, in *Sobranie sochinenii* 1:78–79.

4—Possibilities and Paradoxes of Ownership

1. Stalin, *Sochineniia*, 15:206. The epigraphs are from John Locke, *Second Treatise of Government*, 305–6 (1.5.27); Marx and Engels, *Communist Manifesto*, 235.

2. N. S. Khrushchev, *On the Communist Programme: Report on the Programme of the CPSU to the Twenty-second Congress of the Party, October 18, 1961*, 28.

3. For a critique of binary categories during late socialism (the period following the one covered in this monograph), see Alexei Yurchak, *Everything Was Forever, until It Was No More: The Last Soviet Generation*, 4–8.

4. Elena A. Osokina, "Economic Disobedience under Stalin," 170–200 (200); James R. Millar, "The Little Deal: Brezhnev's Contribution to Acquisitive Socialism," 694–706 (700–701).

5. The concept of permitted autonomy also colors Bradley's analysis of civil society-type organizations in nineteenth-century Russia. See Joseph Bradley, "Subjects into Citizens: Societies, Civil Society, and Autocracy in Tsarist Russia," 1094–123. I do not suggest, however,

that a "civil society" or anything remotely approximating one existed in the USSR.

6. P. Charles Hachten, "Property Relations and the Economic Organization of Soviet Russia, 1941–1948," marks the end of the neglect.

7. This is a blend of concepts outlined in Stephen R. Munzer, *A Theory of Property*; James O. Grunenbaum, *Private Ownership*, ch. 1; Roger J. Smith, *Property Law*, ch. 1.

8. Richard Pipes, *Russia under the Old Regime*, 40–49, 65–71.

9. Ibid., 313. Pipes reiterates that "tsarism respected private property" increasingly from the mid-eighteenth century, with the new word *sobstvennost'* entering the language at the same time as private property rights started to become entrenched. Richard Pipes, *The Russian Revolution, 1899–1919*, 55; also Wortman, *Russian Legal Consciousness*.

10. Richard Pipes, *Property and Freedom*, xi, also ch. 3.

11. Hosking, "Patronage and the Russian State," 303.

12. Edward Keenan, "Muscovite Political Folkways," 115–81 (136, 128).

13. George G. Weickhardt, "The Pre-Petrine Law of Property," 663–79 (665).

14. Pipes, *Under the Old Regime*, 40; Weickhardt, "Law of Property," 668.

15. Richard Hellie, "The Law," 360–86 (361).

16. Nancy Shields Kollmann, "Law and Society," 559–78 (574).

17. Michelle Lamarche Marrese, *A Woman's Kingdom: Noblewomen and the Control of Property in Russia, 1700–1861*; William Wagner, *Marriage, Property, and Law in Late Imperial Russia*. Note that Lee A. Farrow emphasizes limits on nobles' property rights, in *Between Clan and Crown: The Struggle to Define Noble Property Rights in Imperial Russia*.

18. For very distinguished examples of such general works, see Malia, *Soviet Tragedy*, and the various writings of Pipes. Recent historiography that adds subtlety is discussed in the preceding pages. For legal scholarship: a number of academic lawyers in the United States and Britain, working on the Soviet Union in the two postwar decades, recognized the formal importance of individual ownership in the urban housing economy. For example, Harold J. Berman, "Soviet Property in Law and in Plan (with Special Reference to Municipal Land and Housing)," 324–53; Vladimir Gsovski, "Soviet Law of Inheritance," 291–320; Peter B. Maggs, "The Security of Individually Owned Property under Soviet Law," 525–37; Samuel Kucherow, "Property in the Soviet Union," 376–92; Bernard Rudden, "Soviet Housing Law," 591–630, and "Soviet Housing and the New Civil Code," 231–62. The pioneer was John N. Hazard, in *Soviet Housing Law*. The apparent paradox of personal property was first discussed at length by a Western scholar in a dissertation defended in 1968, which used published sources and Marxist rhetoric to present the complex relationship between ideological ideals and practical incentives. Hiroshi Kimura, "Personal Property in the Soviet Union, with Particular Emphasis on the Khrushchev Era: An Ideological, Political, and Economic Dilemma." A more general legal survey on Soviet property that also took the categories of property seriously, Stanislaw J. Sawicki, *Soviet Land and Housing Law: A Historical and Comparative Study*, was published in New York in 1977. More recently, Charles Hachten has skillfully argued that such units as industrial enterprises and households enjoyed substantial status in property relations between 1941 and 1948 and were responsible in part or in whole for major areas of economic activity—including the construction, administration, and ownership of housing. Hachten, "Property Relations."

19. "Departments" included, for example, ministries, enterprises, academies, and unions. Cooperatives were composed of citizen shareholders, often employees of the same institution.

20. For an outline of the house building cooperative, see Andrusz, *Housing and Urban Development*, ch. 4.

21. A decree of 18 December 1917 also abolished private property but allowed for personal property to exist in cities of ten thousand or fewer inhabitants. A decree of 22 May 1922 confirmed the consumption and non-profit-making character of personal property while emphasizing penal sanctions against "speculation." The Civil Code (RSFSR) of October 1922 consolidated the status of personal property. A (Central Committee and Sovnarkom) decree of August 1924 expanded the scope of personal property in bigger cities. Prewar Stalinism strengthened personal property in theory: Article 10 of the 1936 constitution confirmed the force of personal property in general rather than specific terms and underwrote much subsequent legislation and legal commentary. The major Central Committee and Sovnarkom decree of 17 October 1937, "On the preservation of the housing fund and improvement of the housing economies in cities," further consolidated the legal status of personal property.

22. B. K. Komarov, *Zakonodatel'stvo o nasledovanii*, 17.

23. Lovell explores the "particularly ambiguous case" of Soviet dacha ownership in *Summerfolk*, 169.

24. Z. A. Fedotovskaia, *Pravo lichnoi sobstvennosti na zhiloi dom*, 5.

25. L. S. Pavlov, *Kommunizm i lichnaia sobstvennost'*, 3, 39, 47.

26. Pipes, *Under the Bolshevik Regime*, 276, 504.

27. *Narodnoe khoziaistvo SSSR 1922–1982: Iubileinyi statisticheskii ezhegodnik*, 431–32.

28. A. M. Honoré, "Ownership," 107–47 (144–45).

29. Use is made here of Honoré's framework and the underlying structure of his argument rather than the detail of all his incidents, some of which are specifically redundant in the Soviet case.

30. Aristotle, *The Politics*, 2.5.

31. Aquinas, *Summa theologiae*, 2a2ae.66, in St. Thomas Aquinas, *Political Writings*, 208–9.

32. For example, a Sovnarkom decree of 8 August 1921 allowed for the reassessment of what should constitute municipal housing funds, at a time of soviets' acute financial weakness. Skripko et al., *Zhilishchnoe zakonodatel'stvo*, 24.

33. *Vecherniaia Moskva*, 29 August 1945, 1.

34. TsAGM f. 490, op. 1, d. 294, ll. 134–35.

35. For example, see *Vecherniaia Moskva*, 19 September 1945, 2.

36. A. Ia. Koshelev, *Lichnaia sobstvennost' v sotsialisticheskom obshchestve*, 118.

37. Adam Smith, *The Wealth of Nations*, books 4–5, 297–306.

38. James Madison, Federalist Paper No. 10, in Alexander Hamilton, James Madison, and John Jay, *The Federalist*, 41. See also Gordon S. Wood, *The Radicalism of the American Revolution*, 253.

39. J. A. Borkowski and Paul du Plessis, *Textbook on Roman Law*, 157–63.

40. Milovan Djilas, *The New Class: An Analysis of the Communist System*, 44.

41. Smith, *Property Law*, 6.

42. See Xavier Martin, *Human Nature and the French Revolution: From the Enlightenment to the Napoleonic Code*, 259–63. Farrow argues that individual Russian nobles were able to exert more autonomous approaches to the inheritance of property than those fellow Europeans who lived in states governed by Napoleonic-influenced law codes, though the "clan" still exercised influence through the ongoing law of redemption, which extended the rights of family members to reacquire land that had been sold without their permission. See Lee A. Farrow, "The Ties that Bind: The Role of the Russian Clan in Inheritance and Property Law," 13–32.

43. For 1919–1939, calculations are based on Anne Power, *Hovels to High Rise: State Housing in Europe since 1850*, 213. For 1946–1965, calculations are based on Stephen Merrett, *State Housing in Britain*, 239, 248.

44. Dick Urban Vestbro, "Collective Housing Units in Sweden," 3.

45. Bruce Headey, *Housing Policy in the Developed Economy: The United Kingdom, Sweden and the United States*, 45; Lundqvist, *Housing Policy and Tenures in Sweden*.

46. Roger H. Duclaud-Williams, *The Politics of Housing in Britain and France*, 17–19.

47. On West Germany, see Power, *Hovels to High Rise*; Ian D. Turner, ed., *Reconstruction in Post-War Germany: British Occupation Policy and the Western Zones, 1945–1955*.

48. Staemmler, "East Germany," 236.

49. Frank Carter, "Housing Policy in Bulgaria" in Sillince, *Housing Policies*, 170–227 (181).

50. Roland Walter Strobel, "City Planning and Political Ideology in East and West Berlin (Germany), 1949 to 1989: An Examination of the Urban Design of Public Housing on Both Sides of the Wall," 97–99.

51. Virág Eszter Molnar, "Modernity and Memory: The Politics of Architecture in Hungary and East Germany after the Second World War," 82–83.

52. Gábor Locsmándi and John Sillince, "Housing Policy in Hungary" in Sillince, *Housing Policies*, 440–74; Molnar, "Modernity and Memory," 102.

53. Peter Bassin, "Yugoslavia," in Martin Wynn, ed., *Housing in Europe*, 155–77.

54. In some Western European countries, private tenants enjoyed a tradition of very secure occupancy (Austria is a classic example). Yet the level of security was much greater in the USSR, where the tenant held a much more decisive grip on more of the elements of ownership.

5—Individual Ownership, Welfare, and the Soviet Order

1. GARF f. R-5446, op. 59, d. 101, l. 90. The epigraphs for this chapter are from GARF f. 5446, op. 68, d. 51, l. 24; Khrushchev, *Last Testament*, 139.

2. *Konstitutsiia (Osnovnoi zakon) Soiuza Sovetskikh Sotsialisticheskikh Respublik*, 20 (article 44).

3. V. Burmistrov, *Soviet Law and the Citizens' Rights*, 10.

4. V. P. Gribanov and A. Iu. Kabalkin, *Zhilishchnye prava sovetskikh grazhdan*, 18; A. Iu. Kabalkin, *Okhrana zhilishchnykh prav grazhdan*, 3–23.

5. P. P. Gureev, *Zashchita lichnykh i imushchestvennykh prav*, 3. See also N. I. Matuzov, *Sub"ektivnye prava grazhdan SSSR*, 3–4.

6. T. D. Alekseev, *Zhilishchnye l'goty grazhdan SSSR*.

7. As delineated in article 7 of the major Central Committee and Council of Ministers (USSR) decree of 18 October 1937, "On the preservation of the housing fund and improvement of the housing economy in cities," and a decree of the Economic Council (Ekonomsovet) of the Council of People's Commissars, USSR, 26 April 1939. R. I. Kudriavtsev, ed., *Zhilishchnoe zakonodatel'stvo: sbornik ofitsial'nykh materialov*, 494–95.

8. Stephen Kotkin illustrates the privileges associated with house purchase in the 1930s with the example of a Stakhanovite who bought a dwelling for 17,000 rubles, thanks to his very high wages. Kotkin, *Magnetic Mountain*, 210. A postwar refugee described how the director of the "Moscow State Electric Power Station" had "built a beautiful home for himself. He had accumulated great wealth in the bank. So he bought a piece of land [he could not have done this] and built

a fine brick home: eight rooms, two floors. . . . The house cost about fifty thousand rubles" and was built between 1931 and 1934. Refugee no. 1240, in Carolyn Recht, *The Soviet Urban Housing Problem as Reported by Russian Refugees* (part of Harvard Project), 10.

9. Refugee no. 1398, in Recht, *Soviet Urban Housing Problem*, 11.

10. See chapter 1 for an analysis of the decree's impact on reconstruction, where the general analytical concern was to illustrate the course of housing reconstruction and its contribution to the origins of the urban housing program. In this chapter additional evidence is used to bring the specific issue of individual property into sharper focus.

11. *Narodnoe khoziaistvo SSSR 1922–1982*, 425.

12. V. S. Tadevosian, "Nekotorye voprosy zhilishchnogo prava," 43–51 (47).

13. In archival funds, I was only able to locate complete prewar tenurial breakdowns (from which the percentage of personal property holdings in a housing fund can be calculated) for individual cities, not for the USSR as a whole or for the five sample republics. These data are presented in chapter 2. They show that in a comparison of the years 1940 and 1950 (and 1960), the proportion of personal property increased in some city housing funds by more than 10 percent, in some it decreased by more than 10 percent, and in others it remained roughly the same. Published data, meanwhile, suggest that although personal property as a proportion of completed new construction was much higher in the 1946–1950 five-year plan than in that of 1933–1937, the overall proportion of personal property in the urban housing fund was roughly similar in 1940 and in 1950. See *Narodnoe khoziaistvo SSSR v 1958 godu: Statisticheskii ezhegodnik*, 641. However, this last datum reflects a statistical time lag: embedded in the prewar personal property figures are large numbers of old dwellings that were not municipalized in the 1920s. Many of these were destroyed during the war, so the considerable contribution of personal property to postwar reconstruction (see chapters 1, 2, and 4) and the published data on new completions cited above show that many more new houses were entering the personal property fund after 1944. So the absolute stock of personal property was growing. Individual ownership was spreading.

14. Varga-Harris shows how this remained true even in the Khrushchev era in "Constructing the Soviet Hearth," 234.

15. For European analogies, see Paul Betts and David Crowley, eds., *Domestic Dreamworlds: Notions of Home in Post–1945 Europe*, 2; Richard Bessel and Dirk Schumann, eds., *Life after Death: Approaches to a Cultural and Social History of Europe during the 1940s and 1950s*.

16. A foreign scholar writing at the time argued on the basis of legal documents that formal structures for adjudicating such disputes existed and were used even during the wartime emergency. See Donald G. Leitch, "Soviet Housing Administration and the Wartime Evacuation," 180–90.

17. GARF f. R-5446, op. 85, d. 1, l. 113.

18. RGAE f. 9510, op. 3, d. 131, l. 181.

19. GARF f. A-256, op. 6, d. 7785, l. 84.

20. GARF f. R-7523, op. 58, d. 437, ll. 9–12.

21. GARF f. R-5446, op. 68, d. 62, l. 210.

22. Ibid., op. 85, d. 8, ll. 44–46.

23. GARF f. R-7901, op. 3, d. 255, l. 5.

24. GARF f. R-7523, op. 58, d. 114, ll. 132–38.

25. *Vesna na Zarechnoi ulitse*, dir. Marlen Khutsiev and Feliks Mironer.

26. For soviet tenure, see the case of Latyeva: GARF f. R-5446, op. 85, d. 8, ll. 44–46. For departmental tenure, see the example of one G. M. Dymov of Moscow Region and his attempt

to keep control of his dwelling in ibid., d. 9, ll. 78–81. In this case of a wartime returnee, the rights of the individual tenant seemed to trump those of the enterprise that formally owned his housing space.

27. Gennady Fomin, *Housing Construction*, 7.

28. For example, "On the eviction from accommodations belonging to organs of transport of those not involved in transport, and the resettlement of transport employees," TsIK and SNK USSR decree, 13 February 1931 in Kudriavtsev, *Zhilishchnoe zakonodatel'stvo*, 353.

29. For example, *Vecherniaia Moskva*, 18 May 1945, 3; 5 April 1950, 1.

30. TsAGM f. 2852, op. 1, d. 22, l. 53.

31. GARF f. A-259, op. 7, d. 8771, ll. 9ff.

32. They were instead acts of resistance, common sense, and canny manipulation. Cf. Fitzpatrick, *Everyday Stalinism*.

33. Instruktsiia Ministerstva kommunal'nogo khoziaistva RSFSR 30 August 1947 no. 727, in Kudriavtsev, *Zhilishchnoe zakonodatel'stvo*, 237.

34. In Penza in November 1947 the average citizen had 3.7 square meters of housing space. GARF f. A-259, op. 6, d. 4543, l. 16.

35. Kudriavtsev, *Zhilishchnoe zakonodatel'stvo*, 237.

36. GARF f. A-259, op. 6, d. 4577, ll. 1–15.

37. GARF f. R-7523, op. 58, d. 127, ll. 77–78. For another case, see ibid., d. 143, l. 87.

38. Kudriavtsev, *Zhilishchnoe zakonodatel'stvo*, 553.

39. GARF f. R-5446, op. 85, d. 5, ll. 237–39. Malenkov took a personal interest in the case: Karachevtseva was lucky.

40. Kudriavtsev, *Zhilishchnoe zakonodatel'stvo*, 216. However, a law of 1939, reemphasized in a Sovnarkom decree of August 1941, assured veterans and their family members of retaining their housing space. Edele, "Soviet Veterans as an Entitlement Group," 123.

41. GARF f. R-7523, op. 58, d. 115, l. 6.

42. Calculated from *Narodnoe khoziaistvo, statisticheskii ezhegodnik* (1958), 641; (1964), 610.

43. RGAE f. 339, op. 3, d. 370, l. 25.

44. The usual specific features of personal property law, and its considerable difference from private property, would of course still apply.

45. RGAE f. 339, op. 3, d. 554, ll. 236–40.

46. *Narodnoe khoziaistvo, Statisticheskii ezhegodnik* (1964), 605.

47. Here the personal property sector was admittedly unusually small as a proportion of the stock but in absolute terms still amounted to a lot of houses.

48. TsAGM f. 2852, op. 1, d. 102, l. 122.

49. Ibid., d. 114, l. 40.

50. Ibid., d. 116, contains numerous orders and resolutions for requisitions.

51. Slum clearance is briefly discussed in chapter 3. For various European perspectives of the same phenomenon, see Jeffrey Diefendorf, ed., *Rebuilding Europe's Bombed Cities*.

52. GARF f. A-259, op. 45, d. 1086, ll. 45–49.

53. Steven Harris describes the Gor'kii method in "Moving to the Separate Apartment," ch. 3, and makes a case for its significance. He argues that the personal property figures relied greatly on such collective construction, as the dwellings therein were classified as personal property. The legal point is correct, but the proportion of collective construction is not verified empirically. Officials were certainly most concerned about individual builders, and the physical cityscape reflected their policies.

54. These had existed in the 1920s and 1930s, but the major housing decree of 17 October 1937 effectively sidelined them.

55. "On housing construction and dacha construction cooperatives," *Sobranie post-anovlenii i rasporiazhenii pravitel'stva SSSR* 5 (1958): 115.

56. "On individual and cooperative housing construction," ibid., 12 (1962): 283–86 (283).

57. RGAE f. 1562, op. 37, d. 2541, l. 18.

58. Fedotovskaia, *Pravo lichnoi sobstvennosti na zhiloi dom*, 9.

59. Sh. D. Chikvashvili, *Zhilishchno-stroitel'naia kooperatsiia v SSSR*, 16.

60. I. P. Prokopchenko, *Chto dolzhen znat' chlen zhilishchno-stroitel'nogo kooperativa*, 59.

61. M. A. Nechetskii, *Zhilishchno-stroitel'nye kooperativy*, 32.

62. Vladimir Voinovich, *Ivankiada*. Though set in Brezhnev's USSR, this novella captures the paradoxes inherent in the system set up by Khrushchev.

63. TsAGM f. 490, op. 1, d. 268, l. 91.

64. Ibid., d. 294, ll. 73, 166.

65. Ibid., d. 285, ll. 163, 172.

66. GARF f. A-259, op. 45, d. 1087, l. 39.

67. To be fair, the archival record also contains examples of more ordinary-sounding housing cooperatives (for example, TsAGM f. 490, op. 1, d. 285, l. 53), though there is a decided tilt toward cooperatives of prestigious elites with savings and know-how.

68. Koshelev, *Lichnaia sobstvennost' v sotsialisticheskom obshchestve*, 164, 172–73; Pavlov, *Kommunizm i lichnaia sobstvennost'*, 39, 47.

69. RGAE f. 339, op. 3, d. 1046, l. 197.

70. *Programme of the Communist Party of the Soviet Union Adopted . . . October 31, 1961*, 63.

71. A. G. Potiukov, *Zhilishchnye spory v sudebnoi praktike*, 4.

72. Aleksandr Vysokovskii argues for a "sense of ownership" that was emphatically separate from legal right during the late stages of Soviet history, but this underestimates the more complex blend of de jure and de facto elements that composed individual ownership by the end of the Khrushchev era. See Vysokovskii, "Will Domesticity Return?" 271–308 (275).

73. For example, TsAGM f. 2276, op. 1, d. 2, ll. 1–2.

74. GARF f. 5446, op. 68, d. 61, ll. 246–47.

75. TsAGM f. 2276, op. 1, d. 14, l. 17.

76. TsAGM f. 2433, op. 8, d. 48, l. 58.

77. TsAGM f. 2276, op. 1, d. 29, l. 17.

78. Iu. V. Trifonov, *Obmen*, in Iurii Trifonov, *Sobranie sochinenii*, vol. 2.

79. A useful discussion of the published laws as they applied in the immediate postwar period is Gsovski, "Soviet Law of Inheritance."

80. Prokopchenko, *Chto dolzhen znat' chlen zhilishchno-stroitel'nogo kooperativa*, 61–63.

81. Komarov, *Zakonodatel'stvo o nasledovanii*, 4.

82. The apartment would legally become vacant, however, if family members were registered elsewhere at the time of death of the occupier.

83. *Predostavlenie zhiloi ploshchadi i pravo pol'zovaniia eiu*, 31.

84. GARF f. A-259, op. 6, d. 4577, ll. 1–15. 85. A dwelling was therefore to a large extent a family property, which in some ways protected the property rights of individual family members and in other ways reduced them. In combination with the general housing shortage, this had particular effects on the Soviet way of life, forcing divorcees, for example, to continue to cohabit (see also chapter 3). Cf. Field, "Divorce and Conceptions of Private Life."

85. RGANI f. 5, op. 30, d. 192, ll. 57–61.

86. RGAE f. 339, op. 3, d. 1051, l. 30. Buriak, Timofeeva (see chapter 3), and Pokrovskaia (see next note) were all writing to the organizers of the All-Union Conference on City Planning of 1960. Ibid.; ibid., d. 1046, l. 196; ibid., d. 1051, l. 42.

87. Ibid., d. 1051, l. 42.

88. Potiukov, *Zhilishchnye spory v sudebnoi praktike*, 60.

89. Susan E. Reid, "'The Meaning of Home: 'The Only Bit of the World You Can Have to Yourself,'" in Lewis H. Siegelbaum, ed., *Borders of Socialism: Private Spheres of Soviet Russia*, 145–70 (149).

90. See the introduction for distinctions between the USSR and Western welfare states, and for an explanation of the reasons that the USSR was not a welfare state.

91. Rent controls after the war (in Britain, for example) provide an example of redistribution toward private tenants.

92. See chapter 1.

93. Notwithstanding the greater regularization of some of its political and administrative processes; see Gorlizki and Khlevniuk, *Cold Peace*.

94. GARF f. 5446, op. 68, d. 42, ll. 68, 73.

95. In similarly extreme circumstances, however, this might well be a universally human reaction.

96. See chapter 3 for discussion of equality in the urban housing economy between 1958 and 1964, and for detail on the reformed system of appeal.

97. *Predostavlenie zhiloi ploshchadi i pravo pol'zovaniia eiu*, 34.

98. TsAGM f. 2852, op. 1, d. 142, l. 22.

99. RGAE f. 339, op. 3, d. 820, l. 60.

100. Oleg Kharkhordin, *The Collective and the Individual in Russia: A Study of Practices*, 279–80, 286.

101. I acknowledge that the evidence I present does not fully refute Kharkhordin's controversial contentions, with which further engagement is required.

102. A major discussion of internal passports and their relationship to the functioning of the Stalinist system, with particular reference to population movements and the role of the NKVD, is David Shearer, "Elements Near and Alien: Passportization, Policing, and Identity in the Stalinist State, 1932–1952," 835–81. For the historical origins of Soviet mechanisms of control, checking, and information gathering, see Peter Holquist "Information Is the Alpha and Omega of Our Work."

103. GARF f. R-7523, op. 37, d. 16, ll. 123–24.

104. GARF f. R-5446, op. 59, d. 93, l. 84.

105. Note that the argument in chapter 1 about the existence of an "enlightened officialdom" after the war referred to central policy makers rather than local officials, though the harsh effects in this case might have been the unintended consequence of officials covering each other's backs.

106. TsAGM f. 490, op. 1, d. 213, ll. 53, 54.

107. TsAGM f. 2852, op. 1, d. 64, l. 43. The status of the so-called *limitchiki* would be a problematic factor during the rest of the Soviet period and would be an interesting subject of further research.

108. Ibid., d. 129, ll. 17, 18.

Conclusion—Paradise in Grey

1. The epigraph is from *Konstitutsiia (Osnovnoi zakon) SSSR*, 20.

2. *Narodnoe khoziaistvo SSSR za 70 let: Iubileinyi statisticheskii ezhegodnik*, 509. This figure is *obshchaia ploshchad'* and includes kitchen, bathroom, and storage space (unlike most of the data cited in the book). Given that in the 1970s and 1980s apartments were of different types and dimensions than they were earlier, no attempt has been made to convert the figures to the equivalent *zhilaia ploshchad'* using those approximate formulae that generally work for the 1950s and 1960s.

3. Alexander Dedul, *Six Thousand Move In Every Day: A Good Flat for Every Family*.

4. A. S. Seniavskii places later Soviet achievements and shortcomings in the historical context of the earlier period. For his full discussion, see *Rossiiskii gorod v 1960-e–80-e gody*, 202–21.

5. Barry Steven Kotlove, "The Cost of Soviet Housing," 37.

6. Hedrick Smith, *The Russians*, 435; John Simpson, *Strange Places, Questionable People*, 196; Colin Thubron, *Among the Russians: From the Baltic to the Caucasus*, 25; Malcolm Bradbury, *Rates of Exchange*, 76; Margaret Thatcher, *The Downing Street Years*, 479; Simpson, *Strange Places*, 251.

7. Graham Greene, *The Human Factor*, 284; John le Carré, *The Russia House*, 265.

Primary Sources

ARCHIVES

State Archive of the Russian Federation, main depository

(*Gosudarstvennyi Arkhiv Rossiiskoi Federatsii*, GARF "R")
f. R-5446   Council of Ministers (USSR)
f. R-5451   All-Union Central Soviet of Trade Unions (VTsSPS)
f. R-5462   Central Committee (CC) of the Trade Union (TU) of Education Employees
f. R-5475   CC of the TU of Construction Workers and Workers in the Construction
                Materials Industry
f. R-7523   Supreme Soviet (USSR)
f. R-7676   CC of the TU of Transport Mechanical Engineering Workers
f. R-7860   CC of the TU of Workers in the Meat and Dairy Industry
f. R-7901   CC of the TU of Employees of Political-Instructional Institutions and Culture

State Archive of the Russian Federation, RSFSR depository

(*Gosudarstvennyi Arkhiv Rossiiskoi Federatsii*, GARF "A")
f. A-259   Council of Ministers (RSFSR)

Russian State Archive of the Economy

(*Rossiiskii Gosudarstvennyi Arkhiv Ekonomiki*, RGAE)
f. 51   State Committee for Radio-Electronics, Council of Ministers (GKRE)
f. 233   National Council of the Economy (SNKh)
f. 293   Academy of Architecture
f. 339   State Construction Committee, Council of Ministers (Gosstroi)
f. 1562   Central Statistical Administration (TsSU)
f. 4372   State Planning Committee, Council of Ministers (Gosplan)

f. 7733   Ministry of Finance
f. 8216   Ministry of Urban and Rural Construction
f. 8627   Ministry of the Oil Industry
f. 9028   Bank for Financing the Communal and Housing Economy
f. 9166   Ministry of Mechanical Engineering Enterprises
f. 9432   State Architecture Committee, Council of Ministers
f. 9510   Ministry of Urban Construction
(*All bodies all-union*)

Russian State Archive of Social and Political History

(*Rossiiskii Arkhiv Sotsio-Politicheskoi Istorii*, RGASPI)
f. 397   Khrushchev
f. 651   *Stroitel'naia gazeta* editorial papers

Russian State Archive of Contemporary History

(*Rossiiskii Arkhiv Noveishei Istorii*, RGANI)
f. 5   General Committee of the Communist Party

Central Archive of the City of Moscow

(*Tsentral'nyi Arkhiv Goroda Moskvy*, TsAGM)
f. 490   Main Administration of the Housing Economy
f. 534   Main Architectural-Planning Administration
f. 589   Moscow Housing Construction Trust (*Moszhilstroi*)
f. 605   Main Administration for Housing and Civil Construction (*Glavmosstroi*)
f. 716   Main Administration for Construction of Tall Buildings, Ministry of Construction USSR (*Glavvysotstroi*)
f. 2276   Bureau for Housing Exchange of the Administration of Accounts and Distribution of Housing
f. 2433   Administration of Accounts and Distribution of Housing
f. 2852, op. 1   Sverdlovskii Raion Housing Administration
f. 2852, op. 5   Kalininskii Raion Housing Administration

The National Archives, Kew, London (TNA: PRO)

FO 371   Foreign Office: Political Departments, General Correspondence, 1906–1966
FO 418   Foreign Office: Confidential Print, Russia and Soviet Union, 1821–1956
PREM 11   Prime Minister's Office, Correspondence and Papers, 1951–1964

PERIODICALS

Arkhitektura SSSR
Izvestiia
Narodnoe khoziaistvo, statisticheskii ezhegodnik
Pravda

Sobranie postanovlenii i rasporiazhenii pravitel'stva SSSR
Sovetskaia arkhitektura, ezhegodnik
Sovetskoe gosudarstvo i pravo
Stroitel'naia gazeta
Trud
Vecherniaia Moskva
Zhilishchno-kommunal'noe khoziaistvo

DOCUMENT COLLECTIONS AND COMPENDIA

Kesaris, Paul, ed. *CIA Research Reports: The Soviet Union, 1946–1976.* Frederick, MD: University Publications of America, 1982.

Kiselev, A. S., ed. *Moskva poslevoennaia, 1945–1947: Arkhivnye dokumenty i materialy.* Moscow: Mosgorarkhiv, 2000.

Kosenkova, Iu. L. *Sovetskii gorod 1940-kh—pervoi poloviny 1950-kh godov: Ot tvorcheskykh poiskov k praktike stroitel'stva.* Moscow: URSS, 2000.

KPSS v rezoliutsiiakh i resheniiakh s"ezdov, konferentsii i plenumov tsentral'nogo komiteta. Moscow: Izdatel'stvo politicheskoi literatury, 1970 (15 vols.), 1983 (15 vols.).

Lur'e, Lev, and Maliarova, Irina. *1956 god. Seredina veka.* St. Petersburg and Moscow: Neva, 2007.

Mitchell, B. R. *International Historical Statistics: Europe, 1750–2000.* Basingstoke: Palgrave Macmillan, 2003.

Narodnoe khoziaistvo SSSR 1922–1982: Iubileinyi statisticheskii ezhegodnik. Moscow: Finansy i statistika, 1982.

Narodnoe khoziaistvo SSSR za 70 let: Iubileinyi statisticheskii ezhegodnik. Moscow: Finansy i statistika, 1987.

Recht, Carolyn. *The Soviet Urban Housing Problem as Reported by Russian Refugees.* Maxwell Air Force Base, Alabama: Air Research and Development Command Human Resources Research Institute, January 1954.

Statistisk Årsbok för Sverige 1971. Stockholm, 1970.

Zubkova, E. Iu., et al., eds. *Sovetskaia zhizn', 1945–1953.* Moscow: ROSSPEN, 2003.

FICTION

Aksenov, Vasilii. *Sobranie sochinenii.* Vol. 1. Moscow: Iunost', 1994.

Bitov, Andrei. *Sobranie sochinenii.* Vol. 1. Moscow: Molodaia gvardiia, 1991.

Bradbury, Malcolm. *Rates of Exchange.* London: Arena, 1984.

Dudintsev, V. *Ne khlebom edinym. Novyi mir.* 1956, 8:31–118, 9:37–118, 10:21–98.

Greene, Graham. *The Human Factor.* Franklin Center, PA: The Franklin Library First Edition Society, 1978.

Grossman, Vasilii. *Life and Fate.* Translated by Robert Chandler. London: Harvill, 1995.

Le Carré, John. *The Russia House.* London: Hodder and Stoughton, 1989.

Solzhenitsyn, Aleksandr. *The First Circle.* Translated by Max Hayward, Manya Harari, and Michael Glenny. London: Harvill, 1988.

Trifonov, Iurii. *Sobranie sochinenii.* Moscow: Khudozhestvennaia literatura, 1985–1986.

Voinovich, Vladimir. *Ivankiada.* Ann Arbor: Ardis, 1976.

———. *Khochu byt' chestnym: povesti.* Moscow: Moskovskii rabochii, 1989.

FILM

A esli eto liubov'? Directed by Iulii Raizman. Mosfil'm, 1961.
Cheremushki. Directed by Herbert Rappoport. Lenfil'm, 1962.
Dolgie provody. Directed by Kira Muratova. Odesskaia kinostudiia, 1971.
Dom, v kotorom ia zhivu. Directed by Lev Kulidzhanov and Iakov Segel'. Tsentral'naia kinostudiia detskikh i iunosheskikh fil'mov imeni M. Gor'kogo, 1957.
Eshche raz pro liubov'. Directed by Georgii Natanson. Mosfil'm, 1968.
Garazh. Directed by El'dar Riazanov. Mosfil'm, 1979.
Ia shagaiu po Moskve. Directed by Georgii Daneliia. Mosfil'm, 1963.
Ironiia sud'by, ili s legkym parom! Directed by El'dar Riazanov. Mosfil'm, 1975.
Katok i skripka. Directed by Andrei Tarkovskii. Mosfil'm, 1960.
Khrushchevki. ORT, *Sovetskaia imperiia* series, 2004.
Nash dom. Directed by Vasilii Pronin. Mosfil'm, 1965.
Osennii marafon. Directed by Georgii Daneliia. Mosfil'm, 1979.
Vesna na Zarechnoi ulitse. Directed by Marlen Khutsiev and Feliks Mironer. Odesskaia kinostudiia, 1956.
Zastava Il'icha (also known as *Mne dvadtsat' let*). Directed by Marlen Khutsiev. Tsentral'naia kinostudiia detskikh i iunosheskikh fil'mov imeni M. Gor'kogo, 1964.

OTHER PRIMARY SOURCES

Alekseev, T. D. *Zhilishchnye l'goty grazhdan SSSR.* Moscow: Gosiurizdat, 1962.
Aquinas, St. Thomas. *Political Writings.* Edited and translated by R. W. Dyson. Cambridge: Cambridge University Press, 2002.
Arendt, Hannah. *The Origins of Totalitarianism.* London: André Deutsch, 1986.
Aristotle. *The Politics.* London: Penguin, 1992.
Bukharin, N., and E. Preobrazhenskii. *Azbuka kommunizma: populiarnoe ob"iasnenie programmy rossiiskoi kommunisticheskoi partii bol'shevikov.* Moscow: Gosudarstvennoe izdatel'stvo, 1920.
Burmistrov, V. *Soviet Law and the Citizens' Rights.* Moscow: Novosti Press Agency, 1974.
Chikvashvili, Sh. D. *Zhilishchno-stroitel'naia kooperatsiia v SSSR.* Moscow: Iuridicheskaia literatura, 1965.
Davenport-Hines, Richard, ed. *Letters from Oxford: Hugh Trevor Roper to Bernard Berenson.* London: Weidenfield and Nicolson, 2006.
Dedul, Alexander. *Six Thousand Move In Every Day: A Good Flat for Every Family.* Moscow: Novosti, 1979.
Djilas, Milovan. *The New Class: An Analysis of the Communist System.* London: Thames and Hudson, 1957.
Economic Commission for Europe. *Annual Bulletin of Housing and Building Statistics for Europe.* Geneva: United Nations, 1957–1970.
Engels, Friedrich. *The Housing Question.* London: Martin Lawrence, 1935.
Fedotovskaia, Z. A. *Pravo lichnoi sobstvennosti na zhiloi dom.* Moscow: Gosiurizdat, 1963.
Fomin, Gennady N. *Housing Construction.* Moscow: Novosti, 1974.
Friedrich, Carl, and Zbigniew Brzezinski. *Totalitarian Dictatorship and Autocracy.* 1956. Cambridge, MA: Harvard University Press, 1965.
Gribanov, V. P., and A. Iu. Kabalkin. *Zhilishchnye prava sovetskikh grazhdan.* Moscow: Znanie, 1964.

Gureev, P. P. *Zashchita lichnykh i imushchestvennykh prav*. Moscow: Nauka, 1964.

Habermas, Jurgen. *The Structural Transformation of the Public Sphere: An Inquiry into a Category of Bourgeois Society*. Cambridge: Polity, 1989.

Hamilton, Alexander, James Madison, and John Jay. *The Federalist*. Cambridge: Cambridge University Press, 2003.

Harrington, Michael. *The Other America: Poverty in the United States*. New York: Macmillan, 1962.

Iakovlev, Aleksandr. *Omut pamiati: ot Stolypina do Putina*. 2 vols. Moscow: Vagrius, 2001.

Kabalkin, A. Iu. *Okhrana zhilishchnykh prav grazhdan*. Moscow: Gosiurizdat, 1963.

Kharitonova, A. E. "Istoriia razvitiia gorodskogo zhilishchnogo stroitel'stva SSSR (1956–63gg)." Candidate of Historical Sciences dissertation, Moscow, 1965.

———. "Osnovnye etapy zhilishchnogo stroitel'stva v SSSR." *Voprosy istorii* 5 (1965): 50–64.

Khomutetskii, N. F. *Leningrad: ocherk arkhitektury*. Moscow: Gosudarstvénnoe izdatel'stvo literatury po stroitel'stvu i arkhitekture, 1953.

Khrushchev, N. S. *The Last Testament*. Vol. 2 of *Khrushchev Remembers*. Translated and edited by Strobe Talbott. London: Penguin, 1977.

———. *On the Communist Programme: Report on the Programme of the CPSU to the Twenty-second Congress of the Party, October 18, 1961*. Moscow: Foreign Languages Publishing House, 1961.

———. *Vospominaniia: Vremia, liudy, vlast'*. 4 vols. Moscow: Moskovskie novosti, 1999.

Komarov, B. K. *Zakonodatel'stvo o nasledovanii*. Moscow: Gosiurizdat, 1963.

Konstitutsiia (Osnovnoi zakon) Soiuza Sovetskikh Sotsialisticheskikh Respublik. Moscow: Politizdat, 1977.

Koshelev, A. Ia. *Lichnaia sobstvennost' v sotsialisticheskom obshchestve*. Moscow: Izdatel'stvo sotsial'no-ekonomicheskoi literatury, 1963.

Kovaleva, L., ed. *Moskva*. Moscow: Rabochaia Moskva, 1935.

Kravchenko, Victor. *I Chose Freedom: The Personal and Political Life of a Soviet Official*. London: Robert Hale, 1947.

Kudriavtsev, R. I., ed. *Zhilishchnoe zakonodatel'stvo: sbornik ofitsial'nykh materialov*. Moscow: Gosiurizdat, 1950.

Lenin, V. I. *The State and Revolution*. In *Collected Works*, 25:381–492. 47 vols. London: Lawrence and Wishart, 1961.

——— (as N. Lenin). *Will the Bolsheviks Maintain Power?* London: Labour Publishing, 1922.

Levskii, A. A. "Deiatel'nost' Moskovskoi organizatsii KPSS po vypolneniiu reshenii XX s"ezda partii v oblasti uluchsheniia zhilishchnykh uslovii trudiashchikhsia." Candidate of Historical Sciences dissertation, Moscow, 1961.

Lipetsker, Mikhail S. *Property Rights of Soviet Citizens*. London: Soviet News, 1946.

Locke, John. *Second Treatise of Government*. Cambridge: Cambridge University Press, 1971.

Marx, Karl, and Friedrich Engels. *The Communist Manifesto*. London: Penguin, 2002.

Matuzov, N. I. *Sub"ektivnye prava grazhdan SSSR*. Saratov: Privolzhskoe knizhnoe izdatel'stvo, 1966.

Mlynár, Zdeněk. *Night Frost in Prague: The End of Humane Socialism*. London: C. Hurst, 1980.

Nazarbayev, Nursultan. *My Life, My Times, and the Future*. Translated and edited by Peter Conradi. Northants: Pilkington Press, 1998.

Nechetskii, M. A. *Zhilishchno-stroitel'nye kooperativy*. Saratov: Privolzhskoe knizhnoe izdatel'stvo, 1965.

Pavlov, L. S. *Kommunizm i lichnaia sobstvennost'*. Leningrad, 1962.

Posokhin, M. V. *Dorogi zhizni: iz zapisok arkhitektora*. Moscow: Stroizdat, 1995.

Potiukov, A. G. *Zhilishchnye spory v sudebnoi praktike*. Leningrad: Izdatel'stvo Leningradsk-ogo universiteta, 1962.

Predostavlenie zhiloi ploshchadi i pravo pol'zovaniia eiu. Moscow: Gosiurizdat, 1962.

The Programme of the Communist Party of the Soviet Union Adopted by the Twenty-second Congress of the CPSU, October 31, 1961. London: Soviet Booklet no. 83, 1961.

Prokopchenko, I. P. *Chto dolzhen znat' chlen zhilishchno-stroitel'nogo kooperativa*. Moscow, 1964.

Salisbury, Harrison E. *A New Russia?* New York and Evanston: Harper and Row, 1962.

Scott, John. *Behind the Urals: An American Worker in Russia's City of Steel*. Bloomington and Indianapolis: Indiana University Press, 1989.

Shipilov, M. A. *Zhilishchnyi vopros pri kapiltalizme i sotsializme*. Moscow: Izdatel'stvo politicheskoi literatury, 1964.

Simpson, John. *Strange Places, Questionable People*. London: Macmillan, 1998.

Skripko, V. R., I. B. Martkovich, and P. G. Solov'ev. *Zhilishchnoe zakonodatel'stvo v SSSR i RSFSR*. Moscow: Izdatel'stvo literatury po stroitel'stvu, 1965.

Smith, Adam. *The Wealth of Nations*. Books 4–5. London: Penguin, 2003.

Smith, Hedrick. *The Russians*. New York: Ballantine, 1993.

Solzhenitsyn, Aleksandr. *Sobranie sochinenii*. Vols. 5, 7. Paris: YMCA Press, 1980.

Spender, Stephen. *Journals, 1939–1983*. Edited by John Goldsmith. London: Faber and Faber, 1985.

Stalin, I. V. *Sochineniia*. Vols. 14–16. Edited by Robert H. McNeal. Stanford, CA: Hoover Institution, 1967.

Stalingrad: Al'bom dokumental'nykh fotoilliustratsii o gorode-geroe. Moscow: Izogiz, 1956.

Tadevosian, V. S. "Nekotorye voprosy zhilishchnogo prava." *Sovetskoe gosudarstvo i pravo*, 7 (1958): 43–51.

Thatcher, Margaret. *The Downing Street Years*. London: HarperCollins, 1993.

Thubron, Colin. *Among the Russians: From the Baltic to the Caucasus*. London: Penguin, 1983.

Tomsen, A. A. "Zhilishchnyi vopros pri kapitalizme i v SSSR." Candidate of Economic Sciences dissertation, Moscow State Economics Institute, 1959.

Van der Post, Laurens. *Journey into Russia*. London: Penguin, 1971.

Ward, Paul W. *Life in the Soviet Union: Reprinted Articles from the Sun*. Baltimore, MD: The Sun, 1947.

Zhuravlev, V. V. "Nachal'nyi etap resheniia zhilishchnoi problemy v SSSR." *Voprosy istorii* 5 (1978): 33–46.

Zinov'ev, Aleksandr. *Kommunizm kak real'nost'*. Moscow: Eksmo, 2003.

Secondary Sources

Adler, Nanci. *The Gulag Survivor: Beyond the Soviet System*. New Brunswick, NJ: Transaction Publishers, 2002.

Aksiutin, Iurii. *Khrushchevskaia "ottepel'" i obshchestvennye nastroeniia v SSSR 1953–1964gg*. Moscow: ROSSPEN, 2004.

Alterman, Rachelle. *Planning in the Face of Crisis: Land Use, Housing, and Mass Immigration in Israel*. London and New York: Routledge, 2002.

Aly, Götz. *Hitler's Beneficiaries: Plunder, Racial War, and the Nazi Welfare State*. New York: Metropolitan, 2007.

Andrusz, Gregory D. *Housing and Urban Development in the USSR.* London and Basingstoke: Macmillan, 1984.

——. "A Note on the Financing of Housing in the Soviet Union." *Soviet Studies* 42, no. 3 (1990): 555–70.

Attwood, Lynne. *Creating the New Soviet Woman: Women's Magazines as Engineers of Female Identity, 1922–1953.* Basingstoke and New York: Macmillan, 1999.

—— "Housing and the Home in the Khrushchev Era." In *Women in the Khrushchev Era*, ed. Melanie Ilic, Susan E. Reid, and Lynne Attwood. Basingstoke and New York: Palgrave Macmillan, 2004.

Autio-Sarasmo, Sari. "Soviet Economic Modernisation and Transferring Technologies from the West." In Kangaspuro and Smith, *Modernisation in Russia*, 104–23.

Barber, John, and Mark Harrison. *The Soviet Home Front: A Social and Economic History of the USSR in World War II.* London and New York: Longman, 1991.

Barnes, Steven A. "Soviet Society Confined: The Gulag in the Karaganda Region of Kazakhstan." PhD dissertation, Stanford University, 2003.

Baron, Samuel H. *Bloody Saturday in the Soviet Union: Novocherkassk, 1962.* Stanford, CA: Stanford University Press, 2001.

Barraclough, Geoffrey. "Late Socialist Housing: Prefabricated Housing in Leningrad from Khrushchev to Gorbachev." PhD dissertation, University of California, Santa Barbara, 1997.

Bater, James H. *The Soviet City: Ideal and Reality.* London: Edward Arnold, 1980.

Beer, Daniel. "Origins, Modernity, and Resistance in the Historiography of Stalinism." *Journal of Contemporary History* 40, no. 2 (2005): 363–79.

Berliner, Joseph S. *Factory and Manager in the USSR.* Cambridge, MA: Harvard University Press, 1957.

Berman, Harold J. "Soviet Property in Law and in Plan (with Special Reference to Municipal Land and Housing)." *University of Pennsylvania Law Review* (1947–1948): 324–53.

Betts, Paul, and David Crowley, eds. *Domestic Dreamworlds: Notions of Home in Post–1945 Europe.* Special issue of *Journal of Contemporary History* 40 (2005): 2.

Bittner, Stephen V. "Exploring Reform: De-Stalinization in Moscow's Arbat District, 1953–1968." PhD dissertation, University of Chicago, 2000.

——. "Local Soviets, Public Order, and Welfare after Stalin: Appeals from Moscow's Kiev Raion." *Russian Review* 62, no. 2 (2003): 281–93.

——. *The Many Lives of Khrushchev's Thaw: Experience and Memory in Moscow's Arbat.* Ithaca and London: Cornell University Press, 2008.

——. "Remembering the Avant-Garde: Moscow Architects and the 'Rehabilitation' of Constructivism, 1961–1964." *Kritika* 2, no. 3 (2001): 553–76.

Block, Alexander. "Soviet Housing: Some Town Planning Problems." *Soviet Studies* 6, no. 1 (1954): 1–15.

——. "Soviet Housing: The Historical Aspect." *Soviet Studies* 5, no. 3 (1954): 246–77.

——. "Soviet Housing, the Historical Aspect: Some Notes on Problems of Policy. I." *Soviet Studies* 3, no. 1 (1951): 1–15.

——. "Soviet Housing, the Historical Aspect: Some Notes on Problems of Policy. II." *Soviet Studies* 3, no. 3 (1952): 229–57.

Bohn, Thomas. *Minsk—Musterstadt des Sozialismus. Stadtplanung und Urbanisierung in der Sowjetunion nach 1945.* Cologne: Böhlau Verlag, 2008.

Borkowski, J. A., and Paul du Plessis. *Textbook on Roman Law.* Oxford: Oxford University Press, 2005.

Boterbloem, Kees. *Life and Death under Stalin: Kalinin Province, 1945–1953*. Montreal: McGill-Queens University Press, 1999.

Boym, Svetlana. *Common Places: Mythologies of Everyday Life in Russia*. Cambridge, MA: Harvard University Press, 1994.

Bradley, Joseph. "Subjects into Citizens: Societies, Civil Society, and Autocracy in Tsarist Russia." *American Historical Review* 107, no. 4 (2002): 1094–123.

Briggs, Asa. "The Welfare State in Historical Perspective." In *The Welfare State: A Reader*, ed. Christopher Pierson and Francis G. Castles, 18–31. Cambridge: Polity, 2000.

Brooks, Jeffrey. *Thank You Comrade Stalin! Soviet Public Culture from Revolution to Cold War*. Princeton, NJ: Princeton University Press, 1999.

Brumfield, William Craft, and Blair Ruble, eds. *Russian Housing in the Modern Age: Design and Social History*. Cambridge: Cambridge University Press, 1993.

Buchli, Victor. *An Archaeology of Socialism*. Oxford and New York: Berg, 1999.

Buckley, Mary. "The Untold Story of *Obshchestvennitsa* in the 1930s." *Europe-Asia Studies* 48, no. 4 (1996): 569–86.

Carbone, Cristina Maria. "Building Propaganda: Architecture and the American National Exhibition in Moscow of 1959." PhD dissertation, University of California, Santa Barbara, 2001.

Carman, Naomi, and Daniel Czamanski. "Israel." In *International Handbook of Housing Policies and Practices*, ed. William van Vliet, 517–36. New York: Greenwood Press, 1990.

Castillo, Greg. "Domesticating the Cold War: Household Consumption and Propaganda in Marshall Plan Germany." *Journal of Contemporary History* 40, no. 2 (2005): 261–88.

Colton, Timothy J. *Moscow: Governing the Socialist Metropolis*. Cambridge, MA: Belknap Press of Harvard University Press, 1995.

Condee, Nancy. "Cultural Codes of the Thaw." In *Nikita Khrushchev*, ed. William Taubman, Sergei Khrushchev, and Abbott Gleason, 160–76. New Haven and London: Yale University Press, 2000.

Connor, Ian. "The Refugees and the Currency Reform." In Turner, *Reconstruction in Post-War Germany*, 301–24.

Cooke, Catherine, with Susan E. Reid. "Modernity and Realism: Architectural Relations in the Cold War." In *Russian Art and the West: A Century of Dialogue in Painting, Architecture, and the Decorative Arts*, ed. Rosalind P. Blakesley and Susan E. Reid, 172–94. DeKalb, IL: Northern Illinois University Press, 2007.

Danilov, A. A., and A. V. Pyzhikov. *Rozhdenie sverkhderzhavy: SSSR v pervye poslevoennye gody*. Moscow: ROSSPEN, 2001.

Davies, R. W. *Crisis and Progress in the Soviet Economy, 1931–1933*. Basingstoke: Macmillan, 1996.

Davies, R. W., Mark Harrison, and S. G. Wheatcroft, eds. *The Economic Transformation of the Soviet Union, 1913–1945*. Cambridge: Cambridge University Press, 1994.

Davies, R. W., and Melanie Ilic. "From Khrushchev (1935) to Khrushchev (1956–1964): Construction Policy Compared." In *Khrushchev in the Kremlin: Policy and Government in the Soviet Union, 1956–1964*, ed. Jeremy Smith and Melanie Ilic. London: Routledge (forthcoming).

Davies, Sarah. *Popular Opinion in Stalin's Russia: Terror, Propaganda, and Dissent, 1934–1941*. Cambridge: Cambridge University Press, 1997.

Davies, Sarah, and James Harris. *Stalin: A New History*. Cambridge: Cambridge University Press, 2005.

Day, Andrew Elam. "Building Socialism: The Politics of the Soviet Cityscape in the Stalin Era." PhD dissertation, Columbia University, 1998.

De Grazia, Victoria. *Irresistible Empire: America's Advance through Twentieth-Century Europe.* Cambridge and London: Belknap Press of Harvard University Press, 2005.

DeHaan, Heather Diane. "From Nizhnii to Gor'kii: The Reconstruction of a Russian Provincial City in the Stalinist 1930s." PhD dissertation, University of Toronto, 2005.

Diefendorf, Jeffrey M., ed. *Rebuilding Europe's Bombed Cities.* Basingstoke: Macmillan, 1990.

DiMaio, Alfred. *Soviet Urban Housing: Problems and Policies.* New York and London: Praeger, 1974.

Dobson, Miriam. *Khrushchev's Cold Summer: Gulag Returnees, Crime, and the Fate of Reform after Stalin.* Ithaca and London: Cornell University Press, 2009.

Dower, John. *Embracing Defeat: Japan in the Aftermath of World War II.* London: Penguin, 1999.

Duclaud-Williams, Roger H. *The Politics of Housing in Britain and France.* London: Heinemann, 1978.

Dunham, Vera. *In Stalin's Time: Middle-Class Values in Soviet Fiction.* Cambridge: Cambridge University Press, 1976.

Dunleavy, Patrick. *The Politics of Mass Housing in Britain, 1945–1975: A Study of Corporate Power and Professional Influence in the Welfare State.* Oxford: Clarendon Press, 1988.

Dunmore, Timothy. *Soviet Politics, 1945–1953.* London: Macmillan, 1984.

Duskin, J. Eric. *Stalinist Reconstruction and the Confirmation of a New Elite, 1945–1953.* Basingstoke: Palgrave, 2001.

Edele, Mark. "More than just Stalinists: The Political Sentiments of Victors, 1945–1953." In Fürst, *Late Stalinist Russia,* 167–91.

———. "Soviet Society, Social Structure and Everyday Life: Major Frameworks Reconsidered." *Kritika* 8, no. 2 (2007): 349–73.

———. "Soviet Veterans as an Entitlement Group, 1945–1955." *Slavic Review* 65, no. 1 (2006): 111–37.

———. *Soviet Veterans of the Second World War: A Popular Movement in an Authoritarian Society, 1941–1991.* Oxford: Oxford University Press, 2008.

———. "Strange Young Men in Stalin's Moscow: The Birth and Life of the *Stiliagi,* 1945–1953." *Jahrbücher für Geschichte Osteuropas* 50, no. 1 (2002): 37–61.

Edele, Mark, and Michael Geyer. "States of Exception: The Nazi–Soviet War as a System of Violence." In *Beyond Totalitarianism: Stalinism and Nazism Compared,* ed. Michael Geyer and Sheila Fitzpatrick, 345–95. Cambridge: Cambridge University Press, 2009.

Ellman, Michael, and S. Maksudov. "Soviet Deaths in the Great Patriotic War: A Note." *Europe-Asia Studies* 46, no. 4 (1994): 671–80.

Erickson, John. "Soviet War Losses." In *Barbarossa: The Axis and the Allies,* ed. John Erickson and David Dilks. Edinburgh: Edinburgh University Press, 1994.

Farrow, Lee A. *Between Clan and Crown: The Struggle to Define Noble Property Rights in Imperial Russia.* Newark, NJ: University of Delaware Press, 2004.

———. "The Ties that Bind: The Role of the Russian Clan in Inheritance and Property Law." In *Russia in the European Context, 1789–1914: A Member of the Family,* ed. Susan P. McCaffray and Michael Melancon, 13–32. Basingstoke: Palgrave Macmillan, 2005.

Field, Deborah A. "Divorce and Conceptions of Private Life in the Khrushchev Era." *Russian Review* 57, no. 4 (1998): 599–613.

———. *Private Life and Communist Morality in Khrushchev's Russia*. New York: Peter Lang, 2007.

Filtzer, Donald. "From Mobilized to Free Labour: De-Stalinization and the Changing Legal Status of Workers." In Jones, *Dilemmas of De-Stalinization*, 154–70.

———. "The 1947 Food Crisis and Its Aftermath: Worker and Peasant Consumption in Non-famine Regions of the RSFSR." In *A Dream Deferred: New Studies in Russian and Soviet Labour History*, ed. Donald Filtzer, Wendy Z. Goldman, Gijs Kessler, and Simon Pirani, 343–85. Bern: Peter Lang, 2008.

———. "Poisoning the Proletariat: Urban Water Supply and River Pollution in Russia's Industrial Regions during late Stalinism, 1945–1953." *Acta Slavica Iaponica* 26 (2009): 85–108.

———. *Soviet Workers and De-Stalinization: The Consolidation of the Modern System of Soviet Production Relations, 1953–1964*. Cambridge: Cambridge University Press, 1992.

———. *Soviet Workers and Late Stalinism: Labour and the Restoration of the Stalinist System after World War II*. Cambridge: Cambridge University Press, 2002.

———. *Soviet Workers and Stalinist Industrialization: The Formation of Modern Soviet Production Relations*. London: Pluto, 1986.

Fitzpatrick, Sheila. *Everyday Stalinism: Ordinary Life in Extraordinary Times, Soviet Russia in the 1930s*. Oxford: Oxford University Press, 1999.

———. "Revisionism in Retrospect: A Personal View." *Slavic Review* 67, no. 3 (2008): 682–704.

———. "The Soviet Union in the Twenty-First Century." *Journal of European Studies* 37, no. 1 (2007): 51–71.

———. *Tear Off the Masks! Identity and Imposture in Twentieth-Century Russia*. Princeton and Oxford: Princeton University Press, 2005.

Fulbrook, Mary. *The People's State: East German Society from Hitler to Honecker*. New Haven, CT, and London: Yale University Press, 2005.

Fürst, Juliane, ed. *Late Stalinist Russia: Society between Reconstruction and Reinvention*. London: Routledge, 2006.

———. "Prisoners of the Soviet Self? Political Youth Opposition in Late Stalinism." *Europe-Asia Studies* 54, no. 3 (2002): 353–76.

Gerasimova, Ekaterina. "Public Privacy in the Soviet Communal Apartment." In *Socialist Spaces: Sites of Everyday Life in the Eastern Bloc*, ed. David Crowley and Susan E. Reid. Oxford and New York: Berg, 2002.

———. "Sovetskaia kommunal'naia kvartira kak sotsial'nyi institut: istoriko-sotsiologicheskii analiz (na materialakh Peterburga-Leningrada, 1917–1991gg)." Candidate of Sociological Sciences dissertation, European University, St. Petersburg, 2000.

Gildea, Robert. *France since 1945*. Oxford: Oxford University Press, 2002.

Gorlizki, Yoram, and Oleg Khlevniuk. *Cold Peace: Stalin and the Ruling Circle, 1945–1953*. Oxford and New York: Oxford University Press, 2004.

Gregory, Paul R., ed. *Behind the Façade of Stalin's Command Economy: Evidence from the Soviet State and Party Archives*. Stanford, CA: Hoover Institution Press, 2001.

Grunenbaum, James O. *Private Ownership*. London: Routledge and Kegan Paul, 1987.

Gsovski, Vladimir. "Soviet Law of Inheritance." *Michigan Law Review* 45 (1947): 291–320.

Hachten, P. Charles. "Property Relations and the Economic Organization of Soviet Russia, 1941–1948." PhD dissertation, University of Chicago, 2005.

Halfin, Igal, and Jochen Hellbeck. "Rethinking the Stalinist Subject: Stephen Kotkin's *Magnetic Mountain* and the State of Soviet Historical Studies." *Jahrbücher für Geschichte Osteuropas* 44, no. 3 (1996): 456–63.

Hamm, Michael F., ed. *The City in Russian History.* Lexington: University Press of Kentucky, 1976.

Hanson, Philip. *The Rise and Fall of the Soviet Economy.* London: Longman, 2003.

Harris, James. *The Great Urals: Regionalism and the Evolution of the Soviet System.* Ithaca, NY: Cornell University Press, 1999.

Harris, Steven E. "'I Know All the Secrets of My Neighbours': The Quest for Privacy in the Era of the Separate Apartment." In Siegelbaum, *Borders of Socialism,* 171–89.

———. "Moving to the Separate Apartment: Building, Distributing, Furnishing, and Living in Urban Housing in Soviet Russia, 1950s–1960s." PhD dissertation, University of Chicago, 2003.

Hazard, John N. *Soviet Housing Law.* New Haven: Yale University Press, 1939.

Headey, Bruce. *Housing Policy in the Developed Economy: The United Kingdom, Sweden and the United States.* London: Croom Helm, 1978.

Hellie, Richard. "The Law." In *The Cambridge History of Russia,* vol. 1, *From Early Rus' to 1689,* ed. Maureen Perrie, 360–86. Cambridge: Cambridge University Press, 2006.

Hessler, Julie. *A Social History of Soviet Trade: Policy, Retail Practices, and Consumption, 1917–1953.* Princeton and Oxford: Princeton University Press, 2004.

Hoffmann, David L. *Peasant Metropolis: Social Identities in Moscow, 1929–1941.* Ithaca, NY: Cornell University Press, 1994.

———. *Stalinist Values: The Cultural Norms of Soviet Modernity, 1917–1941.* Ithaca, NY, and London: Cornell University Press, 2003.

Hoffmann, David L., and Yanni Kotsonis, eds. *Russian Modernity: Politics, Knowledge, Practices.* Basingstoke: Macmillan, 2000.

Holquist, Peter. "'Information Is the Alpha and Omega of Our Work': Bolshevik Surveillance in Its Pan-European Context." *Journal of Modern History* 69, no. 3 (1997): 415–50.

———. *Making War, Forging Revolution: Russia's Continuum of Crisis, 1914–1921.* Cambridge, MA: Harvard University Press, 2002.

Honoré, A. M. "Ownership." In *Oxford Essays in Jurisprudence,* ed. A. G. Guest, 107–47. Oxford: Oxford University Press, 1961.

Hooper, Cynthia V. "A Darker 'Big Deal': Concealing Party Crimes in the Post–Second World War Era." In Fürst, *Late Stalinist Russia,* 142–63.

Hosking, Geoffrey. *A History of the Soviet Union.* London: Fontana, 1992.

———. "Patronage and the Russian State." *Slavonic and East European Review* 78, no. 2 (2000): 301–30.

———. *Rulers and Victims: The Russians in the Soviet Union.* Cambridge, MA: Belknap Press of Harvard University Press, 2006.

———. *Russia: People and Empire, 1552–1917.* London: HarperCollins, 1997.

Houf, Michael Scott. "The Re-invention of Hong Kong during the Post-War Period." PhD dissertation, Florida State University, 2002.

Hudson, Hugh D. *Blueprints and Blood: The Stalinization of Soviet Architecture, 1917–1937.* Princeton, NJ: Princeton University Press, 1994.

Ikonnikov, Andrei. *Russian Architecture of the Soviet Period.* Moscow: Raduga, 1988.

Inkeles, Alex, and Raymond A. Bauer. *The Soviet Citizen: Daily Life in a Totalitarian Society.* Cambridge, MA: Harvard University Press, 1959.

Jahn, Hubertus F. "The Housing Revolution in Petrograd, 1917–1920." *Jahrbücher für Geschichte Osteuropas* 38, no. 2 (1990): 212–27.

Jones, Jeffrey. "'People without a Definite Occupation': The Illegal Economy and 'Speculators' in Rostov-on-the-Don, 1943–1948." In *Provincial Landscapes: Local Dimensions of Soviet Power, 1917–1953*, ed. Donald J. Raleigh. Pittsburgh, PA, 2001. 236–54.

Jones, Polly. *The Dilemmas of De-Stalinization: Negotiating Cultural and Social Change in the Khrushchev Era*. New York: Routledge, 2006.

———. "From Stalinism to Post-Stalinism: De-mythologizing Stalin, 1953–1956." In *Redefining Stalin*, ed. H. Shukman, 127–48. London: Frank Cass, 2003.

Kangaspuro, Markku, and Jeremy Smith, eds. *Modernisation in Russia since 1900*. Helsinki: Finnish Literature Society, 2006.

Keenan, Edward. "Muscovite Political Folkways." *Russian Review* 45, no. 2 (1986): 115–81.

Kelly, Catriona. *Refining Russia: Advice Literature, Polite Culture, and Gender from Catherine to Yeltsin*. Oxford: Oxford University Press, 2001.

Kharkhordin, Oleg. *The Collective and Individual in Russia: A Study of Practices*. Berkeley and Los Angeles: University of California Press, 1999.

Khazanova, V. E. "Massovoe i unikal'noe v arkhitekture sovetskikh obshchestvennykh sooruzhenii poslevoennogo perioda." In *Voprosy sovetskogo izobrazitel'nogo iskusstva i arkhitektury*, ed. V. E. Khazanova. Moscow: Sovetskii Khudozhnik, 1973.

Kimura, Hiroshi. "Personal Property in the Soviet Union, with Particular Emphasis on the Khrushchev Era: An Ideological, Political, and Economic Dilemma." PhD dissertation, Columbia University, 1968.

Kollmann, Nancy Shields. "Law and Society." In *The Cambridge History of Russia*, vol. 1, *From Early Rus' to 1689*, ed. Maureen Perrie, 559–78. Cambridge: Cambridge University Press, 2006.

Kotkin, Stephen. *Magnetic Mountain: Stalinism as a Civilization*. Berkeley and Los Angeles: University of California Press, 1997.

———. "Modern Times: The Soviet Union and the Interwar Conjuncture." *Kritika* 2, no. 1 (2001): 111–64.

Kotlove, Barry Steven. "The Cost of Soviet Housing." PhD dissertation, University of California, Davis, 1987.

Kozlov, Vladimir. *Neizvestnyi SSSR: Protivostoianie naroda i vlasti, 1953–1985gg*. Moscow: Olma, 2006.

Kucherow, Samuel. "Property in the Soviet Union." *American Journal of Comparative Law* 11, no. 3 (1962): 376–92.

Kulavig, Erik. *Dissent in the Years of Khrushchev: Nine Stories about Disobedient Russians*. Basingstoke: Palgrave Macmillan, 2002.

Kuschpèta, O. *The Banking and Credit System of the USSR*. Leiden: Martinus Nijhoff, 1978.

Lebina, N. B., and A. N. Chistikov. *Obyvatel' i reformy: kartiny povsednevnoi zhizni gorozhan v gody NEPa i khrushchevskogo desiatiletiia*. St Petersburg: Dmitrii Bulanin, 2003.

Lebow, Katherine Anne. "Nowa Huta, 1949–1957: Stalinism and the Transformation of Everyday Life in Poland's First Socialist City." PhD dissertation, Columbia University, 2002.

Ledeneva, Alena. *Russia's Economy of Favours: Blat, Networking, and Informal Exchange*. Cambridge: Cambridge University Press, 1998.

Leitch, Donald G. "Soviet Housing Administration and the Wartime Evacuation." *American Slavonic and East European Review* 9, no. 3 (1950): 180–90.

Lewin, Moshe. *The Making of the Soviet System: Essays in the Social History of Interwar Russia*. New York: Pantheon, 1985.

———. *The Soviet Century*. London and New York: Verso, 2005.

Lincoln, W. Bruce. *In the Vanguard of Reform: Russia's Enlightened Bureaucrats, 1825–1861.* DeKalb, IL: Northern Illinois University Press, 1982.

Lovell, Stephen. *Summerfolk: A History of the Dacha, 1710–2000.* Ithaca and London: Cornell University Press, 2003.

Lowe, Rodney. *The Welfare State in Britain since 1945.* London: Palgrave Macmillan, 2005.

Lundqvist, Lennart J. *Housing Policy and Tenures in Sweden: The Quest for Neutrality.* Aldershot: Avebury, 1988.

Maggs, Peter B. "The Security of Individually Owned Property under Soviet Law." *Duke Law Review* 10 (1961): 525–37.

Malia, Martin. *The Soviet Tragedy: A History of Socialism in Russia, 1917–1991.* New York: Free Press, 1994.

Manley, Rebecca. "The Evacuation and Survival of Soviet Civilians, 1941–1946." PhD dissertation, University of California, Berkeley, 2004.

Markevich, Andrei. "Urban Households in the USSR, 1941–1964: The Legacy of War." In *Urban Households in Russia and the Soviet Union, 1900–2000: Size, Structure, Composition,* ed. Sergey Afontsev et al. Amsterdam: IISH-Research Paper 44, 2005.

Marrese, Michelle Lamarche. *A Woman's Kingdom: Noblewomen and the Control of Property in Russia, 1700–1861.* Ithaca and London: Cornell University Press, 2002.

Martin, Xavier. *Human Nature and the French Revolution: From the Enlightenment to the Napoleonic Code.* New York and Oxford: Berghaus, 2001.

Matsui, Yasuhiro. "Housing Partnerships, ZhAKTy, or Housing Trusts? A Study of Moscow's Housing Management System, 1917–1937." *Acta Slavica Iaponica* 26 (2009): 109–39.

———. "Stalinist Public or Communitarian Project? Housing Organizations and Self-Managed Canteens in Moscow's Frunze Raion." *Europe-Asia Studies* 60, no. 7 (2008): 1223–46.

Matthews, Mervyn. "Social Dimensions in Soviet Urban Housing." *The Socialist City: Spatial Structure and Urban Policy,* ed. R. A. French and F. E. Ian Hamilton, 105–18. Chichester: John Wiley, 1979.

Mawdsley, Evan, and Stephen White. *The Soviet Elite from Lenin to Gorbachev: The Central Committee and Its Members, 1917–1991.* Oxford: Oxford University Press, 2000.

Medvedev, Roi, and Zhores Medvedev. *Khrushchev: The Years in Power.* London: Oxford University Press, 1977.

Meerovich, Mark Grigor'evich. *Kvadratnye metry, opredeliaiushchie soznanie: Gosudarstvennaia zhilishchnaia politika v SSSR, 1921–1941gg.* Stuttgart: ibidem-Verlag, 2005.

Merrett, Stephen. *State Housing in Britain.* London: Routledge and Kegan Paul, 1979.

Mertelsmann, Olaf. "Was There a Stalinist Industrialization in the Baltic Republics? Estonia—an Example." In *The Sovietization of the Baltic States, 1940–1956,* ed. Olaf Mertelsmann, 151–70. Tartu: Kleio, 2003.

Millar, James R. "The Little Deal: Brezhnev's Contribution to Acquisitive Socialism." *Slavic Review* 44, no. 4 (1985): 694–706.

Molnar, Virág Eszter. "Modernity and Memory: The Politics of Architecture in Hungary and East Germany after the Second World War." PhD dissertation, Princeton University, 2005.

Moon, David. *The Russian Peasantry, 1600–1930: The World the Peasants Made.* Harlow: Longman, 1999.

Morcom, Shaun. "The Social Workings of Soviet Power: State-Society Relations in Postwar Russia, 1945–1953." DPhil thesis, University of Oxford, 2006.

Morton, Henry W. "Housing in the Soviet Union." *Proceedings of the Academy of Political Science* 35, no. 3 (1984): 69–80.

———. "Who Gets What, When, and How? Housing in the Soviet Union." *Soviet Studies* 32, no. 2 (1980): 235–59.

Munzer, Stephen R. *A Theory of Property*. Cambridge: Cambridge University Press, 1990.

Nordlander, David. "Origins of a Gulag Capital: Magadan and Stalinist Control in the Early 1930s." *Slavic Review* 57 (1998): 791–812.

Nove, Alec. *Was Stalin Really Necessary? Some Problems of Soviet Political Economy*. London: George Allen and Unwin, 1964.

Nove, Alec, et al. *Problems of Communism* symposium on "Toward a 'Communist Welfare State.'" *Problems of Communism* (1960): 1.

Offe, Claus. *Contradictions of the Welfare State*. Edited by John Keane. London: Hutchinson, 1984.

Offer, Avner. *The Challenge of Affluence: Self-Control and Well-Being in the United States and Britain since 1950*. Oxford: Oxford University Press, 2006.

Osokina, Elena A. "Economic Disobedience under Stalin." In *Contending with Stalinism: Soviet Power and Popular Resistance in the 1930s*, ed. Lynne Viola, 170–200. Ithaca and London: Cornell University Press, 2002.

Overy, Richard. *The Dictators: Hitler's Germany and Stalin's Russia*. London: Allen Lane, 2004.

Paperny, Vladimir. *Architecture in the Age of Stalin: Culture Two*. Cambridge: Cambridge University Press, 2002.

Pikhoia, Rudol'f. *Moskva, Kreml', Vlast': Sorok let posle voiny, 1945–1985*. Moscow: Rus'-Olimp, Astrel', AST, 2007.

Pipes, Richard. *Property and Freedom*. London: Harvill, 1999.

———. *The Russian Revolution, 1899–1919*. London: Harvill, 1990.

——— *Russia under the Bolshevik Regime, 1919–1924*. London: Harvill, 1994.

———. *Russia under the Old Regime*. London: Penguin, 1979.

Pollock, Ethan. *Stalin and the Soviet Science Wars*. Princeton and Oxford: Princeton University Press, 2006.

Potemkina, M. N. *Evakonaselenie v Ural'skom tylu (1941–1948gg)*. Magnitogorsk: MaGU, 2006.

Power, Anne. *Hovels to High Rise: State Housing in Europe since 1850*. London and New York: Routledge, 1993.

Priestland, David. *Stalinism and the Politics of Mobilization: Ideas, Power, and Terror in Interwar Russia*. Oxford: Oxford University Press, 2007.

Pyzhikov, Aleksandr. *Khrushchevskaia "ottepel'."* Moscow: Olma, 2002.

Qualls, Karl D. "Raised from Ruins: Restoring Popular Allegiance through City Planning in Sevastopol, 1943–1954." PhD dissertation, Georgetown University, 1998.

Quine, Maria Sophia. *Italy's Social Revolution: Charity and Welfare from Liberalism to Fascism*. Basingstoke: Palgrave Macmillan, 2005.

Reid, Susan E., ed. "Design, Stalin, and the Thaw." Special issue. *Journal of Design History* 10 (1997): 2.

———"The Khrushchev Kitchen: Domesticating the Scientific-Technological Revolution." *Journal of Contemporary History* 40, no. 2 (2005): 289–316.

———. "The Meaning of Home: 'The Only Bit of the World You Can Have to Yourself.'" In Siegelbaum, *Borders of Socialism*, 145–70.

———. "Who Will Beat Whom? Soviet Popular Reception of the American National Exhibition in Moscow, 1959." *Kritika* 9, no. 4 (2008): 855–904.

———. "Women in the Home." In *Women in the Khrushchev Era*, ed. Melanie Ilic, Susan E.

Reid, and Lynne Attwood, 149–76. Basingstoke and New York: Palgrave Macmillan, 2004.

Remnick, David. *Lenin's Tomb: The Last Days of the Soviet Empire.* London: Penguin, 1994.

Roseman, Mark. "The Uncontrolled Economy: Ruhr Coal Production, 1945–1948." In Turner, *Reconstruction in Post-War Germany*, 93–123.

Rossman, Jeffrey J. *Worker Resistance under Stalin: Class and Revolution on the Shop Floor.* Cambridge, MA: Harvard University Press, 2005.

Ruble, Blair A. "*From khrushchoby* to *korobki.*" In Brumfield and Ruble, *Russian Housing in the Modern Age.*

———. *Leningrad: Shaping a Soviet City.* Berkeley and Los Angeles: University of California Press, 1990.

Rudden, Bernard. "Soviet Housing and the New Civil Code." *International and Comparative Law Quarterly* 15, no. 1 (1966): 231–62.

———. "Soviet Housing Law." *International and Comparative Law Quarterly* 12, no. 2 (1963): 591–630.

Sawicki, Stanislaw J. *Soviet Land and Housing Law: A Historical and Comparative Study.* New York: Praeger, 1977.

Seniavskaia, E. S. *Frontovoe pokolenie: istoriko-psikhologicheskoe issledovanie.* Moscow: Institut rossiiskoi istorii RAN, 1995.

Seniavskii, A. S. *Rossiiskii gorod v 1960-e–80-e gody.* Moscow: RAN, 1995.

Service, Robert. *A History of Modern Russia from Nicholas II to Putin.* London: Penguin, 2003.

———. *Stalin: A Biography.* London: Macmillan, 2004.

Shearer, David. "Elements Near and Alien: Passportization, Policing, and Identity in the Stalinist State, 1932–1952." *Journal of Modern History* 76, no. 4 (2004): 835–81.

Shlapentokh, Victor. *Public and Private Life of the Soviet People: Changing Values in Post-Stalin Russia.* Oxford: Oxford University Press, 1989.

Siegelbaum, Lewis H., ed. *Borders of Socialism: Private Spheres of Soviet Russia.* New York and Basingstoke: Palgrave Macmillan, 2006.

———. *Cars for Comrades: The Life of the Soviet Automobile.* Ithaca and London: Cornell University Press, 2008.

———. *Stakhanovism and the Politics of Productivity in the USSR, 1935–1941.* Cambridge: Cambridge University Press, 1988.

Sillince, J. A. A. *Housing Policies in Eastern Europe and the Soviet Union.* London and New York: Routledge, 1990.

Smith, Jeremy, ed. *Beyond the Limits: The Concept of Space in Russian History and Culture.* Helsinki: SHS, 1999.

———. "Khrushchev and the Path to Modernization through Education." In Kangaspuro and Smith, *Modernisation in Russia*, 221–36.

Smith, Mark B. "Individual Forms of Ownership in the Urban Housing Fund of the Soviet Union, 1944–1964." *Slavonic and East European Review* 86, no. 2 (2008): 283–305.

———. "Khrushchev's Promise to Eliminate the Urban Housing Shortage: Rights, Rationality, and the Communist Future." In *Soviet State and Society under Nikita Khrushchev*, ed. Melanie Ilic and Jeremy Smith. London: Routledge, 2009. 26–45.

Smith, Roger J. *Property Law.* Harlow: Longman, 2003.

Solnick, Steven. *Stealing the State: Control and Collapse in Soviet Institutions.* Cambridge, MA, and London: Harvard University Press, 1998.

Sosnovy, Timothy. *The Housing Problem in the Soviet Union.* New York: Research Program on the USSR, 1954.

———. "Rent in the USSR." *American Slavic and East European Review* 18, no. 2 (1959): 174–81.

———. "The Soviet Housing Situation Today." *Soviet Studies* 11, no. 1 (1959): 1–21.

———. "The Soviet Urban Housing Problem." *American Slavic and East European Review* 11, no. 4 (1952): 288–303.

Spicker, Paul. *The Welfare State: A General Theory.* London: Sage, 2000.

Staemmler, Gorlind. "East Germany (The German Democratic Republic)." In Wynn, *Housing in Europe*, 220–46.

Starr, S. Frederick. "Visionary Town Planning during the Cultural Revolution." In *Cultural Revolution in Russia, 1928–1931*, ed. Sheila Fitzpatrick, 207–40. Bloomington: Indiana University Press, 1978.

Straus, Kenneth M. *Factory and Community in Stalin's Russia: The Making of an Industrial Working Class.* Pittsburgh, PA: University of Pittsburgh Press, 1997.

Strobel, Roland Walter. "City Planning and Political Ideology in East and West Berlin (Germany), 1949 to 1989: An Examination of the Urban Design of Public Housing on Both Sides of the Wall." PhD dissertation, University of South California, 1998.

Stronski, Paul. "Forging a Soviet City: Tashkent, 1937–1966." PhD dissertation, Stanford University, 2003.

Taubman, William. *Khrushchev: The Man and His Era.* London: Free Press, 2003.

Tikhonov, Aleksei, and Paul R. Gregory. "Stalin's Last Plan." In *Behind the Façade of Stalin's Command Economy: Evidence from the Soviet State and Party Archives*, ed. Paul R. Gregory, 159–92. Stanford, CA: Hoover Institution Press, 2001.

Titov, Alexander. "The 1961 Party Program and the Fate of Khrushchev's Reforms." In *Soviet State and Society under Nikita Khrushchev*, ed. Melanie Ilic and Jeremy Smith, 8–25. London: Routledge, 2009.

Tolz, Vera. "Cultural Bosses as Patrons and Clients: The Functioning of the Soviet Creative Unions in the Postwar Period." *Contemporary European History* 11, no. 1 (2002): 87–105.

Tomoff, Kirill. *Creative Union: The Professional Organization of Soviet Composers, 1939–1953.* Ithaca, NY: Cornell University Press, 2006.

Tooze, Adam J. *The Wages of Destruction: The Making and Breaking of the Nazi Economy.* London: Allen Lane, 2006.

Turner, Ian D., ed. *Reconstruction in Post-War Germany: British Occupation Policy and the Western Zones, 1945–1955.* Oxford, New York, and Munich: Berg, 1989.

Varga-Harris, Christina. "Constructing the Soviet Hearth: Home, Citizenship, and Socialism in Russia, 1956–1964." PhD dissertation, University of Illinois at Urbana-Champaign, 2005.

Vestbro, Dick Urban. "Collective Housing Units in Sweden." *Current Sweden* 234 (September 1979).

Volkov, Vadim. "The Concept of *kul'turnost'*: Notes on the Stalinist Civilizing Process." In *Stalinism: New Directions*, ed. Sheila Fitzpatrick, 210–30. Abingdon and New York: Routledge, 2000.

Vysokovskii, Aleksandr. "Will Domesticity Return?" In Brumfield and Ruble, *Russian Housing in the Modern Age*, 271–308.

Wagner, William. *Marriage, Property, and Law in Late Imperial Russia.* Oxford: Clarendon Press, 1994.

Ward, Chris. *Stalin's Russia.* London: Edward Arnold, 1999.

Waswo, Ann. *Housing in Postwar Japan: A Social History.* London: Routledge Curzon, 2002.

Weickhardt, George G. "The Pre-Petrine Law of Property." *Slavic Review* 52, no. 4 (1993): 663–79.

Weiner, Amir, ed. *Landscaping the Human Garden: Twentieth-Century Population Management in a Comparative Framework.* Stanford, CA: Stanford University Press, 2003.

———. *Making Sense of War: The Second World War and the Fate of the Bolshevik Revolution.* Princeton and Oxford: Princeton University Press, 2001.

Wood, Gordon S. *The Radicalism of the American Revolution.* New York: Vintage, 1993.

Wortman, Richard. *The Development of a Russian Legal Consciousness.* Chicago and London: University of Chicago Press, 1976.

Wynn, Martin, ed. *Housing in Europe.* London: Croom Helm, 1984.

Yaney, George. *The Urge to Mobilize: Agrarian Reform in Russia, 1861–1930.* Urbana: University of Illinois Press, 1982.

Yurchak, Alexei. *Everything Was Forever, until It Was No More: The Last Soviet Generation.* Princeton and Oxford: Princeton University Press, 2006.

Zaleski, Eugène. *Stalinist Planning for Economic Growth, 1933–1952.* London: Macmillan, 1980.

Zbarsky, Ilya, and Samuel Hutchinson. *Lenin's Embalmers.* London: Harvill, 1999.

Zubkova, Elena. *Obshchestvo i reformy, 1945–1964.* Moscow: Rossiia molodaia, 1993.

———. *Russia after the War: Hopes, Illusions, and Disappointments, 1945–1957.* Armonk and London: M. E. Sharpe, 1998.

WEBSITE

www.sovarch.ru.

www.ingramcontent.com/pod-product-compliance
Ingram Content Group UK Ltd.
Pitfield, Milton Keynes, MK11 3LW, UK
UKHW040002020225
454465UK00002B/71